Showdown in the Sonoran Desert

Showdown in the Sonoran Desert

Religion, Law, and the Immigration Controversy

Ananda Rose

OXFORD
UNIVERSITY PRESS

OXFORD

UNIVERSITY PRESS

Oxford University Press, Inc., publishes works that further
Oxford University's objective of excellence
in research, scholarship, and education.

Oxford   New York
Auckland   Cape Town   Dar es Salaam   Hong Kong   Karachi
Kuala Lumpur   Madrid   Melbourne   Mexico City   Nairobi
New Delhi   Shanghai   Taipei   Toronto

With offices in
Argentina   Austria   Brazil   Chile   Czech Republic   France   Greece
Guatemala   Hungary   Italy   Japan   Poland   Portugal   Singapore
South Korea   Switzerland   Thailand   Turkey   Ukraine   Vietnam

Published by Oxford University Press, Inc.
198 Madison Avenue, New York, New York 10016

www.oup.com

Oxford is a registered trademark of Oxford University Press

Library of Congress Cataloging-in-Publication Data
Rose, Ananda.
Showdown in the Sonoran Desert : religion, law, and the
immigration controversy / Ananda Rose.
p.   cm.
Includes bibliographical references and index.
ISBN 978–0–19–989093–4 (hardcover : alk. paper)
1. United States—Emigration and immigration—Religious aspects—Christianity.
2. Emigration and immigration—Religious aspects—Christianity.
3. Immigrants—Civil rights—United States.   4. Illegal aliens—United States.
5. United States—Emigration and immigration—Government policy.
6. Mexican-American Border Region—Emigration and immigration.   I. Title.
BR517.R58 2012
261.7—dc23   2011033707

1 3 5 7 9 8 6 4 2
Printed in the United States of America
on acid-free paper

Then the righteous will answer him, "Lord, when was it that we saw you hungry and gave you food, or thirsty and gave you something to drink? And when was it that we saw you a stranger and welcomed you, or naked and gave you clothing? And when was it that we saw you sick or in prison and visited you?" And the king will answer them, "Truly I tell you, just as you did it to one of the least of these who are members of my family, you did it to me."

–Matthew 25:37

CONTENTS

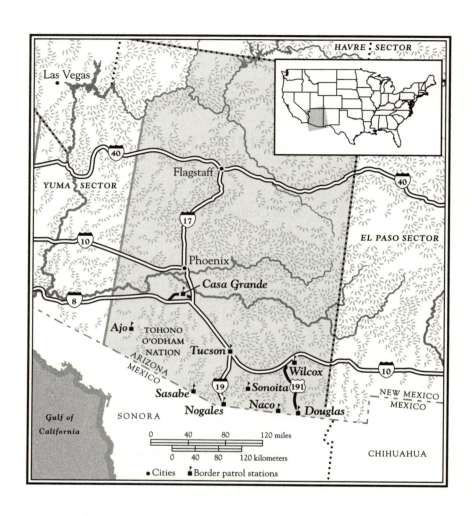

HAVRE SECTOR

Las Vegas

YUMA SECTOR

Flagstaff

EL PASO SECTOR

Phoenix

Casa Grande

Ajo

TOHONO O'ODHAM NATION

Tucson

Wilcox

ARIZONA MEXICO

Sasabe

Sonoita

NEW MEXICO

Nogales

Naco

Douglas

MEXICO

SONORA

Gulf of California

CHIHUAHUA

0   40   80   120 miles

0   40   80   120 kilometers

● Cities   ▪ Border patrol stations

Showdown in the Sonoran Desert

The Immigration Controversy: Religion and Law in Collision

For all of recorded history, people have migrated in search of a better life. They have walked jaw-dropping distances, across ice and desert, mountains and valleys, jungles and plains, hoping to find easier ways to survive in the world. They have gotten into boats and set sail for shores, known and unknown, with little hope of reaching them alive. In part, it is what makes us human: our tireless movement, from here to there and anywhere. "Go from your country and your kindred and your father's house to the land that I will show you," God commands Abraham. And he did so, freely.

But is it a human right to migrate according to need? Or is it a human right for citizens of a sovereign nation to be able to monitor and control their borders? How might a reasonable balance be struck between true compassion and suitable law that guarantees the safety and dignity of all people?

These are questions that are being raised with urgency along the nearly 2,000-mile stretch of border between Mexico and the United States. People from all sides—human rights groups, religious coalitions, law enforcement agencies, legal representatives, ranchers, civil patrol groups, individuals of all ages and political backgrounds—are passionately engaged in the debate.

Grabbing particular attention over the last few years has been the rising numbers of migrant deaths in the Sonoran desert. In the last decade, the remains of approximately 2,000 migrant bodies have been found in this vast desert region, and it is estimated that many hundreds more have perished but have not been found. It is a landscape of striking beauty, with its array of cacti, the largest of them—the native saguaro—growing up to forty-five-feet high; the ironwood trees, which can persist for centuries; mountains jutting dramatically into the stark blue sky; the seemingly infinite expanse of brown and red sands; coyotes slinking through the underbrush; hawks riding the warm vortices of air; lizards and tarantulas scuttling across rocks; roadrunners dashing through the brush; hummingbirds, with stunningly colored wings, flitting about; mountain lions sleeping in the rocky crags of canyons; sunsets that paint the desert purple, imparting a sense of awe to the onlooker. One quickly understands why some Arizonans call themselves "desert rats," why they love the desert and could never imagine leaving it, despite its torrid summers.

Still, the Sonoran desert, and the mountainous area east of it, can pack a deadly punch, especially to migrants, and more rarely to hikers and campers who lose their way in this virtually waterless wilderness. In the summer months, when temperatures easily soar above 100 degrees, death can come in a matter of hours. In the winter months, the temperature can drop so suddenly that death by hyperthermia is not uncommon. *Coalición de Derechos Humanos*, a Tucson-based human rights organization, keeps a record of all the migrant deaths going back to the year 2001. In collaboration with consular records and county medical examiners, the group provides, on its website, the names of all these deceased migrants; their sex; their age; their country of origin; the location where their bodies were recovered; and the cause of death.[1] Sometimes this information is never recovered: the name is left as "unknown," the country and age as "unknown," the cause of death "pending" or "undetermined." But as one glances through the macabre list, one sees that death can come in a variety of ways to unfortunate migrants. We read "gunshot wound of leg," "hyperthermia," "hypothermia," "probable dehydration," "environmental exposure," "blunt force injuries," "undetermined due to skeletal remains," "homicide," "stab wound," and the list goes on.

Southern Arizona is a land of ghosts, so people will tell you. They are not referring to the mesmerizing ghost towns that dot the landscape—the once-booming mining towns now abandoned. Nor are they referring to the famous cowboys shot dead in bar brawls, nor the hanged brothel madams, nor any of the other hapless characters of "the wild west" who are said to haunt the area. They are referring to the ghosts of men, women, and children who over the years—the centuries, really—have succumbed to the unforgiving terrain of the Sonoran desert. From the Spanish explorers and missionaries who first crossed the region, to the gold-seeking forty-niners, many have ventured naïvely into this merciless terrain, only to be overcome by its scorching immensity and to perish of thirst and the elements. But never have so many people died, in such large numbers over so little time, as during the past decade.

Why, so suddenly, has the Sonoran desert turned into a graveyard? Many will argue that the increase in deaths is due to the more stringent border enforcement policies adopted by the U.S. Border Patrol, beginning in the mid-1990s under the Clinton administration. This border "crackdown" included "Operation Hold the Line" (which deployed more troops along the Rio Grande in Texas) and "Operation Gatekeeper" (which bolstered the border in southern California). These operations involved walling off highly trafficked sections of the border, especially the corridor between Tijuana and San Diego; employing high-tech cameras and sensors; greatly increasing the number of Border Patrol agents; implementing checkpoints on U.S. highways; and prosecuting migrants more frequently on the charge of "illegal entry" rather than simply repatriating them under the long-standing policy of "catch and release." Such measures made crossing the border more difficult. As a result, migrants began to venture into more remote and treacherous areas. Rather than taking one of the easier and more conventional routes—by swimming the Rio Grande or dashing across the Tijuana/San Diego divide—they began venturing into the Sonoran desert, the Huachuca and Chiricahua Mountains, and the Coronado National Forest. This became known as "the funnel effect."

The funnel effect quickly turned the Tucson sector into the southwest's deadliest stretch of border. While the Tucson sector, which stretches from Yuma, Arizona, to the New Mexico state line, makes up roughly only 14 percent of the U.S.-Mexican border (a 262-mile stretch), it accounts for half of migrant deaths.[2] "Just over more than half of the deaths occur here in Arizona due to the extreme weather," says Border Patrol Agent Jorge Alejandro Gomez. Moreover, according to official Border Patrol statistics, the Tucson sector is seeing, on average, nearly 50 percent of all "illegal alien apprehensions" in the United States (approximately 317,000 in the 2008–2009 fiscal year).[3] Making matters worse is a confluence of problems: illegal arms being smuggled south to fuel drug cartels and other criminal organizations; the northbound smuggling of illegal substances; America's appetite for cheap labor; and the paradoxes of "free trade" yet "closed borders."

Meanwhile, the northward journey of migrants has become riskier than ever. *Coyotes*, or human smugglers, have been charging exorbitant prices to migrants. Worse still, it is not uncommon for *coyotes* to take advantage of migrants, robbing or raping them, or leaving them stranded in the desert. Just talk to migrants in shelters and they will tell you harrowing stories of survival, of abuse at the hands of *coyotes*, and the despair of being deported. Talk to Border Patrol agents, and they will tell you heartbreaking accounts of migrants they have come across, the ones they have rescued and the ones they could not. Even ranchers will tell stories of sick migrants stumbling across their lands, dazed with dehydration, or of migrants found dead on their properties.

In response to migrant deaths and the overall chaos at the border, people are slipping themselves into ideological wedges. Everyone is demanding change and action. It is the course of action, however, that is a matter of great divide. Broadly speaking, there are those in the Tucson sector (as well as throughout the United States) who turn to religious and ethical claims in attempting to respond to the humanitarian crisis of migrant deaths. Many of these people refer to themselves as "people of faith and conscience," and most espouse some form of the Judeo-Christian concept of radical hospitality. It is a tradition, drawing from the Hebrew Bible and from the New Testament, that exhorts people to exhibit compassion to strangers in need, regardless of kinship or citizenry. In the Tucson sector, "people of faith and conscience" have been trying to live out this principle of biblical hospitality in different ways. Interfaith coalitions have been formed in response to the migrant death spiral. They have been working to provide immediate first aid to migrants in the Sonoran desert in a myriad of ways. Many of these groups also protest what they see as the U.S. government's strategy of further "militarizing" the border, a strategy they deem misguided and ineffectual, ultimately proving deadly to migrants.

On the other ideological shore, there are those who emphasize the need for proper law and order. People on this side—Border Patrol, Minutemen, and many ordinary citizens—have been actively defending the government's position on border enforcement. While the deaths are tragic and the stories of so many migrants are heartbreaking, it is, nonetheless, paramount that the laws of the land be respected. Securing the border is neither inhumane nor draconian they say. It is the right of every nation, and in the best interest of its citizenry, to monitor who is entering and exiting its country. People on this side tend to point to certain statistics, such as the fact that in 2009, 16 percent of "illegal aliens" apprehended in the Tucson sector had criminal records in the United States.[4] Such statistics are used to emphasize the need to vet everyone entering the country. They are also used to defend the heightened security measures—walls, cameras, sensors, extra agents— that "people of faith and conscience" say are pushing migrants too far into the desert. While the majority of men and women entering the country illegally are decent people searching for better lives, says Border Patrol Agent Jorge Alejandro Gomez, it is simply not the case for everyone, and therein lies the problem. Biblically inspired hospitality, while a beautiful ideal, is simply unrealistic in terms of national borders.

And so it goes: the accusations have been flying back and forth. "People of faith and conscience" blame current border enforcement policies for turning the Tucson sector into a graveyard, calling the policies "immoral," "ill conceived," "paranoid," and "racist." At the same time, Border Patrol and their supporters accuse their detractors of being "naïve," "self-righteous," "anarchical," and "unpatriotic."

As the finger pointing goes back and forth and the body count mounts, tensions have been escalating between federal law enforcement agents and "people of faith and conscience" over how to deal with the situation at the border. These are tensions that are reminiscent of the Sanctuary days of the 1980s, when over 500 congregations violated federal law by sheltering illegal immigrants from Central America who were fleeing the ravages of civil war. Those contentious days between law enforcement and interfaith coalitions have been evoked anew over the arrests of faith-based aid workers in the Tucson sector. These high-profile cases—such as that of Shanti Sellz and Daniel Strauss who were accused of "harboring" illegal immigrants (they claimed to be driving three sick migrants to get medical care), or of Dan Millis and Walt Staton who were accused of "littering" on federal lands (they say they were leaving out water jugs for thirsty migrants)—have only widened the gap between factions and exacerbated the mutual acrimony.

What has been shaping up is nothing less than an ideological battle between ordinary Americans forced to grapple with the difficult realities of illegal immigration. It is a confrontation that involves conflicting definitions of certain terms and ideas: What is our moral duty to the stranger in our midst? And what is our moral duty to the nation? How can we respect the integrity of sovereign borders while also respecting the dignity of human beings? How should a border—that seemingly arbitrary line in the sand—be humanely maintained?

Regardless of where one stands, what is clear is that "people of faith and conscience" in the Tucson sector, by confronting federal law enforcement policies, are creating spaces for these sorts of questions to be asked. They are questions that are being asked not just in southern Arizona, or in Texas or California, but throughout the country, from tiny cattle towns in Wyoming to rocky hamlets on the shores of Maine.

And they are questions that lie at the heart of this book. As the Reverend Robin Hoover of Humane Borders says: "In all the major religions, we find accounts of dealing with foreigners, sojourners, strangers. [In the Bible], ways and means were introduced to address the human needs of those who are different, who had permission to be present for an extended time, and who are residents of other lands but who dwelt among the people for a period of time. [In such stories], the principles of rights, dignity, opportunity, and human worth are upheld and enforced."[5] In short, what must be asked is this: How can we "hold up the principles of justice, accommodation, dignity, and even love which have guided the founding of the world's great religions" while also respecting the laws of the land?[6]

How far should one go to follow the "Arab hospitality" of which the poet, Naomi Shihab Nye, writes in her poem "Red Brocade?"[7] Is one meant to open one's house (by extension one's country) unconditionally to a perfect stranger who appears at the door (by extension the border)? Are we meant to feed and tend to that stranger without knowing his story, where he is from, what trouble he has or has not been in; to offer him food, aid, and shelter; and trust that he will bring us (our family, our estate, our home-land) no harm? What are the dangers in offering such an unconditional welcome? Certainly there are both rewards and limits to this kind of radical hospitality.

The following pages are, above all, an attempt to wrestle with this moral dilemma. The people highlighted in them are the ones who come across the thirsty migrants in their backyards, who bandage the wounds, who hear the stories of survival, who search for the dead, who analyze the bones, who track the footprints, who dodge the smugglers' bullets, who fingerprint the apprehended, who, in the most visceral of ways, are confronting the question on a daily basis: How should we treat the strangers who have entered the country illegally?

During months of extensive fieldwork conducted in southern Arizona in 2009, I heard hundreds of stories and testimonies from a range of men and women: migrants, attorneys, Border Patrol agents, ranchers, nuns, pastors, priests, humanitarian aid workers, and members of civil patrol groups. I soon learned that everyone has a story in the borderlands, many stories. You just start talking to people and they start telling you stories. Hearing so many stories strengthened my belief that individual narrative is one of the most compelling and relevant sources of knowledge. Such stories offer a window into the lived experience, lived pain, lived hopes, and lived struggles of others. The issues cannot remain abstract in the face-to-face encounter of such storytelling. By hearing people's struggles firsthand—whether the anger of a rancher over damage done to his property by trespassing migrants, or the migrant who has left three children behind in a violent shantytown north of Mexico City in the hope of providing them with a better life through southbound remittances, or the Border Patrol agent stuck between his loy-alty to law and the pain of finding a baby girl dead in the desert—entrenched partisan views over how to handle immigration, ideally, begin to break down. The stories can act as a catalyst to help each one of us, no matter what strong opinions we may hold, move past the black-and-white divides that plague the current immigration debate.

At best, the stories may help us to *imagine*, if only for a moment, what it is like to be in someone else's shoes. They may help us to think of the problem from a different angle, and to help us move beyond the stereo-types (of the heartless Border Patrol agent, the sanctimonious aid worker, the bigoted Minuteman, the law-breaking immigrant, etc.), so that perhaps, instead of continuing to parrot party lines, everyone can take a small step back and see the problem in a more nuanced, *humanized* light. Even if one does not want to let go of one's strongly held opinions, at the very least, by hearing stories from "the other side," one's own views can be more truly tested.

My aim in these pages has not been to take sides but rather to try to approach the problem in a disinterested fashion; to try to play a bit of the devil's advocate all around; to see the merits and flaws behind clashing philosophies. To this end, I conducted hundreds of interviews with folks in southern Arizona, many of whom held deeply conflicting views. Most of the interviews I conducted were spontaneous and informal. They occurred during long car rides with Border Patrol agents and with faith-based aid workers, in the offices of clergy, at migrant shelters, at musters, and after church meetings. To widen the scope of these stories, I analyzed the writings of key organizations (Humane Borders, No More Deaths, United States Customs and Border Protection, the Minuteman Project, etc.), their brochures, their literature and their websites. I consulted relevant articles in the press, editorials, and theological and political writings on the subject of illegal immigration, especially involving the Tucson sector.

In examining the crisis of migrant deaths in the Sonoran desert, I began to see the problem (like most problems) as one occurring on multiple levels. On the first and most basic level, there are the high-profile squabbles going on between law enforcement agents and faith-based aid workers in the Tucson sector. Take for example the August 2009 arrests of Franciscan priest Jerome Zawada and Quaker activist John Heid at a virtual fence tower site near Sasabe, just twelve miles from the border. The two men said they were praying at the site in protest of the militarization of the border, which they believe is responsible for pushing migrants too far into the desert. They were arrested for trespassing on government property. Or, take the August 2008 confrontation between nearly two dozen Border Patrol agents and No More Deaths members. The confrontation occurred after horse-patrol agents tracked migrant foot-signs to the No More Deaths campsite, where members of the interfaith group base their migrant aid operations. When asked, No More Deaths members said there were no migrants near or at the camp, but a quick search by agents found two migrants. This discovery led to a long and nasty standoff between agents and aid workers. Nor are such confrontations limited to the Tucson sector. In early 2009, for example, Methodist minister John Fanestil was detained for trying to give communion through the border fence at Friendship Park in California. The park had long been a meeting place for relatives and friends who shared meals and conversations through the fence near the San Diego/Tijuana divide.

But in February 2009 the park was closed and a secondary border wall was erected there. Fanestil protested by marching right past Border Patrol barricades, along with dozens of other protestors, and attempting to give communion to folks on the other side of the fence.

These showdowns and others like them point to the larger ideological clash over how to handle the issue of illegal immigration, not just in the Tucson sector but also across the nation. On the one hand, there is the vision of many religious and interfaith activists who turn to a biblically inspired model of hospitality, which stresses love of stranger and a "borderless" sort of compassion. Conflicting with this is the vision of law enforcement, rooted in notions of safety and security, which stresses strict adherence to legal codes and respect for international borders.

The fact that these distinct ways of dealing with the deaths are clashing so fiercely in the Tucson sector points to yet another level: the breakdown, at the federal level, of any sort of constructive immigration reform. In reality, the cause of so many migrant deaths does not lie in the Tucson sector alone but also in the halls of Washington. The unprecedented number of deaths in the Sonoran desert is happening, in large part, because of the U.S. government's inability to envision, compromise on, and enact effective immigration reform. Almost anyone will agree that the current immigration system is shamefully outmoded and inefficient. There has been virtually no movement toward beginning the process of reform at the national level, not only because of the paralyzing partisanship that plagues the debate but also because of the time, money, international collaboration, analysis, dialogue, and vision such reform would require. Immigration reform is not just one issue. It is a set of interconnected issues, each with its own brokenness and inherent complexity. Hence, the rub of trying to "fix" it.

To begin with, how to handle the estimated 11 million undocumented immigrants already living here is a profoundly moral question. There is no shortage of opinions on the matter, from providing legal paths for such immigrants to become citizens; to continuing the raids, incarcerations, and deportations that have marked the last decade; to trying to broker a middle ground between these two core stances. Included in such a debate is the question of family cohesion and/or family reunification, which involves finding acceptable solutions that do not break families apart but that also uphold the integrity of the law. There is also the current visa system, which most say is not adequately working. Some say the U.S. government should issue far more visas and create a proper guest worker program, while others argue against such measures. There is the call for better worker verification programs as well as more advanced systems of vetting, identifying, and tracking immigrants once they are here. These are just some of the short-term questions involved in immigration reform.

The long-term questions are more complicated still and involve, for example, the need to fully understand the intricate and symbiotic economic relationships between Mexico and the United States. They include a certain coming to terms with this country's dependence on cheap labor and the migrant "pull" that such dependence creates. They require acknowledging the harsh disparity of wealth between the two neighboring countries and the concomitant problems of the drug trade, the arms trade, and the illegal human trafficking trade. It is a dizzying web of interconnected problems.

But still, set aside this toxic cocktail of problems (partisanship, economics, drug wars, the human trafficking business, etc.) and there remains another reason the issue of illegal immigration touches such a sensitive nerve in the public at large. That reason points to what I see as the broadest, and most existential level of the equation: our inability (as a nation, perhaps even as a species) to deal with what Jean-Paul Sartre called "the problem of the existence of others." In many ways, at its core, illegal immigration is about this: the threats, perceived or otherwise, that the mere existence of others poses to our well-being. It is about the difficulties inherent in the encounter between self and other, especially when the other is a radical stranger, a noncitizen, an *alien*. While the term "alien" has clear derogatory undertones, it is nonetheless fitting in certain ways, since it expresses the absolute "otherness" of the illegal immigrant's status. For all of history, the "wholly other" has captured our imagination, sparked fear, invoked desire, caused us to commit all sort of acts, both heinous and altruistic. In the end, effective immigration reform and a viable solution to the deaths in the desert will be connected to our ability to admit to the fears, projections, and other existential emotions that others illicit in us.

Since the Tucson sector is my area of focus, I will not, as a result, expound on the topic of national immigration reform or U.S. immigration law, although I will address it where doing so is vital. There are many fine books on these topics to which I must refer the reader. Nor will I tackle the problem from "the Mexican side of things," although it must be stated that the United States is not fully to blame for migrant deaths and migrant suffering. The recent and gruesome massacre of seventy-two migrants south of the border, in Tamaulipas state, at the hands of drug cartel members, is proof that Mexico too must reckon with its shadows. The widespread abuse of migrants, mainly Central American, in Mexico has been well documented by esteemed human rights groups and condemned by countless governments and international organizations. Beyond the official reports of migrant abuse in Mexico (the robbery, rape, murder, and kidnapping at the hands of criminal gangs, human smugglers, and corrupt Mexican officials), sadly, all one need do to verify this abuse is visit a migrant shelter or soup kitchen at the border. Talk to migrants there, and before long a migrant will tell a gut-wrenching story about the terror and abuse he or she experienced on the journey through Mexico.

With these heart-aching complexities in mind, the project has been divided into two parts. The first half is devoted to examining the ways in which Judeo-Christian scripture has inspired a captivating humanitarian movement in the Tucson sector. It looks at how collections of clergy, laity, and other "people of faith and conscience" are responding to the migrant death spiral in the Sonoran desert. Here, as throughout, my methodology is mainly ethnographic. Keeping the ethnographic texture at the forefront of these pages, I begin by highlighting a soup kitchen in the border town of Nogales, Sonora, run by three Mexican Sisters of the Eucharist. Following, I will reflect back on the Sanctuary movement of the 1980s to more closely examine how biblically inspired notions of hospitality clashed with law enforcement then and how they continue to do so now, nearly three decades later. Then I look at two more "migrant ministries" based out of Tucson— Humane Borders and No More Deaths—and examine how these ministries are living out the biblical call "to love stranger as self" in an effort to aid migrants.

In the second half of the project, I take up the viewpoints of those who, while voicing concern for the well-being of migrants, come down on the side of law. I offer some reflections on the unprecedented U.S.-Mexican barrier wall that is being constructed in southern Arizona, as a way of speaking about the logic behind current border enforcement strategies. Following, I describe time spent at a Patriot's Coalition muster and during a Border Patrol ride-along, with the goal of asking, What is everyone so afraid of? What lies behind anti-illegal immigration sentiment? Last, I address Arizona's controversial law, Senate Bill 1070, as a way of discussing larger existential conflicts lying at the heart of the immigration debate before offering some concluding remarks.

The center of this project, it should not be forgotten, is death. At the beginning is death; and at the end, there is death also. The pages in between attempt to examine the role of compassion and the role of law in the immigration controversy in Arizona. But remember, even as you read these words, that someone is almost certainly setting out into the Sonoran desert, taking his or her first footstep into the wilderness. There is someone who has just finished her last water bottle and who is looking out, in all directions, at the endless landscape of cactus and mountain. There is someone tending to his blisters, wondering how to keep on walking. There is someone handing her money to a human smuggler, in Sasabe, or Nogales, or Naco, and praying for safekeeping. And there is someone at the coroner's office in Tucson, examining bones on a gurney.

While the Tucson sector serves as the epicenter of my research, the issue is relevant far beyond the dusty, cactus-strewn confines of Arizona. Places like Malta, Italy, and Spain, for example, are reeling with a similar ethical quandary. In recent years, these southern European countries have seen thousands of illegal immigrants from Africa turn up on their shores. These are immigrants who have risked their lives to cross the sea in rickety boats (as hundreds more perish trying to) in search of better lives. With the recent and continuing political upheaval in North Africa, there will certainly be more migrants undertaking this perilous journey, forcing the citizens of little rocky Mediterranean islands, such as Lampedusa or Malta, to continue to ask themselves eerily similar questions: How do we respond to the stranger at the door, of whom we know nothing, the totally "other"? While law enforcement, under the jurisdiction of the European Union, has been setting up detention camps and other controversial legal mechanisms to deal with the influx in recent years, religious coalitions have been mobilizing to provide the same sort of radical hospitality (to African migrants) that many Tucsonans have been giving (to Latin American migrants) thousands of miles away.

Meanwhile, back in the halls of Washington, immigration reform looms awkwardly on the horizon. Until we as a nation are able to envision and enact more humane and effective immigration policies, the deaths in the desert will continue. The deaths are simply a symptom of a larger crisis. How the United States deals with its borders and with the migrants who cross them has, unfortunately, become a question of life or death. Any solution must be intensely dialogical. It will require respectful, rational, patient, and protracted conversation, not only among politicians and lobbyists in Washington but also among human rights workers, activists, policy makers, clergy and laity, law enforcement officials, academics, economists, business owners, and average citizens living at the U.S.-Mexican border.

"I have always found that mercy bears richer fruits than strict justice," said Abraham Lincoln. If there is one thing everyone agrees with in southern Arizona, it is that the deaths in the desert must stop. The question that remains unresolved is this: How best to stop them? The role of mercy and the role of justice, and the balance forged between, remains unknown.

PART I

God in the Desert: Migrant Deaths and the Rise of Border Ministries

CHAPTER 1

A Window into the Crisis:
Three Nuns and a Soup Kitchen

I n Nogales, Mexico, Sister María Engracia Robles is standing over a large
tin pot filled with beans. With the small bony fingers of her left hand,
she stirs the contents of the pot while simultaneously dishing out rice
with her right hand onto colorful plastic plates. Sister Robles, a member
of the Sisters of the Eucharist, is one of three nuns who runs El Comedor,
a soup kitchen in Nogales, Mexico, just a few hundred feet from the
U.S.-Mexican border. Every day, she and the other two sisters, Alma Delia
Isaías and Imelda Ruiz, feed as many as 300 men, women, and children who
have recently been deported from the United States and left in Nogales to
fend for themselves.

Each dawn, one of the three sisters heads out into the cold desert air and
makes her way to El Comedor. Often, when she arrives to unlock the gate,
there is already a long line of people extending down the sidewalk. Some
are wounded, to varying degrees of severity. Many shiver in place, jumping
up and down to keep warm. As soon as one of the sisters opens the gate,
the migrants pour into El Comedor, gaining access to the soup kitchen by
showing the stub of paper they received from U.S. Immigration and
Customs Enforcement (ICE) upon deportation.

El Comedor is a cramped space, enclosed by a chain-link fence and sheltered from the rain by a few slats of corrugated metal overhead. One can
walk from one end to another in just a few steps. There are several metal
tables and a closet filled with donated goods, mostly clothes, shoes, and
medical supplies. Off to one side is the kitchen, big enough for only two
people to stand in. Somehow, in this minuscule space, the sisters, along
with a volunteer from Guadalajara, Federico Cabrera, manage to cook

impressive amounts of beans, rice, tuna casseroles, and vegetable sautés—depending on what food they receive each day from donors. They serve two meals a day, breakfast and a late lunch, except on Sundays.

"We cook whatever we get," Sister Robles says, as I peer into the kitchen in amazement, watching her prepare for lunch."It's different every day."

Sister Robles is a tiny woman with silver hair, an angular face, and small expressive eyes. But despite her diminutive stature, she is a well of strength and determination. Despite the daily suffering she witnesses, she never tires. Instead, what she sees only fuels her resolve.

Before every meal, Sister Robles turns on a microphone to say a prayer. "Thank you Lord for this food we have received," she begins. Her prayer is peppered with much coughing. Many of the migrants are sick. Sister Robles raises her voice slightly, so that she may be heard above the coughing. "May you guide them safely in their journeys Lord," she booms. She knows as well as anyone that the journey can take them almost anywhere: into the hands of the Border Patrol; or to some far-flung town or city in the United States where they have friends or relatives; or into the hands of a bad *coyote* who might rob or rape them, or leave them stranded in the desert.

El Comedor was opened in 2008 in response to the unprecedented influx of deported migrants arriving in Nogales. This surge was the result of heightened Border Patrol enforcement in the Tucson sector, including construction of the new wall (by order of "The Secure Fence Act of 2006"), high-tech cameras and sensors, the increase in Border Patrol agents, and, in particular, the addition of mass trials. These trials occur daily in the DeConcini Courthouse in Tucson. They are part of a new program known as the Arizona Denial Prosecution Initiative, or, more familiarly, as Operation Streamline. Operation Streamline mirrors similar programs in Texas and California and aims at deterring migrants from trying to illegally reenter the United States. Rather than continuing with the old policy of "voluntary return" (often dubbed "catch and release"), in which migrants are simply returned to Mexico after quickly being processed, now approximately 10 percent of apprehended migrants are brought to trial.[1] In being found guilty of "illegal entry," these migrants are given a criminal record and banned from entering the United States for several years. Many of the migrants have been captured before and hence are tried for the crime of "illegal reentry," resulting in harsher punishments.

Every afternoon, in a special courtroom of the DeConcini Courthouse, roughly seventy migrants are tried at once. The majority of the defendants are male. They sit together on benches, shackled, their chains ringing eerily throughout the courtroom with every slight movement they make. There is a separate bench for women migrants, also heavily shackled. Throughout the courtroom a pungent smell of stale sweat and other body odors permeates the air; most of the migrants are in the same unwashed clothes they were wearing when apprehended by the Border Patrol. The trial for each migrant lasts, on average, thirty seconds. One by one, migrants are identified by the judge, asked if they are citizens of Mexico (or another, usually Central American, nation), if they understand their rights, and finally, how they plead to the charge of illegal entry (or reentry). In almost all cases, they plead, "*culpable*," guilty. Each defendant wears a black headset through which simultaneous translation into Spanish is broadcast. Sometimes, when the defendant's native language is other than Spanish, such as an indigenous language like Nahautl, Mixtec, or Zapotec, an interpreter is present as well.

When the trial is over, the approximately seventy men and women who have been found guilty shuffle, chains rattling, out of the courtroom. Most are loaded onto buses and driven south to the U.S.-Mexican border where they are dropped off, deportation papers in hand. There is no standard port of entry where deportees are left. Some are dropped off in Naco, others in Sasabe, and still others in Nogales. Many are wounded from their long and unsuccessful treks through the desert. Many more are wearing the same clothes they have been in for weeks. Most have nothing to eat, no money, and often no passports or papers. That is how so many end up at the gates of El Comedor in Nogales, looking for food, clean clothes, new sneakers, medical attention, some advice or support.

Along with El Comedor, the three sisters also opened up a small shelter for unaccompanied women and their children: El Albergue Para Mujeres Caminantes (Shelter for Women Migrants). The sisters saw how vulnerable migrant women and children were, especially at night when a confluence of illegal activities—human smuggling, sex trafficking, and drug running—really gets underway. The shelter has eight beds, a small kitchen, and a common area. The shelter and the soup kitchen are part of the Kino Border Initiative, just one of dozens of Christian and interfaith ministries on the border trying to alleviate the suffering of migrants and deportees. The project, which celebrated its official inauguration on January 18, 2009, in a mass in Nogales, is funded by the Jesuit Refugee Service of America and other Catholic service organizations.

"We are trying to respond to what is most needed by migrants," Father Martin McCintosh explained to me on my first visit to El Comedor. He is one of four Jesuit priests who work in tandem with the three sisters on the Kino Border Initiative. He was raised in Tijuana and, having witnessed the plight of migrants on a daily basis all his life, feels called to the work he is doing. "So far, the sisters have set up the soup kitchen and the shelter for women," McCintosh added. "Now we are trying to buy land to open a health clinic. It is sorely needed here in Nogales."

Within five minutes of my first visit to El Comedor, I saw what McCintosh meant by the desperate need for a health clinic. I watched Maryada Vallet, a volunteer for No More Deaths, offer her services as an emergency medical technician (EMT). They are services that are indispensable. Many of those who come to eat are also sick or wounded from the journey and in desperate need of medical attention. Within minutes of my arrival at El Comedor, a young Honduran man flagged Maryada down. He was hunched up and shivering. He had rolled up the right pant leg of his sweatpants, exposing the flesh of his thigh, the length of which was covered by a deep open wound that penetrated down to the muscle and bone.

"Oh my Gosh!" Maryada's long-lashed eyes popped open. "What happened to you?"

"On the train," the man said. "A big piece of metal got me." By the train, he meant one of the freight trains that many Central American migrants ride by the hundreds. The train travels nearly 1,000 miles from the Guatemalan border through the length of Mexico. It is known by those who ride it as *La Bestia*, or the Beast, and more commonly still as El Tren de la Muerte, the Train of Death. Many migrants lose their lives riding atop the boxcars. They fall off, or worse, they are pushed off by gang members, robbed or raped. Many lose limbs in the attempt to mount the train. It is a treacherous journey. In fact, the Honduran man with the gaping wound in his thigh is lucky in certain ways. He did not lose his leg, and he had made it all the way to Nogales. "I'm so close," he said to Maryada, as she bent over him, examining his leg, trying to figure out what to do. "So close to the United States. It's just over the hill, isn't it?"

"Yes," Maryada said as she poured iodine solution over his thigh. It spilled off in thin red rivulets, splashing to the ground. He winced. "But you really should go to a hospital," Maryada urged him. "This is a very bad wound. You could die from it. I don't have any antibiotics for you, and this already looks septic."

The man clicked his tongue and raised his right index finger, waving it in the air, in a gesture that meant: *No, I will not go to the hospital.* Being Honduran, he knew there was a chance that one of the Mexican doctors might report him to the authorities, and that after all his effort, he would be deported back to Honduras.

"But you can't cross like that, *buey*," said another concerned migrant who grimaced as he stared down at the wound. "Really, you should go to the hospital."

Maryada bandaged up the man's thigh and urged him once more to seek medical attention. "I can't," he said, "but thank you." Then he turned, exited El Comedor, and began hopping down the street, his injured leg stiff as a board. It was hard to imagine him walking a block like that, let alone across the desert.

"Good luck!" Maryada called out, but her words were lost on the wind.

There was another man with a wound on the inside of his left forearm, one long slash that ran from wrist to elbow. "I was robbed in the desert by the *coyote*," he explained. He had knife wounds on his face as well, above the lip, between the eyes, and at the hairline near his ear. Maryada disinfected his wounds and moved on to the next problem.

There were blisters to tend to, fevers, coughs, and gastrointestinal problems. There was a man who was recently deported from Bakersville, California, where he had lived for nearly a decade before being arrested in a raid. He was clutching a book to his chest, *Cómo Librarse de la Encarcelación* (How to Get Yourself Out of Prison). His eyes were glassy, his forehead glistening with sweat. He was diabetic, he told Maryada, and he had not received treatment since he was detained. Two of his toes were infected with gangrene. Maryada quickly tested his blood sugar, which, not surprisingly, turned out to be dangerously high.

"I don't know what to do about this guy," Maryada said to me. Suddenly, things were beyond her ken and beyond the resources of the soup kitchen. She called a nurse back in Tucson for advice. But while she was talking to the nurse, the man slipped out of El Comedor unnoticed and disappeared into the streets of Nogales.

By then, it was getting dark. The last of the migrants who had stayed long after mealtime to have their wounds tended, straggled out of the soup kitchen and into the night. The penetrating sunlight of the Sonoran desert had receded; in its place was a biting wind and long shadows. I was amazed at how cold it had become so suddenly, and I understood how it was possible for migrants to die of hypothermia in the desert. I was about to leave the soup kitchen myself, to take the five-minute walk back to the port of legal entry, when Sister Alma Delia Isaías popped into the gate. She had spent the day cleaning up the women's shelter, and had come down the hill to El Comedor to see how the day had gone.

"Busy, busy!" cried out Sister Robles who was cutting yellow squash in the kitchen, preparing for the next day's barrage of deported migrants. "What happened with the woman and her two children?"

"They left," said Sister Isaías. "They are going to try to cross tonight I think."

I asked what woman they were talking about. Sister Isaías explained that it was a migrant who had been staying with them at El Albergue for the past few nights, a single mother and her two young children.

"Doesn't it make you sad to see so much suffering every day?" I asked Sister Isaías.

"Yes, of course," she said.

"How do you make sense of it?" I asked. "I mean, why would God have it this way?" Knowing that she was a woman of faith, I felt compelled to ask how she reconciled suffering and belief.

"God doesn't want it this way," she shook her head, then smiled. "He weeps for his children. That is why it is up to us to help our brothers and sisters however we can. It is God's wish for us to do this."

"So you never get tired of cutting squash?" I called back to Sister Robles in the kitchen.

"Tired to death," she said. "But it feels good to know it makes a difference."

I sat down with Sister Isaías on one of the metal benches and asked her why she chose to become a nun and how she wound up there, in Nogales of all places, tending to migrants. Through the *chop-chop-chop* of squash in the kitchen, in the fading light, she said that she could not fully explain it. She described going on vacation with her family several years earlier, when she was in her early twenties. She described how lucky she felt to be on vacation, in such a lovely spot. For whatever reason—she could not quite say—it made her begin to think about those who were less fortunate. Something about that vacation made her want to become a nun. More specifically, she wanted to take care of migrants. There were shelters all throughout Mexico, she explained, funded and run by different Catholic orders and organizations, a sort of underground railroad for migrants. She had spent several years in two other migrant shelters in Mexico. One shelter in particular had left an impression on her: the one in a small village in southern Mexico, on the highly traveled migrant route taken by many Central Americans. She described the terrible suffering of the Central American migrants that she had helped, how they were abused by Mexican authorities, robbed and raped by Mexican gangs. "If you think the Mexican migrants suffer, you should hear the stories of those coming from Central America," she said.

"Are you happy here in Nogales?" I asked her.

"Yes, I hope to stay here many more years. It is so interesting being so close to the United States. I am even learning a little bit of English," she smiled. Then she stood up. "If you're going back tonight," she said, "you better go now. I know it's a short walk, but it's not safe."

Sister Isaías unlocked the gate of the soup kitchen and let me out. "Good luck with all that squash," I called back to Sister Robles. Then I scurried, heart pounding, toward the port of legal entry. Indeed, the walk was not far, but with the escalation of drug-related violence throughout Mexico, especially in border towns, the sense of threat was palpable. I was relieved, a few minutes later, to see the U.S. customs booths. Before proceeding to them,

I paused to look at the crowd of nervous migrants who had gathered in the darkness on the hill overlooking the chain-link fence dividing the United States from Mexico. They were all getting ready to cross. Some were waiting for the right moment to try to scale the fence; but most were joining up with *coyotes* who would take them further east or west of Nogales and deeper into the desert.

I noticed a car screech to a halt. A woman and her three children scrambled out from the back seat. Immediately a *coyote* whistled in her direction. She grabbed her children (the youngest barely able to walk) and ran in his direction. I could not help wondering how that mother's journey would end. Would she and her children be picked up by the U.S. Border Patrol within minutes of attempting to cross? Would they venture into the desert and walk all through the night, the children too? Would the *coyote* take advantage of her, steal her money, leave her in the desert, or worse? One thing was for sure: If she and her children were deported to Nogales, they would most likely wind up at El Comedor.

One day at El Comedor, one window into the disturbing reality of the immigration crisis. From Tijuana to Brownsville, in the many towns and cities that straddle the troubled divide between the United States and Mexico, one can find dozens of soup kitchens like El Comedor. While the dedication of the nuns is inspiring and the stories migrants tell are heartbreaking, places like El Comedor are, sadly, not unique. At almost any Mexican border town or city, one can find a shelter or a soup kitchen run by nuns, priests, and other religiously inspired men and women who, motivated in part by a biblical tradition of radical hospitality, are trying to alleviate the suffering of migrants in places like Nogales. These sisters, fathers, and other clergy and laity, as well as individual citizens inspired by a sense of moral obligation, do not consider the ways in which crossing the border illegally is a violation of federal laws. They believe that, first and foremost, it is their duty to serve, shelter, and aid migrants in distress.

In fact, during one of my later visits to El Comedor, Sister Isaías lamented that some of the people she had fed that day were most certainly gang members, as evidenced by their tattoos.

"How do you feel about that?" I asked her.

She rolled her eyes with a hint of dismay. "Well," she said, "I can't control what they did in the past. God calls me to help them as they are now. All I can hope is that it makes a difference."

Much of Sister Isaías's motivation is rooted in a biblical principle of hospitality. It is a principle of unconditional service and love to those in need by those of means. Sister Isaías's job is not to weed out God's wayward children. Nor is it to enforce international boundaries, or to judge those who cross them without papers. Her job, like that of the other sisters, is to open the gates of the soup kitchen to one and all, and to feed every stranger with a deportation ticket, without asking who he is, where he's coming from, where he's headed. It is this tradition of unconditional hospitality that motivates women like Sister Robles, Sister Isaías, and Sister Ruiz, all along the U.S.-Mexican border. Thus, let us now examine the biblical roots and principles of this tradition. To do so, it is useful to reflect upon the Sanctuary movement of the 1980s and to see how those Sanctuary days have been evoked anew in recent years along the border.

CHAPTER 2

Sanctuary Old and New: The Biblical Tradition of Radical Hospitality

On July 17, 1980, in his acceptance speech for the Republican nomination for the presidency of the United States, Ronald Reagan asked: "Can we doubt that only a Divine Providence placed this land, this island of freedom here as a refuge for all those people who yearn to breath free?" Only a few days before, some thirty-one Salvadorans were found lost in the vast and scorching wilderness of Organ Pipe Cactus National Monument in southern Arizona.[1] Of those thirty-one, thirteen had perished of dehydration in the triple-digit heat. Those who survived had harrowing stories to tell. They told of slipping through barbed wire fence on the night of July 3, carrying suitcases with Bibles and winter clothes and only a few water jugs.[2] They told how, within hours of sunrise, the desert floor had turned into a blistering inferno. They had blundered about aimlessly, defeated by the monstrous heat. They had drunk perfume and aftershave lotion after their water quickly ran out. They had thrown off their clothes, hallucinated, and eaten sand. In the end, thirteen died while the rest clung perilously to life.

Equally as harrowing were the stories the survivors told after they recovered—stories of what they had left behind in their war-torn homeland. They told of seeing loved ones murdered, villages burned to the ground, women raped, children conscripted into guerilla groups or government forces and of the certain death that awaited them if they were to be deported by the United States government.[3] The survivors were seeking asylum, but since they had entered the country illegally, they were held in jail as U.S. authorities decided what to do with them. Many residents of the Tucson area were upset by the stories of suffering they were hearing from the refugees. In particular, many felt that the United States—their own country—was particularly at fault for the plight of these Central American refugees. In Nicaragua, for example, the war to overthrow the revolutionary socialist party, the Sandinista National Liberation Front (*Frente Sandinista de Liberación Nacional*), was heavily funded by the United States that, immersed in Cold War politics, saw the Sandinistas as a threat to U.S. interests and the pursuit of global democracy. As a result, the United States both funded and trained the oppositional forces known as the Contras. The Contras' counteroffensive measures were known to be brutal, including controversial strategies of terror, propaganda, and conscription. Similarly, in El Salvador, the United States funded the military-led government against left-wing revolutionary groups of the Farabundo Martí National Liberation Front (*Frente Farabundo Martí para la Liberación Nacional,* or *FMLN*). Likewise, El Salvador's U.S.-backed military government was known for brutal tactics of repression, torture, and conscription. In short, the United States' hands were not clean, so to speak, when it came to the realities and suffering of hundreds of thousands of Central American refugees.

Back in Tucson, many wanted to help the Salvadorans who had fled to the United States and who had survived the perilous trek through Organ Pipe. In particular, local clergy and laity joined together and raised $2,000 to free the survivors on bond.[4] In the months, and ultimately the years, that followed, more Salvadorans would pour over the border into southern Arizona with similar accounts of torture and terror. Overnight, Ronald Reagan's pronouncement concerning God's exceptional plan for America as a haven for refugees who "yearn to breathe free" was put to the test. Quickly, however, local law enforcement agencies, under the jurisdiction of the U.S. federal government, began turning Salvadorans away, sending them back to their country.[5] Obviously, some refugees belonged to that Divine Providence while others did not.

Clergy in the Tucson area took particular umbrage with what they deemed a system of biased selectivity in matters of asylum. They cited the United Nations Convention and Protocol Relating to the Status of Refugees, a 1951 international convention (adopted in 1954 and updated in 1967), which defined who was a refugee; the rights of refugees, especially concerning asylum; and the duties and responsibilities of asylum-granting nations. The Convention, signed onto by the United States, defined a refugee as anyone who "owing to well-founded fear of being persecuted for reasons of race, religion, nationality, membership of a particular social group or political opinion, is outside the country of his nationality and is unable or, owing to such fear, is unwilling to avail himself of the protection of that country."[6] The Convention further stated that such refugees not be penalized or deported by receiving nations. Hence, certain political activists in and around Tucson argued that the surviving Salvadorans (and soon, the many more who would also cross the border in search of asylum) should be allowed to stay. Sending the Salvadorans back amounted to a breach of human rights and, essentially, international law, they said.

Adding to the moral outrage of many Tucsonans over the treatment of the Salvadorans was that just months before they crossed the border in search of asylum, President Jimmy Carter had signed into law the Refugee Act of 1980, which reaffirmed the definition of a refugee established by the United Nations High Commissioner for Refugees (UNHCR). In his statement on signing the Act into law, Carter asserted:

> The Refugee Act reflects our long tradition as a haven for people uprooted by persecution and political turmoil. In recent years, the number of refugees has increased greatly. Their suffering touches all and challenges us to help them.... The Refugee Act establishes a new admissions policy that will permit fair and equitable treatment of refugees in the United States, regardless of their country of origin.[7]

But still, in the months and years that followed, many asylum-seeking Central Americans were not given safe haven. They were deported despite their assertions that they would be found and killed for having deserted or having fought for the revolutionary groups into which many were forcibly conscripted. Some U.S. officials argued that these Central Americans did not fit into the definition of a refugee. They cited the section of the UNHCR's Convention and Protocol Relating to the Status of Refugees that anyone who has "committed a crime against peace, a war crime, or a crime against humanity" does not qualify as a refugee.[8] Most of those seeking asylum had been involved in the civil war; many had killed and many, in the eyes of the United States, had been involved with the wrong side, such as with Sandinista rebels, or with FMLN rebels. Hence, many of those seeking asylum did not fall under the UNHCR's definition of a refugee. Nor, as a result, did Carter's 1980 Refugee Act, which proclaimed the equitable treatment of refugees "regardless of their country of origin," seem to apply to most Central Americans.

However, many activists argued that United States refugee policy was simply not neutral. It arbitrarily granted asylum to those refugees who were "of special humanitarian concern to the United States," in effect enabling the government to give preference to certain refugee groups over others.[9] In the end, "cold war politics trumped refugee legislation, and those fleeing right-wing government or military persecution were generally denied refugee or asylum status. In Tucson, clergy observed this hypocrisy when they saw Salvadorans and Guatemalans routinely forced to sign 'voluntary departure' forms, in effect deporting them back to Central America."[10]

Among the clergy who sprang into action in response to the waves of
Central Americans seeking (and being denied) asylum were the Reverend
John Fife of Tucson's Southside Presbyterian church and the Quaker Jim
Corbett. In a short matter of time, these two men became the fulcrum of
what would soon be called the Sanctuary movement. They rounded up
other clergy from diverse faith groups in the Tucson area, forming the
Tucson Ecumenical Council Task Force on Central America. "They began
helping undocumented Guatemalans and Salvadorans who had been
detained by [the Immigration and Naturalization Service; INS] at the
border zone. They posted bond, offered legal assistance with INS
deportation hearings, and prepared asylum applications."[11] When the
government continued deporting the refugees, the Task Force began
providing shelter for them in churches and private homes, effectively
breaking the law.

Members of the task force also began meeting refugees at the border and
finding ways to send them to other churches across the United States and
even into Canada. "They envisioned a new underground railroad for the
'feet people' of Central America, modeled on the nineteenth-century band
of abolitionists and Quakers who smuggled slaves up to freedom from the
antebellum South."[12] Like the underground railroad, which was in "direct
violation of the Fugitive Slave Law of 1850, prohibiting the harboring or
assistance of runaway slaves anywhere in the United States," and similar to
the way, during the Vietnam War, that churches and campuses sheltered
draftees and servicemen who refused to fight in Vietnam "as an act of civil
disobedience, rooted in moral opposition to an unjust war," clergy like Fife
and Corbett had no qualms with going against what they saw as unjust
laws.[13] Theirs was a "political protest dramatizing a conflict between
individual conscience and government."[14] As John Fife wrote:

> In spite of the judgment of the U.N. High Commission on Refugees and every inter-
> national human rights organization, the U.S. government refused to recognize people
> fleeing the conditions of Central America as refugees. The subsequent deportations and
> death squads and massacres confronted the church of North America with a fundamental
> question of ethics and faith.[15]

Motivated by their Christian faith, Fife and Corbett, along with a growing
cadre of religious activists, began to mobilize in the effort to provide safe
haven for Central American refugees. Volunteers involved in the movement
walked many Central Americans across the border. Once across, these refugees were shepherded to churches throughout the United States and
Canada, where they were given a place to stay and often set up with jobs in
the local community. In Tucson, refugees by the dozens were sleeping in

the Southside Presbyterian Church. Meanwhile, John Fife wrote a letter to Attorney General William French Smith, in which he said:

> We are writing to inform you that Southside United Presbyterian Church will publicly violate the Immigration and Nationality Act, Section 274 (A)....We take this action because we believe the current policy and practice of the United States Government with regard to Central American refugees is illegal and immoral....We believe that justice and mercy require that people of conscience actively assert our God-given right to aid anyone fleeing from persecution and murder. The current administration of United States law prohibits us from sheltering refugees from Central America. Therefore, we believe that administration of the law is immoral as well as illegal. We beg of you, in the name of God, to do justice and love mercy in the administration of your office. We ask that "extended voluntary departure" be granted to refugees from Central America and that current deportation proceedings against these victims be stopped. Until such time, we will not cease to extend the sanctuary of the church to undocumented people from Central America. Obedience to God requires this of us all.[16]

Indeed, Fife and Corbett and hundreds of their followers continued to shelter refugees. They did so in the name of their God, citing biblical law over U.S. federal law. This act of defiance raised many questions concerning the limits of religious freedom in America. What was an individual meant to do when he or she deemed the law immoral, as during slavery, the Vietnam War, or the civil wars of Central America? What happened when a group, such as those involved in the Sanctuary movement, justified their actions by claiming the legitimacy of religious law (or the idea of a higher ethical law) over federal law?

In Tucson, I met with the Reverend John Fife to ask him about this question. He explained his decision to break the law as "a moral imperative." A tall, lanky man in cowboy boots and a denim jacket, Fife told me that there was no doubt in his mind about what he needed to do. "When I started hearing stories from these refugees, I thought, 'Hey, we can't just sit here and do nothing.... We can't just let our Central American brothers and sisters die.' So, we started meeting them in Mexico and walking them through the desert into this country and giving them a place to stay. We didn't even really care much about the authorities, although they sure cared a lot about us."[17]

Moreover, Fife explained, he and Corbett came to see that they were not violating corrupt, or morally misguided, laws. In fact, in their opinion the U.S. government was violating its own laws. The government, by not granting asylum to Central American refugees, was in violation of both the UNHCR's Convention and the Refugee Act signed by President Carter. Corbett gave a new term to what the Sanctuary movement was doing.

Unlike "civil disobedience," in which activists deliberately broke unjust laws, Fife and Corbett coined what they were doing as "civil initiative." Civil initiative is defined as "the legal right and the moral responsibility of society to protect the victims of human rights violations when government is the violator." As Fife wrote:

> Since the government had threatened the churches who had declared sanctuary with indictment and prosecution, our assumption was that we were engaging in "civil disobedience" in the tradition of Thoreau, Gandhi, and King. In public statements, sermons, and interviews all these prophets of civil disobedience were quoted freely to explain the Sanctuary movement. A phone call from a human rights lawyer a month later put an end to all of those eloquent quotes from Dr. King. "You are doing more harm to human rights and refugee law than anyone else I know," he began. "Listen carefully! You are not doing civil disobedience. Civil disobedience is [publicly] violating a bad law, and assuming the consequences, in order to change an unjust law. We don't want to change U.S. refugee law. It conforms to international standards. The problem is that the government is violating our own refugee law. The government is doing civil disobedience!"[18]

Protesting what they saw as the U.S. government's breaking of its own laws through "civil initiative," Sanctuary movement participants also found justification for their actions through their shared Judeo-Christian faith. Participants relied on key biblical passages (and their interpretations of them) to justify their breach of immigration law. Concerning the actual act of "harboring" refugees, the movement relied on Numbers 35:11:

> The Lord spoke to Moses, saying: Speak to the Israelites, and say to them: When you cross the Jordan into the land of Canaan, then you shall select cities to be cities of refuge for you, so that a slayer who kills a person without intent may flee there. Then cities shall be for you a refuge from the avenger, so that the slayer may not die until there is a trial before the congregation.[19]

Sanctuary activists cited this quote and others like it "as a kind of ancient model for their movement. Various verses in the Old Testament describe 'cities of refuge,' where someone guilty of causing accidental death can escape the dead man's bloodthirsty relatives."[20] In the case of the Sanctuary movement, some of the men seeking refuge in the United States had been involved with leftist guerrilla groups fighting against the government. Regardless of whether refugees had been involved in the fighting or were simply fleeing the calamities of civil war, activists like Fife and Corbett believed they deserved sanctuary, modeled after the biblical tradition. They knew that "the ancient Hebrews had allowed temples and even whole cities to declare themselves places of refuge for persons accused of a crime, a practice that allowed those wrongfully accused to escape swift and harsh retribution until the matter could be resolved. In the late Roman Empire fugitives could be harbored on the precincts of Christian churches. Later during the medieval period, when canon law rivaled secular authority, churches in England were recognized sanctuaries, offering safe haven for a temporary period to accused wrongdoers."[21]

Concerning the Sanctuary movement of the 1980s, the Reverend Alexia Salvatierra has said, "Central American refugees were unable to receive a fair asylum hearing because different standards were set for asylum-seekers from countries allied with the U.S.... To avoid deportation and the threat of assassination, Central American refugees asked Christian congregations for refuge, provoking the ancient practice of sanctuary. Congregations, upon hearing their stories, agreed that they had received unjust treatment and refused to turn them over to federal immigration agents until they could receive a fair hearing."[22] She says further:

> Human beings have always had a tendency to demonize. In biblical times, when someone died by another's action, even if it was unintentional or unavoidable, the typical reaction was a blood feud. The family of the deceased treated the one responsible for the death as a murderer and sought vengeance right away. But in the book of Numbers, we find a creative strategy for counteracting this human tendency. Those who claimed to have killed another by accident could be protected until they could receive a fair hearing. The people of God created sacred places of refuge, or sanctuary, in which the fugitive could find safety and the assurance of justice. Over the centuries, the church often has recalled the concept of sanctuary.[23]

Needless to say, government officials were not pleased by this "creative strategy" adopted by Tucson clergy and laity. They stressed that not only was the government following its own laws properly, but furthermore, the United States of America was a democracy, not a theocracy. The founding fathers had made it clear that the separation of church and state was paramount to a healthy democratic society. Hence, the act of providing "sanctuary" amounted to breaking federal law, which trumped any religious law.

However, those involved in the Sanctuary movement were not dissuaded. In effect, biblical and sacred texts served as the primary justification for challenging (or breaking, depending on opinion) the law, trumping government authority or cold war rationale. The religious activists were not shy about declaring their religious motivations. David Napier, a biblical scholar and participant in sanctuary, cited the Hebrew Bible as justification for the Sanctuary movement's defiance of U.S. law. He wrote, "Hear the Hebrew Bible: 'Never mind what *they* tell you to do: your peers, the electorate, your governmental prophets and priests. What God requires of you is the doing of justice.' "[24]

But what was it that Sanctuary participants were *hearing* from the Bible? What was it that God required of them in terms of doing justice? Not surprisingly, what they were hearing nearly three decades ago is similar to what those involved in Tucson's current border ministries are hearing today. Of particular import is the biblical tradition of radical hospitality found in both the Hebrew Scriptures and the Christian New Testament. Scripturally, it is a tradition that exhorts the person of faith to give shelter to strangers in need. The tradition originates with the Levitical call to love neighbor as self. "You shall not take vengeance or bear a grudge against any of your people, but you shall love your neighbor as yourself," reads Leviticus 19:18. And further, in Leviticus 19:33: "When an alien resides with you in your land, you shall not oppress the alien. The alien who resides with you shall be to you as the citizen among you; you shall love the alien as yourself, for you were aliens in the land of Egypt."[25]

Underlying this command to love neighbor as self exists an even more basic theological assumption: that every human being is created in the image of God. "Discussion of immigration and government immigration policy must begin with the truth that every human being is made in the image of God (Genesis 1:26–28)," says the National Association of Evangelical's (NAE) 2009 resolution on immigration.[26] Made in the image of God, immigrants "have supreme value with the potential to contribute greatly to society."[27]

The ideal of loving neighbor as self combined with the notion of the divine spark in every human being is what clergy like Fife and Corbett relied upon during the Sanctuary movement. It is also what nuns like those at El Comedor rely upon to inspire them in the daily grind of their mission. This tradition of radical hospitality builds upon biblical revelation concerning the migration of people. It "mines Scripture for guidance," looking at the foundational stories of the Israelites and the stories of the early Christian community.[28] Examples from the Old and New Testaments show, time and again, God's involvement in the movement of people, as well as demonstrating ideal ways (as well as morally dubious ways) for citizens to treat aliens and strangers.[29]

There was no shortage of biblical stories for Sanctuary activists to draw upon for their inspiration. As the Reverend Robin Hoover of Humane Borders says: "One thinks of the parable of the Good Samaritan as told by Jesus in Luke 10. There are many similar stories in other faith traditions. It is a border story. Jesus makes the case that we are to treat our neighbors from other countries well."[30] As New Testament scholar Donald Senior wrote, "Down through biblical history the deepest experiences of Israel are marked by migration. The tortured journey of Jacob and his sons to Egypt in search of food in a time of famine is a migration experience, as is the defining experience of the Exodus—a migration of peoples seeking escape from oppression and the promise of a new land and new future."[31] Senior goes on to detail the many other searing experiences of migration, such as the deportation of the northern tribes by Assyria, or the Babylonian exile, which so famously inspired the tortured lament of Psalm 137: "By the rivers of Babylon there we sat down and there we wept when we remembered Zion." "These markers in the biblical saga—the wanderings of the patriarchs, the Exodus, the exile, the dispersion, and the return— became embedded in the consciousness of the people of Israel and helped define their character as a people and the nature of their relationship to God."[32]

Furthermore, Senior points out, "A similar case can be made for Jesus and the early Christian community." Senior cites the gospel of Luke: "Jesus was born on the road as it were," when his parents were forced to return to Bethlehem to register for the census. In the Gospel of Matthew, Joseph, Mary, and the infant Jesus must flee to Egypt to escape Herod's menacing violence. "In the same vein, all the Gospels portray the adult Jesus as an itinerant," while "the Acts of the Apostles portrays the early Christians as a beleaguered people, often scattered through violent persecution."[33]

Thus, a strong thematic current of forced migration can be traced throughout the scriptures. As the National Association of Evangelical's immigration resolution stated:

> The Bible contains many accounts of God's people who were forced to migrate due to hunger, war, or personal circumstances. Abraham, Isaac, Jacob, and the families of his sons turned to Egypt in search of food. Joseph, Naomi, Ruth, Daniel and his friends, Ezekiel, Ezra, Nehemiah, and Esther all lived in foreign lands. In the New Testament, Joseph and Mary fled with Jesus to escape Herod's anger and became refugees in Egypt. Peter referred to the recipients of his first letter as "aliens" and "strangers," perhaps suggesting that they were exiles within the Roman Empire. These examples from the Old and New Testaments reveal God's hand in the movement of people and are illustrations of faith in God in difficult circumstances[34]

Perhaps the most prominent story in the New Testament used by Sanctuary advocates comes from Luke 10, when the lawyer asks Jesus: "Teacher, what must I do to inherit eternal life?" Jesus answers, "What is written in the law? What do you read there?" The lawyer replies, "You shall love the Lord your God with all your heart, and with all your soul, and with all your strength, and with all your mind; and your neighbor as yourself." But then, most curiously, the lawyer, wanting to make sure he understands what is meant by the term "neighbor" turns to Jesus for clarification and asks: "And who is my neighbor?"[35]

What ensues in response to the lawyer's clarifying question is the story of "The Good Samaritan," whereby a man traveling from Jerusalem to Jericho is robbed and beaten half-dead by bandits on the road. Both a priest and a Levite pass the injured man but do not stop to help him. Then a Samaritan, a foreigner not expected to show such mercy to a Jew, sees the wounded man. Unlike the priest and the Levite before him, he comes to his rescue, and we read: "He went to him and bandaged his wounds, having poured oil and wine on them. Then he put him on his own animal, brought him to an inn, and took care of him. The next day he took out two denarii, gave them to the innkeeper, and said, 'Take care of him; and when I come back, I will repay you whatever more you spend.' "[36]

After telling the story of the Good Samaritan, Jesus then turns to the lawyer and asks, "Which of these three, do you think, was a neighbor to the man who fell into the hands of the robbers?" The lawyer answers, "The one who showed him mercy." Jesus then commands the lawyer, "Go and do likewise."[37]

It is stories like these that inspired Sanctuary participants to challenge, and outright defy, U.S. immigration laws. They interpreted stories like that of the Good Samaritan in ways that justified their actions of "illegally harboring" refugees in their houses and sanctuaries. As they concluded from Luke 10, one's neighbor is not always the person who lives next door; it is not always a fellow tribesman or citizen. The neighbor just as easily can be an injured foreigner, an illegal alien or refugee, someone who harkens from another country, speaks another language, believes in a different God. Hence, when confronted by law enforcement agents about sheltering Salvadoran refugees or of shepherding them across the border and through the desert, Sanctuary participants drew upon such stories for encouragement. They did not back down; they would continue to help their "neighbors," as did the Good Samaritan, regardless of the consequences. Nor did the authorities acquiesce. A statement by Corbett sums up the impasse:

> Because the U.S. government takes the position that aiding undocumented Salvadoran and Guatemalan refugees in this country is a felony, we have no middle ground between collaborating and resistance.... For those of us who would be faithful to our allegiance to the Kingdom, there is also no way to avoid recognizing that in this case collaboration with the government is a betrayal of our faith.... We can serve the Kingdom, or we can serve the kingdoms of this world—but we cannot do both. Maybe as the Gospel suggests, this choice is perennial and basic, but the presence of undocumented refugees here among us makes the definitive nature of our choice particularly clear and concrete.[38]

Ethically and theologically, Sanctuary felt compelled to follow "a higher moral law," grounded, in large part, on their Christian faith. As a result, a series of covert undercover operations were undertaken by federal government agencies to attempt to stop the movement. These operations gathered irrefutable proof of how the activists were breaking civil laws. In particular, the FBI hired a man named Jesus Cruz. Cruz was an old *coyote* who had worked with smugglers and who himself had gotten into trouble with the law. In what would later be a controversial move, the INS extricated him from that legal trouble in a deal that put him to work for them.[39] Cruz infiltrated important Bible study groups and other gatherings led by prominent Sanctuary activists. He learned exactly how Fife, Corbett, and others were smuggling refugees in through Nogales and bringing them to "safe houses" in and around Tucson, or providing them with shelter in private homes and churches. In 1985, with piles of proof in hand, the government brought Fife, Corbett, and other Sanctuary participants to trial.

In the end, Fife, Corbett, and others were convicted of "alien smuggling" and other related charges. But still, they did not regret their decisions. When I spoke to the Reverend Fife so many years later, he told me the story of a nun who was indicted along with him. When the judge told her that he would commute her sentence if she pledged not to continue in the movement, she said thanks but no thanks, explaining that it was against her moral beliefs as a Christian not to help people in such a way.[40]

With these trials and the end to the civil wars in Central America, the original Sanctuary movement eventually simmered down, but it in no way died out.[41] Most recently, it has garnered renewed attention with its latest incarnation: the New Sanctuary movement. In January of 2007, religious leaders from eighteen cities across the nation and representing many different faith traditions convened to discuss ways to protect immigrant families from what they viewed as unjust deportation. Based on that January 2007 meeting, the New Sanctuary movement was officially launched.

The impetus for the new movement came from the growing number of men and women who were being arrested, detained, and deported under the post-9/11 crackdown on illegal immigrants. In particular, New Sanctuary proponents were distressed by the number of families being broken up by these deportations. So many of those being deported, they pointed out, had been here for years, some for decades. They had married U.S. citizens or had had children here, and these children were citizens. They were hardworking men and women who had paid their taxes and who were well integrated into American society. They were not criminals. Their only offense was entering the country illegally.

The poster child of the New Sanctuary movement became Elvira Arellano, a Mexican woman facing deportation. Like so many others, she gave birth to a child while living here illegally. Her son, Saul Arellano, is an American citizen due to the Fourteenth Amendment to the U.S. Constitution, which grants birthright citizenship. In an effort to avoid deportation, Arellano attempted to declare sanctuary in the Adalberto United Methodist Church in Chicago. Arellano lived in the church for several months. Federal agents did not enter the church in Chicago to arrest her. But she was later detained during a trip to Los Angeles and deported to Mexico.

Because of her original breach of the law (i.e., illegal entry), she is barred from entering the United States for up to ten years. Her son is living with his father in Chicago, and the family remains separated. Critics of Arellano say that she can always bring her son to Mexico and raise him there; it is her choice to be separated from him. Arellano claims this is not an option: there are better opportunities for her son in the United States, and he is, after all, an American citizen. Uprooting him from his life in Chicago—his friends, school, extended family—and bringing him to Mexico would be too traumatizing, Arellano argued. Those on the side of Sanctuary say that to separate families like this is simply immoral. "A broken system, breaking families," says the Reverend Alexia Salvatierra, summing up her opinion of current immigration laws. The Reverend Salvatierra is one of the New Sanctuary movement's most pivotal leaders. As Salvatierra knows, the case of Elvira Arellano is all too common.

To illustrate, on my second visit to El Comedor, I sat next to a woman named Araceli. To my surprise, Araceli spoke pristine English. She had a three-year-old son, sitting next to her, and an eight-month-old, Luna, bouncing up and down in her lap. "I came to the States when I was only a month old. My parents brought me to Phoenix where I was raised. I have no memory of that trip. How could I?" Araceli, who was also five months pregnant, was detained by the Border Patrol after taking a trip into Mexico to visit her relatives in Chihuahua. Although she had lived in Phoenix most of her life, she is not a citizen. "Would you believe that I had to learn Spanish?" she said to me. "My two kids are American citizens. Most of my family lives in the States. I never thought it was possible to end up like this." When I asked her what she was going to do, she began to cry. "I don't know," she murmured. "I'll get back somehow. Phoenix is my home."

That same day, I also met Raúl who had lived in Portland for over a decade. He crossed through the desert as a teenager to visit his mother who was sick at the time. Three months after he reunited with her, she died. But he stayed in Portland where he now has two children and an American wife. He was pulled over for running a red light one evening in Portland on his way home from work, detained, and deported. His children and wife are in Portland, and for now, since he entered the country illegally as a teenager, Raul is unsure of how he can get back to them.

Likewise, I met Hector whose one-year-old daughter lives in Utah. He was arrested during a raid at his construction company. Since his arrest and deportation, he has tried to enter the United States three times and failed. One of the unlucky ones, he was tried twice for the crime of illegal entry at the DeConcini courthouse in Tucson. "Now, if I try again," he told me, "I will automatically go to jail for two and a half years. I cannot bear the thought of that. Jail is no place to be. But I just want to see my daughter." When I asked him if he would try to cross again, he sighed and looked at the dirt. "I don't think so," he said after a long pause. "I'm trying to get papers to go to Canada. Then maybe I can enter from there. I don't know... I don't know... I have nothing here for me."

Hearing Araceli's, Raúl's, and Hector's stories, one can begin to imagine the fears that so many millions of undocumented women and men must live with in the United States. You run a red light, and your whole life changes. You go to work one day, there is a raid, and instead of coming home, you are deported. You visit family members, and you wind up in a soup kitchen in a dangerous and unfamiliar border town.

It was in the spirit of Elvira Arellano (and of men and women like Araceli, Raúl, and Hector) that the New Sanctuary movement strategized a plan to "offer sanctuary to a few representative families who would become the face of the immigrant reality—the living story of the families broken by a broken system. [The] framework would be the ancient, ringing moral imperative from the book of Leviticus: Treat the stranger as you would the native born."[42]

As the Reverend Salvatierra further explains, the choice to offer sanctuary to certain families rather than to all "was a carefully discerned response to modern realities. Under the Patriot Act, harboring undocumented persons could have very serious legal consequences, far more serious than under the laws of the 1980s. However, lawyers informed the New Sanctuary movement coalition that they believed the term 'harboring' requires the intent to conceal. If the families told their stories publicly, then the congregations would not be violating any law."[43]

Having learned some lessons from the original Sanctuary movement, the newest band of leaders, inspired by similar ideas of biblical hospitality and similar desires to blend the gospel message with social justice pursuits, employed a different tactic. Rather than going about things covertly, as Fife, Corbett, and others had done, they would go public with their actions. There was no concealment of what the New Sanctuary movement was doing: no sneaking deported migrants across the border, no housing them secretly in churches or the homes of parishioners. Those seeking sanctuary, like Elvira Arellano, would have to go public with their narrative. It was a risk, but in return, people like Arellano had the support of the New Sanctuary coalition, and hence ample legal representation as well as financial and community support. Unfortunately for Arellano, in the end, these measures did not impede her eventual deportation and separation from her family.

Salvatierra, like others in the coalition, argues vehemently that the punishment exacted on people like Elvira Arellano is unnecessarily cruel. The question that many like Salvatierra are asking is, Does the crime (crossing the border illegally) merit the punishment (deportation and banishment from setting foot on U.S. ground for years, the breaking apart of families, and the disruption of settled lives)? Salvatierra answers:

> As a spokesperson for the new Sanctuary movement, I'm often asked why we advocate for undocumented immigrants to stay with their families in the United States after they've entered the country illegally: "Don't you respect the law? They shouldn't have immigrated without documents in the first place!" In response, I recount the passage from Mark 2, when Jesus and his disciples were called out for breaking the Sabbath—a grave breach of Jewish law. Jesus says, "the Sabbath was made for humankind, and not humankind for the Sabbath." When laws fail to justly serve the most basic human needs (as with eating or healing on the Sabbath), they are flawed and incomplete. As religious leaders, we respect the rule of law as a good and holy gift. The core Biblical concept of sanctuary is a response to situations in which the proposed punishment is excessive.[44]

Salvatierra further believes that while religious leaders must respect the law as a "good and holy gift," there are some laws that are unjust and must be broken for society to change (as during the Holocaust or the civil rights movement, or by people such as Rosa Parks). When the law breaks families apart, she says, there is something wrong with the law. Moreover, the longer illegal immigrants have been in the United States, becoming part of the fabric of society, the less claim the law has in deporting them. As Joseph Carens argues:

> The moral right of states to apprehend and deport [illegal immigrants] erodes with the passage of time. As [they] become more and more settled, their membership in society grows in moral importance, and the fact that they settled without authorization becomes correspondingly less relevant. At some point a threshold is crossed, and [illegal immigrants] acquire a moral claim to have their actual social membership legally recognized.[45]

Nonetheless, there are many who are not swayed by the arguments of the New Sanctuary movement. In answer to the question, does the punishment fit the crime, many say: Yes, it does. Opponents to the New Sanctuary movement point out that if laws are not taken seriously, there is a danger that the system will disintegrate. There must be respect for the law, and for those who break it, there must be adequate punishment. If an immigrant's first act upon coming to this country is to break the law (entering illegally), the act should not be rewarded with any form of amnesty.[46] Moreover, to reward illegal entrants is also unfair to those who have been waiting for a long time to enter the United States legally. Yes, compassion, or love of strangers (*philoxenia*), should be considered, opponents argue. But it should be properly weighed against "other values such as fairness (some people wait for years to enter) and the integrity of national borders."[47]

Another complaint against the Sanctuary movement is the issue of prooftexting. Jean Bethke Elshtain, a professor at the University of Chicago Divinity School, questions what she sees as the way Sanctuary leaders "cherry-pick" biblical quotes, sometimes out of historical context, in order to claim scriptural or moral authority for their movement. She does not believe that the Bible mandates Sanctuary participation. She writes that the prooftexts used by Sanctuary participants refer to situations in which "there is a terrified, perhaps bleeding, usually hungry person at one's door and one takes him or her in. It has nothing to do with countries or nation states, and once one starts to move to big collectivities it gets much trickier.[48] Elshtain does admit that there are cases in which denying entry to groups of immigrants is flat wrong, such as Franklin Roosevelt's unwillingness to admit a boatload of Jewish refugees from the Third Reich. But this, she writes, 'is completely different from uncontrolled border crossing by people whose motivations are not life and death.' "[49]

Taking passages out of context to claim scriptural authority is a very real problem. Moreover, the tendency to prooftext can work both ways. In the immigration debate, some Christians who side with law enforcement, also cherry-pick Bible quotes to justify their positions. Most frequently, they refer to Romans 13:

> Let every person be subject to the governing authorities; for there is no authority except from God, and those authorities that exist have been instituted by God. Therefore whoever resists authority resists what God has appointed, and those who resist will incur judgment. For rulers are not a terror to good conduct, but to bad. Do you wish to have no fear of the authority? Then do what is good, and you will receive its approval; for it is God's servant for your good. But if you do what is wrong, you should be afraid, for the authority does not bear the sword in vain![50]

This quote seems to fall unequivocally on the side of law. It points to the divine origins of government rule and emphasizes that no one is exempt from obeying the laws of the land. Thus, following the law is interpreted as a holy duty: to respect the law is to respect God.

Still, many theologians would argue that this reading of Romans 13 is simply too superficial. Interpreting Romans 13 in this literalistic fashion remains problematic, for to do so leads to the conclusion that all authorities are good and all laws are to be obeyed. What does this mean when one considers the governments of Hitler or Stalin, Pol Pot, the laws of South Africa's apartheid rule, Saddam Hussein's Ba'ath Party, the Jim Crow laws of the South? Certainly, these were neither good nor holy.

It seems, however, that Christian groups that fall wholly on the side of law, following Romans 13, are in the minority. Even more conservative Christian factions, such as the National Association of Evangelicals, advocate that its members

> temper the tendency to limit discussions on immigration reform to Romans 13 and a simplistic defense of "the rule of law." God has established the nations (Deut. 32:8; Acts 17:26), and their laws should be respected. Nevertheless, policies must be evaluated to reflect that immigrants are made in the image of God and demonstrate biblical grace to the foreigner.[51]

As Mark Galli points out, "Surely Christians . . . should recognize that there are moments when law-and-order is not 'supreme.'" He writes that the ability to recognize when laws are blessed, and when they are not, is itself a biblical principle. This biblical principle is witnessed

> in Daniel's determination to worship his God despite "the laws of the Medes and Persians," in Rahab's betrayal of her people to help Israeli spies, in Jesus' unwillingness to submit to Sabbath laws when they harmed people, in the early apostles' refusal to cease preaching despite the authorities' command. As Peter put it to them, "Judge for yourselves whether it is right in God's sight to obey you rather than God" (Acts 4:19). In each instance, the law of man was superseded by the law of love—of God and of neighbor.[52]

Interestingly, the issue of immigration has united Christian groups who are quick to disagree on other issues, such as abortion or gay marriage. It makes allies of those who otherwise stand, passionately and obstinately, on opposite sides of the political spectrum.[53] What unites them, at least in theory, "is the biblical teaching to extend hospitality to the stranger and succor to the suffering."[54]

But is all this talk about biblical hospitality, Christian love, and succor to the suffering still prooftexting? Perhaps the more important question remains: How much does it matter whether or not, or to what extent, Sanctuary advocates and their detractors invoke certain Bible passages to justify their causes? After all, realistically speaking, it is not possible for everyone to know the philological nuances and the exegetical discrepancies of every biblical passage. One does not have the privilege of time to learn the Hebrew and the Greek of the original text, to pore over historical annals and archaeological findings that elucidate deeper sociohistorical truths concerning given passages, or to trace the millennia of commentary concerning a word, verse, or chapter. It is not that this work, often left to theologians and scholars, is not of great value. It is simply that the phenomenon of prooftexting is happening all the time, and not only in matters of immigration. Quotes from sacred books are always being cited, often out of context, to justify or repudiate any number of causes, from terrorism to abortion, stem cell research to gay marriage, capital punishment to the right to migrate. The list of biblically sanctioned causes is lengthy.

When it comes down to it, what seems most important is not always perhaps the full exegetical truth of a given passage's context but rather how a certain interpretation of that passage is played out in public life; how that theology is *lived* and *promoted*. There will always be warring interpretations and causes backed up by holy books (not to mention secular documents, such as the U.S. Constitution). It is the *effect* those interpretations have on the larger public stage that seems to matter most.

The Sanctuary movement is a complex example of how certain interpretations of scripture can filter down into public life. Take the example of so-called sanctuary cities. Over the last two decades, and beginning in the 1980s, cities and towns throughout the United States (inspired by the language and rhetoric of the Sanctuary movement) chose to become "sanctuary cities." This choice meant that cities like Los Angeles, New York City, Washington, DC, Chicago, San Francisco, Phoenix, Houston, Dallas, Austin, Detroit, Miami, among many others, put certain protections in place for illegal immigrants. The most common protection involved prohibiting municipal workers from inquiring into anyone's immigration status.

In short, sanctuary policies state that "city employees, including the police, are not required to report illegal immigrants to federal authorities."[55] The choice to become a "sanctuary city" was seen as a way of protecting illegal immigrants and honoring their contributions. Take the policy resolution of Cambridge, Massachusetts, reaffirming its status as a "sanctuary city." The "Policy Order Resolution," dated May 8, 2006, states:

> WHEREAS: The City of Cambridge has been enriched and built by generations of immigrants; and WHEREAS: Cambridge has a proud history as a sanctuary city, as declared by City Council Order Number 4 of April 8, 1985; and WHEREAS: There are now approximately 12 million undocumented immigrants in the United States who have been systematically denied the opportunity enjoyed by past generations of immigrants to become legal permanent residents or citizens of this country; and WHEREAS

over the past two decades, immigration policy has become even more restrictive than punitive and closed off avenues previously available for immigrants to obtain legal permanent residency, while the US-Mexico border has been further militarized.[56]

The Resolution continues to detail, in crisp yet eloquent legal prose, the migrant deaths in the desert, the increased poverty and lack of opportunities facing immigrants, the inefficacies of current U.S. immigration policy (and the need for humane reform), the contributions of immigrants to the U.S. economy, the xenophobic nature of current immigration discourse, and the detrimental effects of increased raids on immigrants. It goes on to resolve that "The city of Cambridge reaffirm[s] its commitment as a Sanctuary City" and urges a moratorium on raids until "the US Congress comes to an agreement on comprehensive immigration reform so that the debate can be carried out in good faith, rather than against a backdrop of fear, repression and intimidation." The Policy Order concludes: "RESOLVED: That the City of Cambridge affirms the basic human rights and dignity of every human being; and be it further RESOLVED: That the City of Cambridge rejects the use of the word 'illegal' to describe human beings."[57]

Not surprisingly, with the seemingly irreconcilable partisanship divisions over immigration reform, and post-9/11 fears of illegal foreigners (in particular, terrorists and other criminals), the concept of "sanctuary cities" has come under increasing scrutiny in recent years. In many cases, cities working to repeal sanctuary ordinances have been doing so in response to some high-profile crime involving an illegal immigrant. Take San Francisco, one of the nation's most socially and politically liberal cities. Even so, most recently it has been trying to repeal its "sanctuary" status, in large part owing to the brutal killings of Tony Bologna and his two sons. They were murdered by an illegal El Salvadoran, Edwin Ramos, a member of the *Marasalvatrucha* gang (also known as the MS-13 gang). Ramos gunned down Bologna and his two sons, who were returning from a picnic, in the Excelsior district of San Francisco. It is believed that Ramos mistook them for rival gang members. In the wake of the murders, people blamed "the city's voter-approved sanctuary ordinance, under which police officers and other city employees are prohibited from inquiring into immigration status."[58] Ramos had had other run-ins with the law, and his gang-member affiliation was well documented. However, because of "San Francisco's sanctuary city status, instead of being reported to federal immigration authorities and deported, Ramos was allowed to continue to roam the streets of San Francisco until his arrest for the Bologna killings."[59]

As a result of this murder and others like it, the mayor of San Francisco, Gavin Newsom, has created much tougher immigration policies, turning the image of "the liberal enclave, and so-called sanctuary city" into one that resembles "many other cities in the United States: deeply conflicted over how to cope with the fallout of illegal immigration."[60] In the *New York Times*, Newsom is quoted as saying: "If we start harboring criminals as a sanctuary city, this entire system is in peril." He says that he is working "to balance safety and rights."[61] This is the precarious balance that has certain groups at loggerheads over illegal immigration, both in the Tucson sector and across the nation: How to ensure safety while also respecting basic human rights?

As Cinnamon Stillwell, a writer for the *San Francisco Gate*, stated:

> Supporters of San Francisco's sanctuary city policies, which include members of the local faith community who inspired the original ordinance, argue that the current approach is the only humane solution. In its 2007 pledge, the New Sanctuary movement, describing immigration raids, stated that "We cannot in good conscience ignore such suffering and injustice." But where is the compassion for the injustice inflicted upon American citizens? ... While San Francisco's sanctuary city ordinance may have been well-intentioned, it has resulted in an untenable and anarchic situation that is taking its toll on city residents and surrounding counties alike. Providing sanctuary for law-breakers at the expense of law-abiding citizens is neither a compassionate nor a moral approach. The issue is not one of callousness towards illegal immigrants, but rather, the duty owed American citizens by their government.[62]

Stillwell's words indicate that the finger-pointing going on between local faith communities and law enforcement groups over the complexities of illegal immigration is not limited to the Tucson sector alone.

This same tension—between safety and rights, security and hospitality— was taken up by Mexican and U.S. Catholic bishops in a 2003 letter entitled, "Strangers No Longer: Together on the Journey of Hope." The letter states:

> The Church recognizes the right of a sovereign state to control its borders in further-ance of the common good. It also recognizes the right of human persons to migrate so that they can realize their God-given rights. These teachings complement each other. While a sovereign state may impose reasonable limits on immigration, the common good is not served when the basic human rights of the individual are vio-lated. In the current condition of the world, in which global poverty and persecution are rampant, the presumption is that persons must migrate in order to support and protect themselves, and the nations who are able to receive them should do so when-ever possible.[63]

This is the general stance of the Catholic Church and of many Protestant coalitions along the border: Not only is it not *illegal* to migrate according to need; it is a "God-given" right. When the basic necessities for living a genuine human life are unavailable, it is no longer a question of legality but of dignity.

The letter of Catholic bishops acknowledges the right of a sovereign nation to monitor its borders "in furtherance of the common good," but it simultaneously promotes the right of every human being to migrate when material circumstances become untenable. The question that remains unanswered is, How can the protection of borders and the right to migrate be harmonized? While the letter eloquently details the plight of migrants in their home countries and the harrowing journeys undertaken in search of better lives, it does not propose any systematic mechanism by which sovereign states can reconcile these two teachings, which the letter says "complement each other." As National Association of Evangelical's most recent immigration resolution says: "The Bible does not offer a blueprint for modern legislation, but it can serve as a moral compass and shape the attitudes of those who believe in God."[64] It is this moral compass that Sanctuary movement participants, old and new, along with a majority of Christian leaders, liberal and conservative, have invoked in calls for more humane border policies and an effective overhaul of U.S. immigration policy. It is a moral compass that points to stories and commandments in the Judeo-Christian scriptures that speak of loving neighbor as self, of the age-old realities of migration, and of the duties of citizens to treat foreigners, especially refugees and migrants, with hospitality.

Furthermore, in "Strangers No Longer," U.S. and Mexican bishops address the unfolding tragedy of migrant deaths in the Sonoran desert, ultimately placing the blame on border enforcement policies.

> Of particular concern are the border enforcement policies pursued by both governments that have contributed to the abuse and even deaths of migrants in both Mexico and the United States. Along the United States-Mexico border, the U.S. government has launched several border-blockade initiatives in the past decade designed to discourage undocumented migrants from entering the country.... Rather than significantly reducing illegal crossings, such initiatives have instead driven migrants into remote and dangerous areas in the southwest region of the United States, leading to an alarming number of migrant deaths.[65]

Some, like the Reverend Robin Hoover of Humane Borders, believe that the current suffering of migrants is as acute as, if not worse than, that of the Central American refugees of the 1980s. "The human rights violations of migrants, documented or not," writes the Reverend Hoover, "are now beginning to dwarf the violations of human rights observed during the massive Central American Exodus of more than a generation ago."[66] It seems that, sadly, those thirteen Salvadoran men and women who lost their lives in Organ Pipe Cactus National Monument in July 1980 only presaged a much larger tragedy to come: the one that would ensue decades later, in which hundreds of thousands of migrants would pour into the Sonoran desert, and in which many thousands would lose their lives.

After spending years in Arizona in the 1980s researching and writing about the Sanctuary movement, then *New York Times* journalist, Ann Crittenden, was led to ask a very foreboding question:

> Finally, how is the United States going to deal with a fundamental shift in its history as a refugee nation? The refugees of the future are not likely to be abstractions, huddled in camps thousands of miles and an ocean away, but our own neighbors, knocking at our very gates. The Salvadorans today may be the Mexicans of tomorrow. One of the lessons of the sanctuary story is the need, completely unaddressed by the immigration reform of 1986, to put into place a coherent refugee policy at our borders.[67]

Indeed, the Salvadoran refugees of yesterday are the Mexican and Central American migrants of today. They are far from abstractions; they are, literally, our neighbors. Crittenden's prescient words, from over two decades ago, were written in an attempt to glean lessons from the Sanctuary story. Those lessons concluded that if immigration reform and a coherent refugee policy at our borders were not made an absolute priority, another tragedy, and another collision between faith communities and law enforcement, would surely ensue. She could not have been closer to the truth.

Following is a closer examination of the current tragedy and of the equally contentious showdown between religious activists and federal officials in the Tucson sector. As they did during the 1980s, these religious coalitions have responded to the migrant deaths in their back yards by drawing upon similar ideas, rooted in scripture, of unconditional hospitality and neighborly love. With this in mind, I turn to two of Tucson's most vibrant and controversial border ministries, Humane Borders and No More Deaths.

CHAPTER 3

A Theology of Water: Humane Borders and the Reverend Robin Hoover

The white 4×4 driven by Doug Ruopp, a volunteer for Humane Borders, has come to a halt somewhere past Three Points in the valley below Baboquivari Peak. Ruopp has driven miles down dusty dirt roads, weaving around voracious potholes, past the ranches that hug the Tohono O'odham Reservation.[1] Atop the truck are several blue plastic barrels. Once these barrels were used to deliver the sweetener for Coca-Cola. Now they are filled with water, a precious commodity here in the desert, especially for those who have walked for days through this unforgiving landscape and who have run out of it.

Ruopp hops out of the truck and begins examining the dry mangled brush that surround two more blue barrels, these ones on the desert floor. A blue flag flaps in the wind thirty feet above the barrels. The flag is a signal to migrants that there is a Humane Borders water station here. "*Hola amigos, amigas,*" Ruopp calls out. "*No tengan miedo. No somos la patrulla. Somos amigos. Queremos ayudar. ¡Tenemos agua!*" ("Hi friends. Don't be afraid. We are not the Border Patrol. We are friends. We want to help. We have water!") Ruopp checks around the barrels for human tracks, which he finds. It rained the night before, and hence, the tracks are fresh. Nearby is a backpack in the sand, a lone sneaker, several empty water bottles, and a sweatshirt dangling from a mesquite tree. Although no one emerges from the brush, there are clear traces of lives that have passed through here within the past few hours. There is also a bottle in the sand that is full. Ruopp bends down to pick up the full bottle. He unscrews the cap and sniffs the contents. "Urine," he says.

"Urine?" I ask.

Ruopp explains that sometimes when their water bottles go empty, migrants collect their urine in case of drastic situations. "Worst case scenario," Ruopp says, "urine is better than nothing."

As horrible as it seems, this is the sort of moment that makes Ruopp and other Humane Borders volunteers feel like their hard work has paid off. "It's good to know that whoever left this bottle here got a good drink of water from one of our barrels," he says.

The mission of Humane Borders is just that: to provide water for thirsty migrants who might otherwise perish of dehydration. The water station just described is only one of nearly a hundred others like it. They are scattered throughout southern Arizona in some of the most desolate outposts of the Sonoran desert. Most are not far from heavily traveled migrant trails. The blue flag that soars thirty feet into the air alerts migrants of water from miles away.

Keeping these tanks up and running is no easy business. "The politics of water stations is complex," says the Reverend Robin Hoover, founder of Humane Borders. "There are permits, trucks, insurance, equipment, maintenance, media, vandalism, donors, on and on."[2] The cost of maintaining one typical water station alone (two tanks, one flag) for one year is $1,500. All this money comes from donations. That is not to mention the cost of gasoline (some volunteers must travel up to four hours to reach a water station) and the maintenance of the trucks, which take some hard beatings on a good day.

The story of how Humane Borders came to be is one, in part, of serendipity and vision. When the Reverend Robin Hoover and his wife, Sue Anne Goodman, a university fund-raiser, moved to Tucson from Texas, they had little idea what was in store for them. Hoover had come to Tucson to take over the pastorate of First Christian Church. As Ken Ellingwood writes:

> Hoover now had to get to know an unfamiliar congregation—and introduce himself to his new 350-member flock—in a state where he had never lived before. Even for a man of his considerable energy, the last thing he had come seeking in Arizona was a crusade to add to his busy life. It didn't take long, though, for the crusade to find him.[3]

As it turned out, that crusade would be one of water. The idea for the mission came to Hoover in the summer of 2000, while he was still busy settling into his new life as pastor of the First Christian Church on Tucson's Speedway Boulevard. It came in response to the sudden increase in migrant deaths that occurred over that blistering summer. Until then, the number of migrant deaths in Arizona, while on the increase, was still not as alarming as that summer, when stories of dead migrants hit the news almost daily.

This sudden trend of desert deaths shows up alarmingly on graphs like the one from the "Humane Borders fact sheet." The fact sheet shows that in 1994 there were only two recorded deaths and none in 1995. But since 1995, there has been a steady increase in fatalities: twelve in 1996, thirteen in 1997, seventeen in 1998, twenty-one in 1999, and forty-four in 2000, the year Hoover arrived in Tucson.[4] From there, things grew even grimmer: 78 in 2001, 163 in 2002, 190 in 2003, 221 in 2004, and a high of 279 in 2005.

The majority of migrant deaths in Arizona were from lack of water. These people were migrants like Yolanda Gonzalez, who perished in the desert after giving her baby her last sip of water. It was Gonzalez's death that fueled the founding of Humane Borders. In response to her death and others like it, clergy members from several of Tucson's religious communities came together to discuss the crisis and to brainstorm possible ways of addressing it. On June 11, 2000, Pentecost Sunday, Hoover and eighty-five other religiously inspired folk met at the Pima Friends meeting house in Tucson. At that meeting, they asked two central questions: "First, how can we respond with compassion to the migrants who are risking their lives crossing the deserts along the U.S.-Mexican border? Second, how can we work to change the U.S. immigration policies that place these persons at risk in the desert?"[5]

The idea that struck Hoover as the most pragmatic and humanitarian came from the example of a California man named John Hunter. Hunter, during that same deadly summer of 2000, "launched his own one-man mercy campaign by installing water stations in the desert stretches of Imperial County."[6] Hunter "was no weak-kneed liberal, either. . . . But as he watched the news about migrants dying in southern California's deserts, Hunter decided to act. This had nothing to do with whether the country's immigration policy should be tightened or loosened, he reasoned. This was a more fundamental matter. If lives are being lost in the desert, then you must go to the desert to save them."[7]

Hunter began leaving large jugs of water out in bunches and placing blue banners atop thirty-foot poles. Hoover found Hunter's example an effective response to the crisis. He invited Hunter to talk to his growing coalition about his "water effort" in the hope that they might be able to undertake a similar project. As Hoover saw it, "placing drinking water along well-traveled migrant corridors in the desert was an act with utilitarian and symbolic value. On a religious level, it displayed the Judeo-Christian belief in compassion and tolerance, the same kind shown in the biblical parable of the good Samaritan and elsewhere in exhortations of Jesus: 'For whosoever shall give you a cup of water in my name, because ye belong to Christ, verily I say unto you, he shall not lose the reward.'"[8]

Hoover's plan, however, was much more complicated than Hunter's. He envisioned not just clusters of water jugs but large tanks, set up in strategic locations based on the places where migrants were dying most frequently. He knew many of these tanks would have to be in very remote locations, and this would require a sophisticated network of trucks and tanks, and a hefty sum of money (to be raised through drives and donations). Moreover, Hoover wanted to undertake this "migrant ministry" with full legal approval from the appropriate federal agencies. Although deeply inspired by his Sanctuary predecessors, Hoover wanted to make sure that whatever his group did was done within "the law of the land." He wanted to find a way to both act with the compassion and hospitality that his faith required of him and also to respect the law. As Hoover says, "Humane Borders currently provides passive humanitarian assistance by erecting and maintaining water stations in remote, strategic desert areas on both sides of the border where most migrants travel and where, unfortunately, most migrants die."[9] The use of the word "passive" is key, since it emphasizes Humane Border's non-combative approach.

Choosing to work within the confines of the law, however, was a double-edged sword. On the one hand, in cooperating with Border Patrol, Hoover was able to acquire vital statistics from them. The statistics showed where clusters of migrants were dying and provided Hoover with an idea of where to begin putting out water stations. Not only did the Border Patrol aid him in identifying the most perilous migrant corridors, but equally as important, they granted him permits so that he could place water stations on federal land. It was an uneasy but necessary alliance in Hoover's eyes.

Still, in public, Hoover never held back in decrying what he deemed the "immoral" strategies of the Border Patrol. He believed, in no uncertain terms, that border enforcement policy was to blame for the spike in migrant deaths. The statistics proved it, he said. Before 1994, before the border crackdown, migrants were dying only rarely. "The large, expensive deployment of personnel, technologies, and strategies have resulted in record numbers of migrant deaths," Hoover believed. "Since 1994, migrants have been intentionally pushed into the open desert as a result of consciously chosen public policy. A number of related U.S. border policies have caused exponentially rising death rates and untold human suffering among those seeking a better life and, in many cases, mere survival.... Through our eyes, we conclude that borders, border policies, and border law enforcement should not kill people, freeze them, shoot them, run over them in high speed pursuits, dehydrate them, confine them, or drive them into medical distress. Yet through informed eyes, we see that the policies of the United States have done just this for far too many years."[10]

In both criticizing U.S. border policies and in promoting more humane ones, Hoover drew upon the Judeo-Christian tradition of hospitality. As its motto, Humane Borders adopted the quote from Isaiah 49:10: "They shall not hunger or thirst, neither scorching wind nor sun shall strike them down, for he who has pity on them will lead them, and by springs of water guide them."[11] This motto pointed to the biblically inspired nature of the group's mission. As Reverend Hoover said, "Humane Borders is a strategic faith response to the rising numbers of migrant deaths. Both strategy and faith were present in the founding of Humane Borders, the writing of the mission statement, the early organization of the corporation, and in the unfolding history since those days."[12]

In many ways, there was nobody better suited to deal with the crisis in the desert than Hoover himself. He had spent the previous decade thinking about the connections between religion and public policy and the realm of political theology. In particular, he had dedicated his Ph.D. dissertation to studying the politics of faith-based groups working in immigration policy. Before that, he had earned his Master's of Divinity degree from Brite Divinity School, focusing on social ethics, and is currently writing a book, with the working titled, *Humane Borders: The Moral Argument for Policy Reform*.

Hoover calls himself a "a postmodern liberal critic" and can throw around ideas, in his sonorous Texan drawl, in a cogent and charismatic manner, concerning just about anything. He is full of quips and has no shortage of opinions. Best of all, he will usually keep you laughing as he tosses out jokes like darts. The humor is refreshing, especially since so many of the stories he tells—stories of migrant deaths—can be so chilling.

He calls his work part of "the migrant ministry business," and roots his inspiration in the Christian story. As he says, "What happens to the weeping, sorrowful, hurting, marginalized, and dying is the ultimate test of a social system, be it religious, governmental, or cultural. As a Christian, I use the Christian language of 'the least of these.'"[13] The simple act of providing water to migrants is, for Hoover, not only a moral endeavor but also an act of faith and a witness to the life, work, and message of Christ. "Those who work on immigration issues from the faith perspective," writes Hoover, "turn often to Matthew 25, which is a judgment of the nations for not taking care of the most basic need (material and spiritual) of the 'least of these.' The migrants all fit the profile of those who are far too often without food, water, clothes, welcome, healthcare, or visitation."[14]

Following this call to serve "the least of these," Humane Borders drafted its mission statement in June 2000. It reads:

Humane Borders, motivated by faith, will work to create a just and humane border environment. Members will respond with humanitarian assistance to those who are risking
their lives and safety crossing the United States border with Mexico. We encourage the
creation of public policies toward a humane, non-militarized border with legalized work
opportunities for migrants in the U.S. and legitimate economic opportunities in
migrants' countries of origin. We welcome all persons of good faith.[15]

The aim of the platform was twofold. Most immediately, Humane Borders
would respond with humanitarian assistance by placing water tanks in the
desert. Second, the group would work to lobby for effective and humane
immigration reform at the national level. In undertaking the project, the
group came up with a logo: the North Star and the seven stars of the Big
Dipper filled with water. It is meant to incorporate the "drinking gourd"
from the abolitionist movement, symbolizing Humane Borders' commitment to humanitarian assistance.

With their logo, mission statement, and biblical inspiration, Humane
Borders deployed its first water station in November 2000. Within just a
few years, the organization has progressed from leaving out a few of those
blue tanks of water here and there to having nearly one hundred spaced
throughout the desert. In the group's January–March 2009 newsletter,
Desert Fountain, Hoover wrote:

We're already setting records this fiscal year for recovering human remains from the
desert. Approximately 25—mostly skeletonized—remains were discovered in December
and January alone.... Fortunately, our members have risen to the needs of this organization repeatedly, and we continue to receive more and more water station locations.
Before the calendar year 2009 ends, I'm predicting we will have 115 water stations. Some
of these are in incredibly remote locations but very strategic sites as determined by our
mapping technologies.[16]

To get each of those water stations up and running is no small thing. As
Hoover says, many of the water stations are put up in "incredibly remote
locations." To reach these locations requires confronting the physical challenges of the terrain—the mountains, the rough roads, the lonesome torrid
outposts of the Sonoran desert. For this reason, every truck is equipped
with food packs, first aid kits, satellite telephones, and global positioning
systems (GPS), in case volunteers run into trouble or encounter migrants
in distress.

Even more challenging are the negotiations that must take place to get
permission to put up every station. In each case, Humane Borders works
closely, creatively, and persuasively with ranchers, landowners, and federal
groups to secure permits. Many of the stations are placed on state and

federal land (only 17.5 percent of Arizona land is privately owned).[17] As a result, Hoover and his organization must seek the proper permits from the right agencies. Often, there is a lot of wrangling. Hoover must prove the necessity for setting up a water station at a given spot. He must go into talks with federal officials armed with his maps that show where migrants are dying, and he must convince them that it is in everyone's best interest to have water tanks available for migrants in a certain location.

This last point cannot be glossed over. It is not just the migrant who suffers from the absence of water in the desert, but it is the public as well. As Hoover says, "millions of dollars will be expended by county governments in southern Arizona to re-hydrate, dialyze, and rehabilitate many migrants brought in from the desert. These funds are not reimbursed by the federal government."[18] As a result of the life-saving care that Tucson medical facilities have been providing to sick migrants in recent years, such facilities are running deficits so large that some are talking of closing their doors. Water stations, Hoover argues, are cost-effective responses that keep migrants out of the hospitals and off the medical examiner's table.

If Humane Borders is not wrangling for permission from federal officials, they are doing so with individual citizens (most often ranchers), asking to place stations on their land. This process can be no less difficult. While some ranchers give swift approval, may others give a categorical, "No." Not only do such ranchers refuse to have water tanks placed on their land but they also vociferously oppose the "water effort." In large part, their refusal stems from the outrage they feel over the deleterious effects human migration patterns are having on their land. Hoover is the first to agree that ranchers have a right to complain: their fences are cut by migrants and *coyotes*; their water systems are disturbed; migrant trash costs money to clean up, and even worse, the trash can be lethal to livestock that eat it; bundles of illicit drugs are often hidden or found on ranchers' lands; theft or break-ins are not uncommon.

Another obstacle to the "water effort" in recent years has come from the Tohono O'odham Nation. The Nation's reservation sees a staggering number of migrant deaths each year. In recent years, the Nation has seen close to half the number of deaths that occur in Arizona. Despite these deaths, however, the Tohono O'odham tribal government has refused to allow any Humane Borders' water tanks to be placed on its land. The reasons for this denial reflect the complicated relations between the Tohono O'odham people and immigration and border matters. Many tribal members live in fear of migrants and smugglers. The vast number of migrants passing through O'odham lands mean no harm, but as migration patterns have shifted to their territory, these Native Americans have experienced more incidents of theft on tribal lands. Tribal members have also been affected by human and drug smuggling operations. Since average yearly income for many of the registered 28,000 O'odham is near or below poverty levels, some members have become involved in smuggling. It is quick and easy money. "You see some people driving around the Nation in fancy cars," one tribal member told me, "and you know they have no visible means to pay for such things. They're involved in smuggling. There may not be a lot of O'odham involved in the business, but it is more than it ever was in the past. It makes everyone more wary of the whole immigration thing."

Moreover, as more migrants began traveling through O'odham land, more Border Patrol agents were deployed to the reservation. Since part of this land actually extends into Mexico (approximately 1,500 members live on Mexican O'odham land), the Nation was literally cut in half with the construction of fencing in certain places. "The Border Crossed Us," is a common refrain there. Some members, such as Ofelia Rivas, declare the Border Patrol to be an "occupying army." Others see the need for the Border Patrol to manage the chaos but lament the fact that the Nation is so caught in the middle. These factors, to name only a few, have contributed to the Nation's unwillingness to cooperate with Humane Borders. This has greatly disheartened Hoover's organization over the years. There are some tribal members, such as Mike Wilson, who have publicly decried the Nation's stance concerning the water effort. Wilson began leaving jugs of water on reservation land anyway, even though he was forbidden to do so in certain districts by tribal government. "I understand people's fears," Wilson told me. "I understand their frustration. Are migrants breaking the law by entering illegally? Sure, but there is a higher moral law. It requires me to help my brother and sister in need. It requires me to put out water."[19]

Each Humane Borders water tank that goes up is cause for the organization to celebrate. An even greater cause of joy for volunteers is the proven success that such water tanks have had. Through the use of maps, Hoover's organization can demonstrate that where there are water stations, there are significantly fewer migrant deaths in that area. They have the maps from before the stations were erected, and the maps from after. The results fall clearly in Humane Borders' favor. Such success has allowed the organization to argue for the need for further stations. As Hoover wrote, "We know the water tanks are effective because we can walk into church shelters in Nogales, into churches housing migrants, and other places and ask, 'How many of you have gotten water from a tank beneath a blue flag?' We get lots of *yes* responses along with gratitude and blessings."[20] Sometimes volunteers find notes from migrants left near a water tank, notes like the one found on September 5, 2009, at a tank in Organ Pipe Cactus National Monument, which read: "God bless you. You saved my life. Gracias. An imigrant [*sic*] looking for his American dream."[21]

Still, with all its successes, Humane Borders is not without its enemies. There are those who believe that "providing water to people who were knowingly entering the United States illegally was at best 'a feel-good service.' At worst, it was anti-American."[22] Such factions, including some ranchers and members of civil patrol groups, have accused Humane Borders of being misguided and naïve: Didn't the organization ever stop to think that leaving water out in the desert would give undocumented migrants more incentive to try to cross? Or did they understand that not all the people taking water were decent folks, that some were criminals and drug smugglers? At the core, providing such water rewarded illegal behavior, certain people argued. But Hoover and his volunteer corps always argued back: those who were crossing were going to do it anyway, with or without water. Who in his or her right mind, Hoover retorted, wanted to leave country and family behind, risk rape and robbery, dehydration or hyperthermia imprisonment and death? By the time people decide to cross, there was little convincing them to reconsider. Whether or not there were some barrels of water sitting out in the desert had no bearing on someone who was desperate enough to undertake the perilous journey in the first place. "Contrary to what some people may fear, providing water in the desert will not increase undocumented migration," says the Humane Borders fact sheet. "People do not cross the border to obtain water; they cross the border for jobs."[23]

In fact, Humane Borders has created maps and posters to warn migrants about the dangers of crossing and to try to dissuade them. These posters and maps are placed in shelters and churches along the border in Mexico. The posters read in emphatic lettering: ¡No vaya Ud! ¡No hay suficiente agua! ¡No vale la pena! ¡No arriesga su vida! ¡Puede Ud morir! (Don't go! There is not enough water! It's not worth it! Don't risk your life! You can die!). In smaller lettering, and in Spanish, one can read additional advisory information: "Crossing the border walking through the desert is dangerous and can end in death; if you decide to cross the border by foot be well prepared." Such posters also advise migrants not to cross the desert between May and August, when temperatures are dangerously high; to bring identifying documents; to carry enough water and food; to know and trust the people they are crossing with; and to know the distances they will walk on foot before beginning.

This last point, concerning the reality of distances facing migrants, is emphasized in the map that accompanies the warnings. "Sometimes, migrants have no idea how long they must walk to get where they want to go," the Reverend Hoover told me. "I've seen women in high heels trying to cross. They think Tucson is just a short walk from Nogales; or that Phoenix is just an afternoon of walking."[24] But what the map shows is just how far someone (in good health) can walk from Nogales in one day, two days, three days, and more. As shown, after three days of walking (without getting lost, sick, or being abandoned by a *coyote*), a person is barely halfway to Tucson.

As I was driving through the desert with Doug Ruopp that warm Sunday in January, he pointed to the line of mountains demarcating Tohono O'odham land and said, "If only migrants could stand on top of mountains like that and look out in all directions, I think they would not try to cross. When they realized that they would have to walk all that way, endless miles of the same desert landscape, I think they would give up and go home." This is what the map tries to impart: the immensity and monotony of the landscape, and the all-too-real danger, although, as Hoover believes, in all likelihood such information dissuades very few.

While saving lives by providing water is the priority of Humane Borders, the organization also works on more long-term problem solving. Migrant deaths, the organization believes, are connected to the absence of effective, humane, and realistic immigration policies. During its weekly meetings at the First Christian Church on Wednesday nights, the group brainstorms ways to try to lobby for immigration reform at the national level. As Hoover says, the deaths in the desert are a symptom of the larger problem. That problem comes from the U.S. government's inability to envision, compromise on, and enact proper immigration reform. In short, Hoover advocates national immigration reform that includes some form of amnesty for those millions of undocumented immigrants already here, a viable guest worker program going forward, and a closer look at how the effects of globalization are creating such patterns of migration. He writes:

> As a matter of justice the first priority is to extend a legal status to those who are living in the United States of America without the basic legal recognition or protection. Rational people can disagree as to what that status would be, whether it would lead to citizenship, and for what period of time.... The second thing is to provide legal work opportunities for those who wish to work in the U.S. Again, rational people can have significant differences on how this gets accomplished, but the organized work opportunities for up to 750,000 persons a year should be made available to foreign nationals who are not participating in other programs. Visas would go directly to the migrants to seek employment in certain sectors of the U.S. economy at will. Migrants could organize, have their families follow them, and be able to move from employer to employer at will to avoid Bracero-style working conditions.... Finally, there should be concerted efforts to work cooperatively between nations to provide for economic development in the migrants' countries of origin. Globalization is here to stay. Many of the unjust effects occur in the most marginalized, sending communities and must be addressed by all nations participating in the new realities of inter-dependent political economies.[25]

It is no surprise that, all along, Hoover has had his fill of opponents, not just in Arizona but all across the nation. Recent polls suggest that more than half of Americans do not support the idea of amnesty nor a guest worker program. Nonetheless, Hoover believes that until such immigration reform occurs, the deaths in the desert will continue. Meanwhile, trying to wall off the border is not a humane solution, he asserts. It will only continue to force migrants to take increasingly drastic measures to enter the United States.

This does not mean, Hoover emphasizes, that the United States should have open or porous borders. As he often says, "Our organization is called Humane Borders, not open borders, or no borders, or something else like that."[26] Nations should have the right to control their borders and monitor who comes and goes. It is imperative for national safety. But without proper immigration reform, migrants will continue to evade ports of entry, and the death toll will mount. Until that day comes, Hoover believes that he and his organization have to come up with the best temporary solution: water.

"All this work," Hoover laments, "is just a Band-Aid over the problem."[27] He does not see any substantive change coming anytime soon. The water is just "an interim moral response," he says, as well as a way to draw attention to the humanitarian crisis at the southern border.[28] Nonetheless, Hoover talks a lot about hope. He is in "the hope business" as he calls it. "Hope is the greatest political force we have," Hoover said to me with a wistful shrug of his shoulders the last time we met in his office.

What makes Robin Hoover particularly admirable is his ability to collaborate extensively with individuals, groups, and agencies with whom he disagrees. As he says:

> We have pointed to death in the desert, declared that what is happening there is immoral, and invited anyone with warrant and wisdom on this issue to come to the table, . . . such as the Border Patrol, federal land managers, health care providers, elected officials, and others, to discern viable means of changing what we see. At that table . . . , we have chosen to speak with all interested parties in a non-adversarial way. Each time a decision has been taken and actions undertaken, everything Humane Borders officers and volunteers have done has been public, open, transparent, and within the bounds of law.[29]

Hoover may not agree with all aspects of the law. He may, in fact, vehemently disagree. But he believes in respecting and trying to work within its bounds.

For all of his hard work—his vision, resolve, patience, and willingness to compromise—the Reverend Hoover was awarded (among other honors) Mexico's most prestigious human rights awards, given to him by Mexico's president, Felipe Calderón. In 2010, roughly ten years after launching

Humane Borders, Hoover stepped down as president of the organization, both to complete his book and to undertake new "migrant ministries." His most recent migrant safety initiative is called Project Find Me! (*Proyecto Rescátame!*). The project's aim is to provide Personal Location Beacons to groups of migrants crossing southern Arizona. The beacon uses GPS technology to send emergency signals, activated by migrants in distress in the desert. Through satellite systems, these beacons alert Search and Rescue teams to migrants' calls for help.[30]

For as long as people have been migrating, they have done so across deserts. It is no surprise that so many biblical stories tell of great transformations in the desert: the voice of God is heard; angels appear; Satan tempts men with all the world; sons are sacrificed, or nearly so; covenants are made and broken; idols are fashioned and smashed. It is a place of extremes, a perilous expanse that over the centuries has tested the faith and endurance of many, especially migrants.

In many biblical chronicles of forced journeys across the desert, water becomes a protagonist. Consider Exodus 17, when the Israelites are overcome with thirst in the wilderness. "Give us water to drink," they demand of Moses who in turn cries out to the Lord, "What shall I do with these people? They are almost ready to stone me."[31] The Lord leads Moses to the rock at Horeb, which Moses strikes with his staff, producing a font of life-saving water. Or consider the story of Hagar and Ishmael cast out into the wilderness of Beer-sheba: after their skins of water run dry and the boy is on the verge of death by dehydration, Hagar throws her son under a bush, so as not to watch him die. As she weeps for her child, God speaks to her and leads her to a well of water; mother and child are restored.

These stories, while age-old, are in no way obsolete. They have been playing out in the southwest desert of the United States over the past decade. Rather than Hagar and Ishmael, it may be a mother like Yolanda Gonzalez and her infant baby. Rather than Moses, it may be a bricklayer from Michoacán, or a single mother from Tegucicalpa, heading north in search of a better life in another land. Rather than a spring at the rock at Horeb, it may just be a big blue water tank underneath a high blue flag.

This is why Robin Hoover and his cadre of volunteers do it. It is why they drive the hundreds of miles into the desert with barrels of water; why they negotiate tirelessly with their detractors; why they raise the money to keep the whole operation up and running. Because they know that a little bit of water can save so many lives.

There is a painting by Jean-François Millet entitled "Hagar and Ishmael." It is a stark rendering of mother and child on the brink of death. In the foreground, Hagar lies on the barren yellow ground, clutching her forehead, the expression on her face one of horror and helplessness. Behind her lies her son, listless, naked, the bones of his ribs protruding, his little arm draped over his face, eyes closed. Between them lies a red skin of water, empty and overturned. Aside from that, there is nothing else: a brutal monotony of yellow terrain. Millet has condensed the story of Hagar and Ishmael to its raw tragic core.

It is this core—this anguished mother and her dying son, without water in the desert—that Humane Borders picks up on. As long as there are mothers or sons, fathers or daughters, children or grandparents, dying in the desert of thirst, Humane Borders, inspired by the biblical injunction to care for the stranger, will keep sending out its trucks to the farthest, dustiest, driest corners of the Sonoran desert.

CHAPTER 4

Transcending Borders: No More Deaths and a Higher Moral Law

There is always a story to tell. Tonight, the story concerns a stretcher that was found in the desert next to the body of a dead female migrant. It was found near Ruby Road, southwest of Tucson, by one of No More Death's most dedicated volunteers, Jim Walsh. It was a makeshift stretcher made from scraps of desert wood and woven together with strips of cloth from other migrants' shirts. It was made in an attempt to carry the dying woman out of the desert. Sadly, she did not survive. It is an all too familiar story. She had grown ill from lack of food and water and the general hardships of the journey. When she was no longer able to walk, her fellow migrants did what they could to bring her to safety, but in vain. Walsh came across the woman's lifeless body during one of No More Deaths' routine humanitarian desert runs. Instead of delivering food and water to the woman, Walsh had to make the heartbreaking call to Border Patrol informing them of her dead body.

At the meeting that night, Walsh, in his straw Guatemalan hat and old dirty jeans, tears up as he remembers finding the woman, and beside her, the stretcher.[1] What Walsh wants to convey to the other members of the group is how touched he was by the actions of those who made the stretcher. "It shows how much generosity and compassion fellow migrants can feel for each other," Walsh says. "We do not always stop to consider the sacrifices that migrants make for the perfect strangers traveling with them."

The discussion of the stretcher is taking place at St. Mark's Presbyterian Church in Tucson, where No More Deaths volunteers meet every Monday to discuss the week's events. At every meeting, there is a different agenda. This evening, on a white eraser board, written in blue capital letters, one reads "STRETCHER." Oddly, the stretcher was found two years ago. But the story has emerged again, as the focus of tonight's meeting, because one of No More Deaths' members recently removed it from the place where it was found. She had taken the stretcher (without consulting the group) to her home but was unsure what to do with it. The stretcher had begun to disintegrate due to the elements, and she wanted to preserve it. She thought that it could be placed somewhere, such as a museum, or in a church or a public building, as an artifact and a reminder of the ongoing struggle of migrants; it could also be a way, she thought, to honor and not forget the dead woman.

The majority of the group present that night, however, believe differently. They think it is best to return the stretcher back to where it was found (a small memorial had been set up at the site in the desert already). John Fife, one of No More Deaths' founders, is present at the meeting and raises the question, "anthropological in nature," as to whether removing the stretcher from the desert is akin to removing a sacred artifact from tribal lands and placing it in a museum. Fife does not give his outright opinion, but he wants to raise the ethical questions involving the removal of the stretcher on which the woman died. By the end of the meeting, there is no resolution of the issue.

While every weekly meeting is different in scope, the overall mission of No More Deaths, or *No Más Muertes* as it is called in Spanish, is to end the death and suffering on the U.S.-Mexican border by providing direct aid to migrants and by raising consciousness about border issues in the public sphere. As No More Deaths explains in its preamble,

> We come together as communities of faith and people of conscience to express our indignation and sadness over the continued death of hundreds of migrants attempting to cross the US-Mexico border each year. We believe that such death and suffering diminish us all. We share a faith and a moral imperative that transcends borders, celebrates the contributions immigrant peoples bring, and compels us to build relationships that are grounded in justice and love.[2]

It is interesting to compare the similarities and differences between No More Deaths and the group discussed in the preceding chapter, Humane Borders. The two share similar missions: to end the suffering and death of migrants.[3] They also share a similar theological impetus, locating inspiration for their work in the biblical tradition of radical hospitality. Still, the ways they execute their missions are quite different in nature. While Humane Borders is primarily a ministry of water, the mission of No More Deaths is much more varied in scope. Moreover, while the approach of Humane Borders is defined by the Reverend Hoover as primarily "passive," attempting to work within the confines of civil law, the approach of No More Deaths is more confrontational, actively engaging in campaigns of "civil disobedience" and "civil initiative" that directly challenge law enforcement policies. No More Deaths points to this difference of mission when, in describing the group's genesis, they write:

> A morally intolerable situation inspired a remarkable humanitarian movement in Southern Arizona in the fall of 2003. At that point more than 2,000 men, women and children had died trying to cross the U.S./Mexico border since 1998, driven by economic inequality and ill-conceived U.S. immigration policy. Most deaths were occurring in the desert's brutal summer months, where the average temperature reaches 110 degrees regularly. The death toll continued to rise, in spite of the efforts of well-organized humanitarian aid groups like Humane Borders and The Samaritan Patrols. With another summer of inevitable deaths looming, diverse faith-based communities, social activists, and concerned individuals felt compelled to find another way to stop unnecessary suffering and save lives. The result was the convergence of hundreds of local, regional, and national volunteers who came together to work for one common goal: No Más Muertes—No More Deaths.[4]

In effect, while No More Deaths expresses an appreciation for the work of Humane Borders, they believe that "the water effort" is not enough. "There were a lot of gaps to be filled still, a lot more to be done," explained Sarah Roberts, an active member of No More Deaths, "and that's how No More Deaths came into being: trying to respond to other migrant needs."[5]

In the fall of 2003, the incipient group began brainstorming ways to "fill in those gaps." In the following five years, No More Deaths would come up with four core projects, which became known as (1) Arks of the Covenant, (2) Humanitarian Aid Is Never a Crime, (3) Migrant Aid Centers, and (4) Abuse Documentation. Each one of these projects, in one way or another, has directly challenged U.S. federal law and border policies and sparked much public controversy. They have led to high drama court cases and tenacious bitterness between No More Deaths members and law enforcement agents.

The first idea that took hold of the group's imagination in 2003 was something they called "Arks of the Covenant." When members began brainstorming ways to provide aid to migrants, they thought of setting up base camps in the desert. From these camps, volunteers would embark into the desert (loaded with food, water, medical supplies, GPS tracking devices, and satellite phones) in search of migrants in distress. Referencing the Israelites' journey through the desert toward the Promised Land, No More Deaths decided to call these camps "Arks of the Covenant," or simply "Ark Sites." As stated on the No More Deaths website, these camps would provide "an around-the-clock, non-violent, humanitarian physical presence in the desert [and] would be the single most effective approach" in aiding migrants.[6]

The "Ark Sites" were set up on privately owned land. The site that quickly gained the most media attention was the Arivaca camp. The camp is located on the land of an eighty-five-year-old woman named Byrd Baylor. Baylor, the author of several children's books and a self-proclaimed "tree-hugging dirt worshiper and desert druid," lives just eleven miles from the border.[7] There is a shrine on her property at the No More Deaths campsite. The shrine, erected by migrants who have passed through her land, is a hodge-podge of votive candles and white wooden crosses, old sneakers, discarded backpacks, bottles of water, rosary beads, Bibles, prayer books, and other discarded belongings from migrants.[8]

Ark Sites, like the one near Arivaca, have led to much conflict between No More Deaths members and Border Patrol agents. On the surface, the conflict is mostly related to the issue of "harboring." Below the surface, however, lie even greater philosophical and theological differences regarding how to deal with the hundreds of thousands of migrants entering the country illegally every year. Concerning the issue of "harboring," of which several No More Deaths members have been accused (and brought to trial over), a few legal details must be mentioned. According to U.S. federal law:

> Any person who ... knowing or in reckless disregard of the fact that an alien has come to, entered, or remains in the United States in violation of law, transports, or moves or attempts to transport or move such alien within the United States [ii] [or who] ... conceals, harbors, or shields from detection, or attempts to conceal, harbor, or shield from detection, such alien in any place, including any building or any means of transportation [iii] [or] encourages or induces an alien to come to, enter, or reside in the United States, knowing or in reckless disregard of the fact that such coming to, entry, or residence is or will be in violation of law [iv] ... shall be punished.[9]

The punishment for harboring, concealing, or transporting "illegal aliens" ranges in severity, from small fines to years of imprisonment, depending on the nuances of each case and the subtleties of the law.

In several instances over the years, No More Deaths members have been accused of knowingly harboring and of concealing and transporting migrants. In every case, the accused members have claimed that they were simply helping migrants in distress, not breaking the law. This divide points to the emerging differences under the surface of the conflict: where members feel they are providing "hospitality," federal law sees them as "harboring"; where members believe they are following a higher moral law (when they provide food and water for migrants in the desert), federal law sees them as "encouraging" migrants, or even "concealing" them.

Case in point: in a recent interview, Byrd Baylor tells of two migrants, a woman and her nephew, who showed up at her house dehydrated. She tells of giving each of them a teaspoon of water (anymore would provoke dangerous vomiting). She says that, at the request of the woman who was too sick to go on, she called the Border Patrol. But when agents arrived at her house, they accused her of "harboring." Byrd told them that she was simply providing humanitarian aid to migrants in distress, and that doing so was no crime. While no charges were pressed, the alleged accusation points to the ongoing tensions between No More Deaths members and federal agents.[10]

This debate, over "harboring" versus "humanitarian aid," has become a heated one in the Tucson sector. Such incidents like the one Byrd describes led to the inception of No More Deaths' second campaign, which the group called: "Humanitarian Aid Is Never a Crime." In large part, this second campaign was sparked after two of the group's volunteers, Shanti Sellz and Daniel Strauss, were stopped in July 2005 by Border Patrol agents and arrested for "transporting" three illegal immigrants in their car. Sellz and Strauss both argued that they were not "harboring" or "illegally transporting" anyone. Instead, they said that they had come upon three sick migrants on the side of the road and were taking them to get medical attention. According to an Amnesty International report:

> On July 9, 2005 Daniel [Strauss] and Shanti [Sellz] were transporting three migrants reported to have been suffering from extreme thirst and hunger, resulting in persistent vomiting. The migrants had also developed severe, crippling blisters during their long walks in the desert....Daniel and Shanti were driving the three men to get treatment by volunteer medical professionals in Tucson when they were stopped by the United States Border Patrol and arrested.[11]

Both Strauss and Sellz were charged with two felonies under federal law: transporting illegal immigrants and conspiring to do so. Legal protocol required them to call Border Patrol as soon as they found the sick migrants. But Sellz and Strauss said that there was no phone coverage where they found the migrants. As a result of their choice to transport the ailing migrants, Sellz and Strauss faced a possible fifteen years in prison and $500,000 in fines. In the court proceedings that followed, both defendants pointed out that it was not uncommon to find migrants in distress in remote desert areas south of Tucson. Unable to call ambulances or Border Patrol, Sellz and Strauss chose to drive the migrants for proper medical treatment themselves. What were they supposed to do, they asked, leave the three migrants on the side of the road in such a terrible state?

Although the case dragged on for months, it was eventually dismissed. During the process, however, No More Death launched its "Humanitarian Aid Is Never a Crime" campaign. The group began handing out signs and bumper stickers, which are now seen all over Tucson, in windows, on cars, on T-shirts, and on stakes in front lawns. The message of the campaign was clear: acting to save lives like Sellz and Strauss did is *not* a crime; it is, above all, a moral duty.

The Sellz and Strauss case was only the beginning of what would become a laundry list of confrontations between No More Deaths volunteers and federal and state law enforcement agencies. In August 2008, for example, more than twenty-five federal agents surrounded the area around the Arivaca "Ark Site." Mike Scioli, a sector spokesman, said that horse-patrol agents had followed migrant foot tracks that led to the No More Deaths campsite. Scioli reports that "when asked if there were any migrants there, [No More Deaths volunteers] said no. A search of the area discovered two individuals."[12] The two migrants found at the site were taken into custody while No More Deaths volunteers and Border Patrol agents argued intensely for hours. "Visiting the camp that day was Dr. Miguel De La Torre, a seminary professor at Denver's Iliff School of Theology, and several of his students. 'What I found frustrating,' Dr. La Torre says, 'is that here we were providing medical attention, providing food and water for people in the desert, and that somehow, this is a crime. As Christians, we're practicing our faith, and we're detained for it in this country. When a law says that we can't give basic medical attention to somebody, then that's not the law.' "[13]

Dr. La Torre's comment points straight to the ideological rift at the center of such controversies. In part, the fractious relationship between law enforcement and faith-based humanitarian coalitions like No More Deaths stems from divergent understandings of what is meant by the "law," or what concept of "law" one believes should be privileged. For the Border Patrol and other law enforcement agents, it is "civil law" that must be followed, whereas others, like certain members of No More Deaths (and their supporters) believe that, in some cases, when civil laws seem inhumane or ill-conceived, there is a higher "moral law" to follow. Sometimes, this "moral law" is directly informed by another notion of law, that of "biblical law," derived from the Judeo-Christian scriptures. Sometimes, say some faith-based activists at the border, the "law of man" is simply inferior to "the law of God." Such activists believe that providing humanitarian aid to migrants can never be a breach of law, especially when read in light of key biblical passages that deal with providing hospitality to strangers. If helping migrants in distress is breaking the law, they say, then the law is misguided, and a higher moral law must be followed.[14]

More recent in the list of run-ins between No More Deaths members and law enforcement agents have been the "littering convictions" of two No More Death's volunteers: Dan Millis and Walt Staton. The most recent "littering" debacle involved the twenty-seven-year-old Walt Staton. On December 4, 2008, Staton was leaving plastic water jugs for migrants in the Buenos Aires National Wildlife Refuge southwest of Tucson when he was cited for littering by a U.S. Fish and Wildlife officer. Staton refused to pay the $175 citation issued by the officer because he believed he was not littering. What he was doing, he says, was trying to save lives. The case went to court on June 3, 2009 (Staton faced a possible $10,000 fine and up to a year in prison). In court testimony, Staton explained to the jury that his decision to leave out water was inspired by his faith and also by personally witnessing so many dehydrated migrants over the years; he could not see how leaving out lifesaving water could possibly be a crime. In his closing statement, Staton's lawyer, Bill Walker, held up a jug of water and said, "When the government tells you this case isn't about water or this isn't about saving lives, they're wrong! This is valuable, life-sustaining water."[15] Meanwhile, "prosecutors argued it shouldn't matter what Staton's intentions were, or a person's motives for committing a crime would matter in other cases. 'Every bank robber would come in here and say they did it to save their dying grandmother,' Assistant U.S. Attorney Lawrence Lee said."[16]

"The whole thing is ridiculous," Staton said to me outside the courthouse before his earlier hearing in March 2009. "It is a government ploy. They know I was not littering. They're just trying to prove a point. They don't care about saving lives. Believe it or not, along with leaving out water jugs, I was actually picking up trash. I had a couple trash bags full of garbage in the back of my truck when they stopped me. Apparently, Border Patrol had been monitoring me for a while, from land and from helicopters. They want to confiscate my passport and monitor my travels, all for putting out some water."[17]

It was not the first time that a No More Deaths volunteer had been convicted of littering in the Buenos Aires National Wildlife Refuge. Dan Millis, another volunteer, was found guilty of "littering" in September 2008, just a few months before Staton. Two days before he was cited, Millis came across the dead body of a fourteen-year-old El Salvadoran girl, Josseline Jamileth Hernandez Quinteros, in the Buenos Aires Refuge. Two days after discovering her remains, Millis returned with jugs of water to the spot where he found Quinteros. That is when he was stopped by officials and cited for littering. A camp coordinator for No More Deaths, Steve Johnston, tells the story about Quinteros:

Her parents live in L.A. They've been there for some years. So she and her younger brother were traveling to L.A., to meet up with her parents. On the way, she got injured or sick, I don't know which, and they left her. The brother continued. When her brother got in touch with the parents, they called the Mexican consulate, and the consulate called Derechos Humanos, and Derechos Humanos called us [No More Deaths]. We started looking for her.... She was in between two trails [in the Buenos Aires Refuge]. We walked within a quarter mile of her. It was February—cold, cold. Froze every night. She had been alone out there for two weeks, with no food, no water. She had taken off her shoes. When she was found, her feet were in a little puddle of water, and her shoes were neatly next to her.[18]

Originally, Millis was found guilty, by U.S. Magistrate Judge Bernardo Velasco, of the Class B misdemeanor offense of littering on a National Wildlife Refuge, where Quinteros died, although Millis's sentence was suspended. He would not have to spend time in jail or pay any fines. In a written response to the verdict, Millis wrote,

Yard signs and stickers all around Tucson and beyond assert that "Humanitarian Aid Is Never a Crime." Rather, it is an act of compassion and basic decency, like jumping in a pool after a drowning baby. It's a no-brainer. And to say it shouldn't be punished? Duh! Humanitarian aid should be valued, congratulated, practiced, preached, and, most importantly, funded. Even this "guilty" verdict has a conscience, and can't quite bring itself to levee a penalty.[19]

Millis's littering conviction would eventually (not until September 2, 2010) be overturned, but his case stoked the fire for Walt Staton's case, which was treated more severely by officials. Whereas Millis was only charged with "littering," Staton was charged with "knowingly littering," which is punishable by a year in prison rather than just six months.

In the end, Staton was convicted by a twelve-member jury of "knowingly littering garbage or other debris." After Staton's guilty verdict was announced, No More Deaths released a statement saying:

This is a sad day for human rights and for all of us in Southern Arizona. By penalizing life-saving work, the United States is showing callous disregard for the lives of their neighbors to the south, whose only crime is to seek a better life. No More Deaths will continue to provide life-saving aid to those in need, and to do our part to clean up the desert. The era of border enforcement that uses death and human rights abuses as a deterrent must come to an end.[20]

In response to Staton's guilty verdict, letters of support poured into the No More Deaths website. "If you have saved even one life your work is rewarded tenfold," wrote Barbara and Ed Hook. "All human life is sacred regardless of a person's country. God has no borders in showing love and care to other human beings," wrote P. J. Boone-Edgerton Longoni. "This is indeed a governmental ploy to keep humanitarians from helping those who need aid. Shame on the US border patrol!" Amanda Koplin wrote. "Litterbugs of conscience unite!" wrote Michael Stancliff, professor of rhetoric and composition at Arizona State University. "It is an abuse of human rights to prevent people from carrying out humanitarian aid," wrote Ceil Roeger of the Dominican sisters of Houston. "In my daughter's dictionary 'litter' equates with 'bits or scraps of paper or other garbage scattered around uselessly.' When Walt and other No More Deaths volunteers carefully placed containers of life-giving water in areas where they are most likely to be opened and consumed by thirsty and suffering human beings, they are not littering but purposely providing humanitarian aid," said Laura Dravenstoft. Still others quoted at length from the gospel of Matthew, Exodus, Leviticus, and Deuteronomy.[21]

No More Deaths, which had stopped leaving out jugs of water on the wildlife refuge after Staton's citation in December 2008, chose to begin doing so once again, as a way of protesting his guilty conviction. Despite the likely repercussions, the Reverend Gene Lefebvre, a retired Presbyterian minister, informed Mike Hawkes, the refuge manager, that the group would be resuming its practice of leaving out water. In a public statement Lefebvre said:

> The time has come for us as a people of faith and conscience. Tomorrow, we will place water on the wildlife refuge as we have done in the past. We are doing this not as an act of defiance to you, or your agency. But because sometimes bureaucracy and its rules get in the way, distort truth and cause deaths. We invite you to be responsible to human life, as well as wildlife. Come join us tomorrow.[22]

The day after the statement was released, thirteen people were cited for littering in the refuge, including two ministers and one Franciscan priest.[23] This act only further escalated tensions between factions. Both sides kept to their party line. No More Deaths repeated its refrain: it is lifesaving water we are leaving out; saving lives is not a crime; the government is to blame for the deaths in the first place. Law enforcement kept to its tune: there are three Humane Borders water tanks in the refuge already; it is unlawful to leave plastic jugs of any sort in a wildlife reserve; there is already too much migrant trash in the refuge, and it is killing animals that eat it, many of which are endangered.

Clearly, there was much more at stake than simply a few bottles of water. In reality, the volatility surrounding the case concerns conflicting views over immigration policy; the water has served as a vehicle for each side to point an accusatory finger at the other. As Ashley Powers of the *Los Angeles*

Times wrote, "as the legal proceedings progressed, each side has essentially accused the other of staging a show trial to bolster its view of U.S. border policy."[24] Similarly, the *Arizona Daily Star* published an editorial concluding that both sides—law enforcement and members of No More Deaths— wound up looking bad. "Refuge officials," stated the editorial, "are coming across as heartless bureaucrats for confiscating water bottles that could potentially save lives.... No More Deaths, meanwhile, is coming off as a bunch of activists who refuse to follow the law."[25] The editorial goes on to say that "both sides make compelling arguments for their actions." While No More Deaths claims its mission is simply to save lives by making water available on remote migrant trails, law enforcement argues that "there's already plenty of water. In addition to three water tanks placed there by Humane Borders, Michael Hawkes [manager of the Buenos Aires Wildlife Refuge] said the refuge has more than 30 water sites available for border crossers, 14 of which are directly tied to drinking-water systems."[26] Moreover, Hawkes stressed, the empty bottles are a danger to the wildlife that the sanctuary is meant to protect. "Stray bottles can endanger mule deer, moun- tain lions and other wildlife, which might eat chunks of plastic or catch their antlers or paws in them, he says. The refuge, which also harbors the endangered masked bobwhite quail, is often strewn with backpacks, T-shirts, pants and a stadium's worth of water bottles, mainly from border crossers, Hawkes says. He has suggested that No More Deaths chain jugs to trees so border crossers—thought to each leave 5 to 8 pounds of trash— can refill their water bottles, not dump them for new ones."[27] Hawkes said, "It was like they [No More Deaths] had blinders on: 'Put water bottles on the trail, that's all we can do.' "[28]

When it came to sentencing Staton, the government wrote a memo to the judge pointing out that No More Deaths volunteers often write "*buena suerte*" (good luck) on the plastic water jugs. "The obvious conclusion," says the memo, "is that the defendant and No More Deaths wish to aid illegal aliens in their entry attempt," adding further: "His actions are not about humanitarian efforts, but about protesting the immigration policies of the United States."[29]

On August 11, 2009, with dozens of No More Death supporters crowd- ing the courtroom, "Staton was sentenced to 300 hours of community ser- vice [picking up trash] and 1 year unsupervised probation. Staton was also banned from entering the refuge for one year."[30] In response to the sentence, Staton's lawyer, Bill Walker, who quickly appealed the conviction, said:

> I think the judge was very brave in not inflicting the kind of punishment the U.S. attorney recommended. She didn't impose a harsh fine, nor did she give five years probation, which is what they wanted. The U.S. Attorney's office, on the other hand, was awful in

the way they conducted themselves throughout the proceedings. They politicized this case, and made significant misrepresentations in their statements to the Court. They spent untold thousands of dollars prosecuting this case when they should be going after terrorists and others who threaten our communities. There is no reason for them to have gone after somebody who was simply doing humanitarian work, the way they did.[31]

The *New York Times* editorial staff also weighed in on the case. Like the *Arizona Daily Star*, it opined that neither side behaved admirably. However, it seemed to lay the blame neither on No More Deaths nor on the Buenos Aires Refuge officials, but rather on the U.S. government and the Department of Homeland Security:

Mr. Staton, who has been barred from returning to the refuge for a year, might have done better to play by the rules, finding acceptable ways to leave more water for more people—maybe by securing water jugs to trees, so migrants could refill their own bottles instead of tossing them away.

But we also know that common sense has a way of evaporating in the dangerously surreal setting of the Arizona desert. Plastic litter is a threat to the environment, but so is the strategically dubious border fence, which disrupts migration and feeding for rare and endangered animals along hundreds of miles of remote wilderness. We also know that criminal border violators—gun runners heading south, drug traffickers and human smugglers coming north—are a far more dire threat than littering humanitarians.

Janet Napolitano, the homeland security secretary, gave a speech last week reinforcing her hawkish commitment to border security even as President Obama suggested that he would defer to next year the only real solution to the border problem—immigration reform that gives people an alternative. When the government cracks down on illegal crossings while refusing to establish a safe, sane alternative, funneling people into the remotest stretches of a burning desert, it shares responsibility for the awful results. One of those results is plastic bottles. Another is corpses.[32]

Not everyone would agree, of course, with the *New York Times*'s scathing analysis, which places the blame—the trash, the corpses, and the high-profile squabbles between law enforcement and humanitarian aid workers—on failed U.S. border policies. Nonetheless, the extremely charged "littering" debacle has provided a compelling look into how many faith-based activists and law enforcement agents are simply unable to see eye to eye in matters of immigration.

This contentious relationship only grew as No More Deaths expanded its mission to include a third project: Migrant Aid Stations. The idea was to open up migrant aid centers in Mexican border towns to serve recently deported migrants. No More Deaths saw these aid stations as another means to provide humanitarian aid. Thousands of men, women, and children were being deported daily from southern Arizona. They were being dropped off, at random, No More Deaths claimed, in terrible conditions (often wounded, hungry, sick, traumatized), at all times of day and night. Most migrants came from central and southern Mexican states, hundreds and thousands of miles away, with no money or means of homeward transportation. The goal of the aid station, No More Deaths said, was to provide basic care to migrants and others repatriated across the U.S.-Mexican border, including medical attention, food, water, and clothing.

No More Deaths could not provide the aid they wanted on the U.S. side of the border, but, if they got the right permission, they could do so on the Mexican side. That is exactly what the organization did. The group received permission from the Mexican government to open up its first migrant aid center, in Nogales, Sonora, in the summer of 2006. The aid station is located about one and one-third of a mile west of downtown Nogales, at the Mariposa Port of Entry. The Mariposa Port of Entry is one of Arizona's principal gateways for international trade, with trucks often lined up into the distance. Entering Mexico on foot at the Mariposa Port of Entry, the first thing one sees is the No More Deaths aid station. At the station, there is a big red tent with a No More Deaths banner hanging from it, and under the tent, large tin pots of food and canisters of water. Next to the tent is a dilapidated camping van stocked with donated clothes, and hanging from the van is a white eraser board, which has written on it, in large red lettering: *Personas Extraviadas* ("Missing Persons"). Scrawled across this board are the names of people who have gone missing in the desert and the dates they were last seen. To the right of the tent is an unhitched truck trailer, which has been converted into a modest medical supply center. It is packed with basic first aid equipment. Whenever possible, No More Deaths volunteers, who are also registered nurses or licensed EMTs, come to the station and tend to the sick.

There are benches at the site and groups of migrants sitting on them. Most of the migrants say very little. Many are waiting for dusk to attempt to cross; some are waiting to meet up with a *coyote*; others have just been deported and are weighing whether or not to try their luck again. There is a tense, tired feel to the place. Several feet in front of the tent, on a little dirt mound looking straight down at the fence dividing the United States from Mexico, there are *coyotes* mulling about, even in the daylight. "That little mound is their territory," a No More Deaths volunteer explained to me during one of my visits to the aid station. "Do not ever step onto it. I was once shot at from up there," he pointed to a hill behind him. "I could hear the bullet whizz past me. *Coyotes* are often at war with each other, competing for business, for drugs and for people to smuggle." His warning captured the intensity of the place, the visceral feel of danger and human desperation.

No More Death says that in its first two years, they served more than 250,000 people at the Mariposa aid station in Nogales.[33] The number is mind boggling. With such success, the organization worked to open another aid station in Naco, Sonora, with a similar goal of providing aid, and with similar success. As a result of spending so much time with recently deported migrants at the station in Nogales, No More Deaths volunteers realized they had another mission, a fourth campaign: to document the stories they were hearing from migrants about their time in short-term U.S. custody. In particular, they wanted to document stories of improper treatment by the Border Patrol and other ICE officials. No More Deaths members had been hearing eerily similar complaints from migrants held in short-term detention. The complaints concerned experiences of physical or verbal abuse, lack of sanitary conditions, denial of food and water, and confiscation of personal belongings, among other offenses. No More Deaths began systematically documenting these testimonies by conducting and recording uniform interviews with migrants at the aid stations in Nogales and Naco. After two years of "systematic documentation (2006–2007) by medical professionals and trained volunteers working in migrant centers," No More Deaths released its findings in a report entitled *Crossing the Line: Human Rights Abuses of Migrants in Short-Term Custody on the Arizona/Sonora Border*.[34] The report documents "the daily violations of human and civil rights that result from ICE and border patrol practices during short-term (up to 72 hours) apprehension, processing and repatriation."[35]

Not surprisingly, especially given No More Death's vehement public criticism of U.S. border policies, the report is extremely damning of Border Patrol practices. "We regularly encounter migrants who have been denied food and water and who have been separated from their family members during the repatriation process. We hear accounts of physical and verbal abuse, or injuries sustained while in Border Patrol custody, denial of urgent medical care, and of possessions that are not returned," states the report.[36] The data in the report are categorized into "twelve areas of concern." These areas of concern include the routine failure of the Border Patrol to provide food and water to migrants, verbal and physical abuse, denial of medical treatment, failure to return belongings to migrants, the separation of family members, and the repatriation of women and children at night.

The report is rife with examples of such abuses. Crack it open, and you will find stories of women repatriated after dark, of mothers and babies left on the street after midnight, families going hungry while in detention, pregnant women denied water, sexual harassment and verbal abuse, men beaten with batons, and so forth. One reads, for example:

200. Nogales: 5/1/2007, 1pm.

A young woman, age 17, reported being touched inappropriately while in Border Patrol custody. She was searched by male agents who touched her chest and thighs and reached into her pockets. She was additionally given insufficient water and food and separated from her family at the processing center. Border Patrol agents found them after they had been walking for a week. They were told that if they ran, the agents would order Border Patrol dogs to attack them. The woman witnessed a dog attack a young boy.[37]

210. 8/3/2006, 10:20 am.

Aurelio, age 36, from Guerrero, Mexico reported being pulled out of a car and kicked in the back by Border Patrol agents. An agent grabbed Aurelio again and threw him on the ground and punched him in the right upper chest. The agent kicked him three more times and then hand-cuffed him.[38]

261. Nogales 8/16/2006, 8:50 am

Twelve men and two women were repatriated; after five days of walking they were held for 24 hours and given only water and crackers. The 17-year old nephew of one man was separated from him; one woman was two months pregnant, nauseated and alone with two children; her husband had been killed in the desert previously.[39]

The report goes on for pages in such a manner. While there is no hard proof that such abuses occurred (it is all word of mouth), the group says they believe the testimonies they hear. They stress that the report is qualitative, not quantitative, saying: "The aim is to shed light on and publicize the systematic human rights abuses that thousands suffer at the hands of U.S. immigration law enforcement agents, using testimonies of the individuals who've experienced these abuses firsthand."[40]

The downfall of the documentation is that none of the abuses can be proven. There is no one to testify, for example, that Aurelio was kicked in the back or punched in the chest by a Border Patrol agent. Nor is there any way to know if Aurelio might have done something to instigate such treatment (was Aurelio threatening a law enforcement officer or behaving strangely?). Neither is there any way to verify that those twelve men and two women were given nothing but water and crackers for twenty-four hours; nor can we prove that the woman was touched inappropriately (it is standard procedure to frisk all migrants, since some, especially *coyotes* and drug smugglers, do carry arms), nor that the young boy was attacked by a dog.

Still, folks like Jim Walsh, the man who found the deceased female migrant beside the stretcher, says he hears the same stories enough to know they are real. In a written update for No More Deaths, Walsh describes being at the aid station as several buses, contracted by the Border Patrol, dropped off migrants:

We had the chance to speak with a number of migrants and heard much the same story that we have been hearing since the beginning...only crackers and water, abusive language and humiliating treatment from BP/detention personnel, disregarding of requests for food and medical attention. We fed some very hungry people who had been held since Monday on crackers and water...they told us they saw signs reading "ask if you need food, water or medical attention," but were told to shut up when they asked....I guess the signs are just window dressing.

Badly blistered feet and sprained ankles were treated for the first time at the Mariposa aid station...and the most heart-breaking story of the night was that of Angeles, a woman from Chiapas who fractured bones in her back climbing over the wall near Agua Prieta...she was in severe pain when she was made to walk back over the line from the...bus. We were able to provide her with extra strength Tylenol and a place to lie down for the night (the NMD trailer), but she faces a difficult time as she recovers.[41]

Perhaps, it is not so much about who is right and who is wrong (Border Patrol or No More Deaths), who is telling the truth, or how such truth can be proven. What seems most noteworthy is the fact that the No More Deaths crusade to document the suffering of migrants, and the alleged role of Border Patrol and ICE agents points, once again, to the unremitting antagonism between factions over how to handle the crisis in southern Arizona.

Furthermore, based on their findings, No More Deaths drafted a follow-up document filled with recommendations for Border Patrol short-term custody standards. The standards are meant to regulate Border Patrol procedures carried out with migrants who are detained for short periods of time (up to seventy-two hours), with the aim of "protecting the rights of all individuals detained by the Border Patrol."[42] The number of recommendations is extensive and includes seventy proposals. For example, the document is replete with very sound and possible recommendations ("Agents and DHS subcontractors will provide potable water to each migrant immediately after the initial contact"; "Children shall never be separated from their family"; "Holding cells shall not exceed the maximum capacity as posted inside the facility"; "Women in active labor shall not be handcuffed either en route to, or while in, a hospital," etc.). However, interspersed within such sound proposals are some that may be interpreted as superfluous, and still others that may sound downright insulting to the Border Patrol—for example, "Transportation shall always be at a safe speed that takes into account road and weather conditions." Such a recommendation may sound condescending, as it seems to imply that some, if not many, Border Patrol agents are careless drivers.

Moreover, while No More Deaths gives many decent recommendations, there is no mention of how to implement them. For example: "Each migrant will be medically screened at no cost by a licensed medical professional." This would of course be ideal, but who is going to pay for hundreds of daily health screenings, especially when a significant portion of the American public does not even receive such care themselves? Or, "Searches shall always be conducted by an agent of the same gender as the migrant." Again, this would be ideal. But the reality is that the majority of migrants and agents are male; agents often apprehend groups of migrants in extremely remote areas; for their own safety, agents must check migrants for weapons, but can they wait the hour or two it might take a female agent to arrive on the scene if there is a female migrant in the group?

On a certain level, these questions, and others like them, highlight the depth of disconnect between groups like No More Deaths and the Border Patrol, their mutual inability to understand each other's situation, logic, or justification. Neither in documents such as "Recommendations for Border Patrol Short-Term Custody" nor elsewhere does No More Deaths publicly consider the difficult and often dangerous work facing Border Patrol agents. There is little acknowledgment of the logistical complexities involved in trying to contain, or even just monitor, hundreds of thousands of men, women, and children entering the Tucson sector illegally. Nor is there any sort of expression of respect for the work of Border Patrol agents, even if the group may disagree with its policies.

Nearly three years after the release of *Crossing the Line*, in September 2011, No More Deaths released an even more scathing report, *A Culture of Cruelty: Abuse and Impunity in Short-Term U.S. Border Patrol Custody*. The follow-up report claims twelve times as many interviews with migrants (as there were in *Crossing the Line*), "detailing more than 30,000 incidents of abuse and mistreatment." The group explains that it entitled the report *Culture of Cruelty*

> because we believe our findings demonstrate that the abuse, neglect, and dehumaniza-
> tion of migrants is part of the institutional culture of the Border Patrol, reinforced by an
> absence of meaningful accountability mechanisms. This systematic abuse must be con-
> fronted aggressively at the institutional level, not denied or dismissed as a series of aber-
> rational incidents attributable to a few rogue agents. Until then we can expect this culture
> of cruelty to continue to deprive individuals in Border Patrol custody of their most
> fundamental rights.[43]

Once again, with their latest report, it seems that No More Deaths and Border Patrol could not be further apart. While No More Deaths goes so far as to accuse many common Border Patrol practices as "plainly meeting the definition of torture under international law,"[44] the Border Patrol adamantly defends its practices as humane and reasonable. Like members of No More

Deaths, most Border Patrol agents have their hearts in the right place; they feel that they are serving their country, trying to make it safer, trying to do the right thing for and by others. The fact that both agents and activists have earnest and well-meaning intentions makes the situation even more tragic, as it speaks to the near total breakdown of dialogue. Without dialogue, it is difficult to hope for reconciliation between groups. Without reconciliation, there will be no collaboration. It seems that faith-based activists and law enforcement will simply be unable to forge any common ground in Arizona—or anywhere else along the border for that matter.

When I spoke with Agent Mario Escalante, spokesperson for the Border Patrol's Tucson sector about this breakdown in dialogue, he said the Border Patrol has tried to negotiate over the years with No More Deaths. "Look," he said, "We try to work with them. We invite them to come talk with us. But time and again, they turn their backs on us and just do their own thing, blaming us for it all. It is very frustrating."[45]

Part of the breakdown stems from the fact that No More Deaths (like Humane Borders and others in "the migrant ministry business") believes that U.S. border enforcement policy is absolutely misguided and utterly inhumane. They see it as a strategy of "militarization" that deliberately pushes migrants into the desert. In fact, the first principle of No More Deaths' "faith-based principles for immigration reform" calls for people to "recognize that the current Militarized Border Enforcement Strategy is an ill-conceived policy."[46] As the Reverend John Fife, founder and leading voice of No More Deaths, says:

> That strategy has deliberately channeled the migration of workers into the most hazardous, isolated, and deadly areas of the borderlands. The resulting deaths of over 5,000 poor workers, their wives, and their children, and the suffering of untold hundreds of thousands of migrants in the desert is not just a failed strategy. It is also a continuing violation of human rights and international law.[47]

Fife goes on to cite the Inter-American Court of Human Rights, the United Nations Human Rights Commission, and Amnesty International, all of whom, in recent years, have stated that the death of migrants and many border enforcement policies are "the strongest evidence that the United States has violated and continues to violate human rights."[48]

Meanwhile, Border Patrol agents and their supporters see current strategies as extremely successful. Even President Obama, in speeches given in 2010 and 2011, has declared the border safer and more secure than ever. Border Patrol numbers point to this success. While there were 317,000 "illegal alien apprehensions" in 2008–2009, that number dropped to 212,000 in 2009–2010. Part of the drop can be blamed on the economic recession, federal agents say, but much of it is the result of an effective border strategy.

Similarly, Chris Cox, former president of the Arizona chapter of the Minutemen Civil Defense Corps, believes that the militarized border strategy has greatly improved the situation on the border. "You should've seen how bad things were five years ago," he said during a phone interview. "We'd camp out on the border and in a weekend, we'd see hundreds of illegals running across. Now, we only see a few. There's no doubt that the wall, the increase in agents, the prosecutions, and other such measures have kept the numbers down. Don't get me wrong. I don't mind people coming to this country, as long as they do so in a lawful way. But you see what happens when you don't abide by the laws? You get all this misery: The drug smugglers, the human smugglers. It's just a real mess. But things are better with the current strategy."[49]

Still, many will say that fewer migrants does not equal fewer deaths. As Tohono O'odham tribal member Mike Wilson said, "In the reservation we are seeing less migrants but more deaths. So many migrants are going to extremes."

No More Deaths doesn't just blame the deaths on what they see as a failed border strategy. They also pin the deaths on the lack of effective immigration reform at the federal level. The group's preamble to its faith-based principles for immigration reform reads:

> As religious leaders from numerous and diverse faith traditions, we set forth the following principles by which immigration policy is to be comprehensively reformed. We believe that using these principles—listed from the most imminent threat to life to the deepest systemic policy problems—will significantly reduce, if not eliminate, deaths in the desert borderlands.[50]

These faith-based principles are, in order: (1) Recognize that the current Militarized Border Enforcement is an ill-conceived policy. (2) Address the status of undocumented persons currently living in the United States. (3) Make family unity and reunification the cornerstone of the U.S. immigration system. (4) Allow workers and their families to enter the United States to live and work in a safe, legal, orderly, and humane manner through an Employment-Focused immigration program. (5) Recognize that the root causes of immigration lie in environmental, economic, and trade inequalities.[51]

As the Reverend Fife explained, No More Deaths' vision of comprehensive immigration reform must include "short-term and long-term fixes." In the short term, Fife says, the U.S. government must find a way "to legalize the status of folks living here already. We must give those people documents so they don't have to live in the shadows, and so that they can be recognized as contributing members of our society."[52] He says further, "we must also establish legal means for workers to cross the border, guest worker programs and such. Mexico would have to cooperate by doing criminal background checks, and both governments would have to work closely with each other, especially to see what economic needs there were." In the long term, Fife says, we must look at the ways NAFTA and other "elite capitalist measures" are creating poverty and a shameful disparity of wealth, enabling inhumane work situations (such as at sweatshops), forcing people to migrate, and causing families to separate.[53]

The critique of NAFTA (a common theme among No More Deaths members) is part of the group's quest to address the "root causes" of migration. As Douglass Massey points out: "Although Mexico's 1997 GNP per capita of $3,700 places it in the upper tier of developing nations, it pales in comparison to the U.S. figure of $29,000, and nowhere else on earth is there such a sharp contrast along the border, much less one that is two thousand miles long."[54] Further, Massey writes:

> A full understanding of international migration requires facing up to four basic questions: What are the forces in sending societies that promote out-migration, and how do they operate? What are the forces in receiving societies that create a demand for immigrant workers, and how do they function? What are the motivations, goals, and aspirations of the people who respond to these forces by migrating internationally? And what are the social and economic structures that arise in the course of migration to connect sending and receiving societies?[55]

These are the sorts of "holistic" questions that members of No More Deaths try to examine during their weekly meetings at St. Mark's Presbyterian Church. In particular, they place significant blame on what they see as NAFTA's "politics of contradiction." It is a politics that simultaneously seeks to move "toward integration while insisting on separation. In time-honored fashion, the United States sought to have its cake and eat it too—to move headlong toward a consolidation of markets for capital, goods, commodities, and information, but...to prevent the integration of one particular market: that for labor."[56] No More Deaths could not agree more with Massey's assessment: the United States' reliance on cheap labor, while simultaneously preventing the integration of that labor, plays a tremendous role in keeping the cogs of illegal immigration turning.

In the final analysis, it seems there will be little compromise between No More Deaths and law enforcement agents. Reverend Fife, paraphrasing "Jim Corbett's ethical call to churches in 1982," wrote:

For those of us who would be faithful in our allegiance to the Kingdom of God, there is no way to avoid recognizing that collaboration with a government that violates human rights is a betrayal to our faith, even if it is a passive or even loudly protesting collaboration that tolerates the deaths of thousands of poor migrant workers. When a government uses the crucifixion of entire peoples in the desert as a border strategy, we have no middle ground between collaboration and resistance. We can take our stand with the oppressed, or we can take our stand with organized oppression—but we cannot do both.[57]

It is a divisive statement, but it expresses the passion and conviction behind No More Deaths.

In the end, neither side is completely blameless. Both law enforcement agents and No More Deaths members have shown shades of righteousness and a sad inability to compromise. Nonetheless, it is hard not to admire the doggedness of this small grassroots organization that meets in a sparse church hall every Monday night. Moreover, the fact that the group has caused such a stir in the public sphere, whether through "harboring" or "littering" trials, confrontational abuse documentation and policy recommendations, desert campsites and migrant aid stations, is testimony to their power. Each trial, each campaign, each new initiative gets people's attention and puts the focus where they want it: on the suffering and death of migrants.

No matter what side one takes, it is clear that what has been heating up in the Sonoran desert over the past decade between federal officials and faith-based activists is a fierce battle of ideas over differing views on immigration policy. Each week, tensions between factions seem to escalate. No one is willing to bend; the acrimony goes back and forth: the barbs, the mutual accusations, the provocations, the symbolic punches and counter punches. Where it will lead, how it will intensify, no one can say for sure. What one can say, however, is that, for the moment, "people of faith and conscience" are not backing down.

CHAPTER 5

Postscript: Riding with the Samaritans

On a warm January afternoon, I travel to Ruby, Arizona, with "The Samaritans," another of Tucson's faith-based aid groups. The Samaritans was founded in 2002. Members describe themselves as "people of faith and conscience who are responding directly, practically and passionately to the crisis at the U.S.-Mexican border...a diverse group of volunteers that are united in our desire to relieve suffering among our brothers and sisters and to honor human dignity."[1] Their mission involves providing emergency medical assistance, food, and water to migrants crossing the Sonoran desert. They call these missions "Samaritan patrols." On the day I go out with them, they are delivering bright orange blankets, along with water and packets of food to Ruby's only resident, a man who goes by the name Sun Dog.

Ruby is a gem of a ghost town, located in the mountainous area northwest of Nogales in Coronado National Park. Due to its desolate location, migrants and their *coyotes* often pass through the town. Because so many migrants have been coming through Ruby, Samaritan volunteers have been leaving supplies with Sun Dog who doles them out to migrants. If they need a place to sleep, Sun Dog says he directs them to the town's abandoned mining shaft and provides them with blankets.

Sun Dog invites us into his ramshackle house and offers us some deer meat. "Sometimes I wind up in Mexico when I'm hunting deer," he explains. Sun Dog has bright blue eyes and a beard that makes Grizzly Adams's beard seem tame in comparison. "There's no way of knowing when you're in Mexico and when you're in the States in these parts," he adds.

Then he tells me the story of a woman named Maricela. "One day this woman came screaming over the hills," Sun Dog says, "running for her life. Behind her was a *coyote*, close at her heels. Well, she just stumbled into my arms, by sheer luck, sheer luck! The *coyote* had brutally raped her friend and was coming after Maricela next. So Maricela ran without knowing that Ruby was just over the hills."

"So Sun Dog called my wife back in Tucson who is a doctor," Walt Collins, one of the Samaritans pipes in, "and she came down to Ruby and looked over her. Then we brought Maricela to a safe house. Now she's living somewhere in New Jersey."

"What ever happened to her friend?" I ask Sun Dog.

There is an ominous silence. "No one ever heard from her," Sun Dog shakes his head.

Such violence, one quickly learns, is not uncommon. Women risk the most trying to cross into the United States. "Among the dangers migrant women face, sexual violence, due to the frequency of its occurrence and the degree of suffering it necessarily inflicts, occupies a singular and terrifying place."[2] The incidences of rape are so widespread that many women report getting birth control pills before setting out on the journey north.

An interesting point to take note of in this ghastly story is that the Samaritans took Maricela to "a safe house." Later, when Collins was driving me back to Tucson, as we passed through the small town of Arivaca, he pointed to the "safe house." It was nothing more than a dilapidated trailer with boarded up windows. I chose not to ask Collins about the discrepancy that exists between the group's proclaimed adherence to federal laws and Collins' admission that they had taken Maricela to "a safe house," an act that would, of course, amount to the crime of "harboring." Better not ask, better not to know, I thought. To this day, I still wonder.

On its website, the group is clear: "Samaritans is an entirely overt organization committed to a protocol of aid that Border Patrol is aware of."[3] Yet, the act of taking Maricela to a safe house, which allowed her to complete her journey to New Jersey, seems to contradict this claim of transparency. This is not a critique; if anything, it simply points to the many complexities and moral struggles facing everyone involved in the border crisis. Perhaps Collins and those with him felt that after all she had suffered, Maricela deserved a break. Perhaps there was some other part of the story that I was not aware of, that might explain things. In the end, it does not seem to really matter. The incident was years ago, and, sadly, Maricela's is just another story among hundreds of thousands of stories that, in one way or another, resemble it.[4]

As we approached the outskirts of Tucson that day, I remembered my meeting with Dr. Bruce Parks, Pima County's chief medical examiner. Parks said to me, "When I got into this business, I had no idea what was in store for me. When I took the job here in Tucson all those years ago, I did not plan for this."[5] By *this,* he meant all the dead migrants that have been found over the years. Usually, their remains are transported to his office so that he and his colleagues and interns can perform the autopsy to discern the cause of death, along with other information such as sex or age. Sometimes the remains come to him in such a terrible state, he said, that it is impossible to tell exactly how the person died. "Back when I started there was only the occasional migrant death Now, the bodies don't stop coming. The children and the pregnant women are the worst," Parks added.

When Collins dropped me off in the parking lot of Tucson's Southside Presbyterian church, I found myself wondering, as the sun set over the Santa Catalina Mountains, casting an ethereal purple glow over the city, if there is any solution to the crisis at our southern border.

As the death toll rises, faith-based activists keep mobilizing. And they keep pointing the finger at federal law enforcement. Their harsh policies are responsible for the deaths, they say. Before the wall, before the high-tech equipment, before the beefing up of the border, people weren't dying like this.

In his address to the World Council of Churches, the Reverend Robin Hoover said:

> All along the migrant trails, faith communities, representatives of civil society, and human rights groups gather and organize to systematically provide a number of goods and services to target populations. Our help will never be sufficient, but still, we help with water stations for migrants crossing deserts, aid stations for persons in medical distress, shelters in Mexico for rest and rehabilitation to aid migrants being repatriated, and finally, counseling and legal services where appropriate. All of this is still needed, but totally inadequate to human need for the millions of migrants who move across our lands. The crisis we experience in the desert southwest and beyond in both directions is a need that can only adequately be addressed with the resources and resolve of the states.[6]

Because the federal government is not providing these resources, Hoover says, the work of border ministries is necessary. Those involved in them believe it is a moral duty to respond to the suffering strangers in our midst. It is our moral duty to leave out tanks of water in the desert; to provide soup kitchens and beds for the deported; to search for stranded migrants lost or dehydrated in remote areas; to offer medical assistance to the wounded. Not to do so is inhumane. Not to do so is to deny the message of radical hospitality that is so prominent in the Judeo-Christian scriptures, a message that commands us to feed, clothe, and welcome "the least of these," without asking who he or she is, where he or she is from, or where he or she is headed.

"As my country aspires to achieve national security, to benefit from stable labor markets, to expand human rights, and to reduce the amount of political noise associated with migration, it will be unable to achieve those goals unless it meets the basic needs of the migrants who are staring at us from our deserts," Hoover said, summing up the sentiment of activists at the border.[7]

One thing seems certain: until the governments of Mexico and the United States make immigration reform a top priority, until the complex machinery of immigration and border enforcement policies are properly evaluated, it seems that little will change. People like Doug Ruopp will continue checking the water tanks in the desert. Robin Hoover will continue wrangling with federal officials to put out more. Maryada Vallet will keep patching up people with subpar medical supplies at El Comedor. Folks like Walt Staton and Dan Millis will keep leaving out water, despite the consequences. Women like Maricela will keep running for their lives. And nuns like Sister Robles will keep waking up at dawn and dishing out beans and rice onto colorful plastic plates for hundreds of deportees.

PART II

Law in the Desert: Security, Sovereignty, and the Natural Rights of the State

CHAPTER 6

Fencing Arizona: Meditations on a Wall

I have come to the tiny town of Sasabe, Arizona, on a bright January afternoon to see the "new wall." "New," because only a few years ago there was just a line of thin barbed wire dividing the twin towns of Sasabe—Arizona and Mexico—just enough wire to keep the cows from crossing from the United States into Mexico, and vice versa.[1] Now, where the barbed wire once was, there are high steel pylons spanning the stark desert floor for several miles east and west of both Sasabes. There is not much in Sasabe, Arizona, which seems almost like a ghost town—nothing except a convenience store (with a "closed" sign dangling from the pink door), a few squat houses, and in the distance some ranches. The road through Sasabe comes to a screeching halt at the wall, where there is a small and somnolent border station, manned by a few droopy-eyed guards.

What is perhaps strangest about the new wall is that it stretches only a few miles, after which it comes to a sudden halt. One can see where the wall, both east and west of the station, simply ceases to exist at the foot of scrubby hills not far in the distance. Such a sudden ending might cause one to pause and wonder, What is the point of such a wall? Migrants need only walk a few extra miles, around the wall, before making their attempted entry.

Moreover, adding to the surreal effect of a wall in the middle of nowhere was the remarkable play of shadow and light occurring at the time of my visit. It was a few hours past noon, and the sun had fallen slightly behind the wall. The image that emerged was not only of the high wall but also of the shadow the wall cast into the sand, fanning out across the dusty road used by Border Patrol vehicles. The one wall had become two: a wall of steel and a wall of shadow.

Standing in the wall of shadows, I wrapped my hands around the thick steel bars and glanced into Mexico, just inches from my nose. On the Mexican side, there were hundreds of empty bottles scattered among the palo verde trees, bottles of Red Bull, water, Pedialyte, Coca-Cola, Fanta, and other drinks, evidence that despite the wall, large numbers of migrants had been there and were still attempting to cross.

Why, one might wonder, is there a wall at Sasabe, in such a desolate and sluggish town? The reason lies precisely in the remoteness of the place, as well as in the fact that sixty miles south of Sasabe is the "migrant hub" of Altar, Mexico. As migrants have been redirected to more desolate areas (due to heightened border enforcement policies, which have made more conventional crossings in urban areas increasingly difficult), Altar has become the Grand Central Station, so to speak, of border crossings. It is the place where hundreds, sometimes thousands, of migrants congregate daily before departing on their desert trek. From Altar, they are squeezed into the backs of pickup trucks, which travel the dangerous dirt road up to Sasabe, Sonora. It is a road used heavily by warring drug traffickers, and is, as a result, a lawless stretch. Rapes, robberies, and murders are not uncommon on the road. Once in Sasabe, most migrants meet up with *coyotes*, putting their lives and trust (and usually the rest of their money) in the hands of these smugglers. From there, it is a short walk to the hills at the wall's edge, where if they are lucky, they will dash across and slip into the rough and wild hands of the desert.

The wall at Sasabe is just one of many newly constructed segments of physical barrier that have been erected along the U.S.-Mexican border since the late 1990s. While Congress has been mired in a stalemate over immigration reform, "one area of immigration policy that is proceeding, despite the political stalemate [is] the building of the border fence between the U.S. and Mexico."[2] Since 2005, some \$2.4 billion has been spent on the fence, mostly in Arizona.[3] This costly and concerted effort was made possible through the Secure Fence Act, passed by Congress in 2006. The act was passed "to establish operational control over the international land and maritime borders of the United States" by which was "meant the prevention of all unlawful entries into the United States, including entries by terrorists, other unlawful aliens, instruments of terrorism, narcotics and other contraband."[4] Operational control was to be achieved "not later than 18 months, after the date of the enactment of this Act," and was to involve systematic surveillance "through more effective use of personnel and technology, such as unmanned aerial vehicles, ground-based sensor, satellites, radar coverage, and cameras; and physical structure enhancements to prevent unlawful entry by aliens into the United States."[5]

Hence, border security was divided into three main categories: personnel, technology, and infrastructure. "Infrastructure" referred mainly to the construction of at "least 2 layers of reinforced fencing," which was to cover over 700 miles of "priority areas," or approximately one-third of the border. This effort to construct a U.S.-Mexican border fence is not only unprecedented but is also a recently new endeavor. In 1971, when first lady Pat Nixon inaugurated Border Field State Park in Imperial Beach, California, a park that is adjacent to the U.S.-Mexican border at the San Diego/Tijuana divide, she remarked, "I hate to see a fence anywhere." She was referring to the barbed wire barrier of the park, separating the two countries. The first lady had someone cut a piece of the barbed wire fencing so she could cross over into Mexico and greet onlookers. "I hope there won't be a fence here too long," she said as she did. Her wish would not come true.

In 1990, the first substantial effort to construct adequate fencing along the U.S.-Mexican border occurred there, at the San Diego/Tijuana divide, where, at the time, the majority of undocumented migrants were crossing. This fencing effort, at the most southwest corner of the border, far surpassed the bits of barbed wire, placed here and there, that previously served as deterrents to migrants. Instead, the steel wall near San Diego (made in part with military landing mats) marked the beginning of a new era of more intentional and rigorous border security infrastructure. During the Clinton administration, and later, in the wake of 9/11, geographically specific operations were undertaken in which physical barricading became more commonplace. However, it was the Secure Fence Act of 2006 that made fence building an integral and more systematic component in the attempt to "achieve operational control over the border."

In tandem with "physical infrastructure enhancements," that is, nearly 700 miles of additional fencing, the Secure Fence Act also called for improved personnel and technology mechanisms. In the Tucson sector, for example, one can see these additions all over. There are the Boeing-built surveillance towers ascending like giant sentinels from the desert floor, the checkpoints on heavily traveled interstate highways bringing all traffic to a halt, Border Patrol trucks constantly whizzing by, agents arresting migrants on the side of the road, the blackhawk helicopters overhead, the Wackenhut buses loaded with migrants being deported to Mexico, as well as the detention centers tucked away from the public eye and the courtrooms where the mass trials of Operation Streamline occur every weekday. All these measures serve the aim of gaining control. True control, as the Department of Homeland Security explains, means that "continuous detection and interdiction resources [exist] at the immediate border with [consequent] high probability of apprehension upon [illegal] entry."[6]

In the high-stakes drama to gain control, the emerging barrier wall has become a sort of protagonist in its own right: a strange, often shocking, larger-than-life character. The wall speaks volumes about the uneasy history between the United States and Mexico, about the breakdown of multiple interconnected systems (economic, diplomatic, political), and about a certain uncontainable fear and frustration. The wall also asserts a certain ideology, in this case, that of border security, the supremacy of law, respect of sovereign borders, and the value of order and control.

There is nothing as irrefutable as a steel wall, rising up from the sands of the desert, so starkly dividing two countries, to send a message, a sequence of messages, to one's neighbors, to the world, and to one's own citizens. While walls may be built in good faith, in an attempt to regulate relationships between two parties—whether two individuals, or two nations— they are more likely an admission of some sort of failure, a sign of an uncontainable conflict, or the collapse of effectual dialogue. They are often characterized by a disparity in wealth or power: there is one party, with more resources, trying to wall out the party with lesser means.

Mostly, though, walls are constructed as acts of desperation when other strategies have not worked. The U.S.-Mexican barrier fence is no exception. Almost every day on the news, there is another story of drug violence, of illegal weapon stashes, of human smuggling tragedies. No matter what viewpoint one takes concerning the U.S.-Mexican border, there is little disagreement that the situation is untenable.

Admittedly, by nature, border areas tend to be chaotic and conflictual. They are erratic convergence zones. Where national borders run up against each other, so do national laws. Within a stone's throw, different sets of rules apply, creating zones of opportunity, rebellion, lawlessness, and danger. The border is a place where many come to test the limits of the law, to go beyond them, or simply to enjoy certain freedoms that do not exist on one side or the other. Hence, it can quickly become a hotbed of illegal activity and of consequent violence. Not just during Prohibition, when Americans flocked over the border to purchase alcohol, but today more than ever, this violence and illegal activity is part of the fabric of border towns: American teenagers slip over the border to drink, people teem south to pay for sex with greater ease or to purchase drugs or cheap pharmaceuticals; drug cartel members smuggle weapons south into Mexico, while northward go the bundles of drugs or the hundreds of thousands of migrants without papers. It is this sort of "chaos" that Homeland Security is trying to contain through the unprecedented construction of a border wall.

As Charles Bowden wrote:

Borders everywhere attract violence, violence prompts fences, and eventually fences mutate into walls. Then everyone pays attention because a wall turns a legal distinction into a visual slap in the face. We seem to love walls, but are embarrassed by them because they say something unpleasant about the neighbors—and us. They flow from two sources: fear and desire for control. Just as our houses have doors and locks, so do borders call forth garrison, customs officials, and, now and then, big walls. They give us divided feelings because we do not like to admit we need them.[7]

The U.S.-Mexico border, from its inception, has been a historically contested space. Going back to the Mexican American War (1846–1848), sparked when the United States annexed Texas, the American southwest has always been a place of blended cultures, languages, and identities. When Mexico admitted defeat after the Mexican American war, it also gave up nearly half a million square miles. Through the treaty of Guadalupe Hidalgo, the United States acquired parts of what are today Colorado, Arizona, New Mexico, and Wyoming, along with all of California, Nevada, and Utah. A few years later, in 1853, through the Gadsden Purchase, the United States acquired further lands—what is today southern Arizona and southern New Mexico. Purchased primarily for the purpose of building a transcontinental railroad, the Gadsden Purchase created the U.S.-Mexican border as we know it today. As the text of the Gadsden Purchase reads:

> The Mexican Republic agrees to designate the following as her true limits with the United States for the future: retaining the same dividing line between the two Californias as already defined and established, according to the 5th article of the treaty of Guadalupe Hidalgo, the limits between the two republics shall be as follows: Beginning in the Gulf of Mexico, three leagues from land, opposite the mouth of the Rio Grande, as provided in the 5th article of the treaty of Guadalupe Hidalgo; thence, as defined in the said article, up the middle of that river to the point where the parallel of 31° 47' north latitude crosses the same; thence due west one hundred miles; thence south to the parallel of 31° 20' north latitude; thence along the said parallel of 31° 20' to the 111th meridian of longitude west of Greenwich; thence in a straight line to a point on the Colorado River twenty English miles below the junction of the Gila and Colorado rivers; thence up the middle of the said river Colorado until it intersects the present line between the United States and Mexico.[8]

With these words, the "true limits" of the U.S.-Mexican border were finalized. Not surprisingly, however, these "lines in the sand" remained deeply contested. Today, over a century and a half later, much rancor and frustration remain among certain groups living at the border. Tohono O'odham tribal lands, for example, were divided nearly in half through the Gadsden Purchase, and today, many tribal members (both Mexican O'odham and American O'odham) use the refrain "the border crossed us."

The continued construction of the U.S.-Mexican barrier wall has only added salt to these wounds. For those who were already deeply ambivalent or downright angry about the border to begin with, such measures as the Secure Fence Act are seen as inhumane, imperialistic, or, at best, quixotic.

By April 2009, over 600 miles of new border fencing had been constructed at various locations, with a concerted focus on "hotspots" in southern Arizona. So far, however, the "fencing effort" has proven harder than expected. The difficulties are evident both in the piecemeal process by which the wall has come into existence as well as in the mishmash of materials used, not to mention the cost of maintenance (an estimated $6.5 billion in upkeep over the next two decades, according to a report from the U.S. Government Accountability office [GAO]) and the overall price tag of construction so far: $2.4 billion.

The patchwork nature of the wall has many skeptics asking how effective it really is. In Sasabe, for example, the wall is made of a uniform line of high steel pillars spilling out across the sands for several miles. But travel farther east to Nogales and you will see quite a different affair: a mix of steel pillars and barbed wire fencing and, in the city center, a stretch of fence made out of surplus helicopter landing mats from the Vietnam War.[9] Travel farther east still, toward the tiny town of Naco, and you can find places where, within a short half-mile stretch, the wall is made up of eclectic and stunningly different materials—nothing like the double reinforced fencing suggested by the Secure Fence Act. I found a place just west of Naco where, within a few hundred steps, high steel pillars gave way to a stretch of crossed railroad tracks, which, a few hundred feet later, turned to barbed wire at a dry wash, which, at the other end of the wash, merged with metal mesh.

While walking that stretch of "wall" west of Naco, I was approached by a Border Patrol agent who had gotten wind of my presence. After verifying that I was not there to "meet" any migrants or "help" anyone across, he turned cheerful and talkative. He talked about how "boring" his job had become with all the heightened border enforcement. "Nowadays, it's rare for anyone to try crossing in the daylight hours." When I asked the agent what he thought of the wall, he said he thought it definitely deterred many migrants and smugglers. Then I pointed west, to the Coronado Mountains and asked the agent if he thought it was possible to build a wall across such rugged terrain.

"That's what the virtual wall is for," he answered.

By the "virtual wall," he meant the suite of technology—cameras, sensors, and radar—that were employed both where a wall could not be built because of difficult terrain or as a backup to the wall itself. Formally referred to as SBI-Net (Secure Border Initiative Network technology program), the project was contracted to Boeing, which commenced a pilot project in the Tucson sector covering twenty-eight miles. In particular, the pilot project used "a multi-application tower system equipped with commercially available camera and radar sensors and communications equipment...and unattended ground sensors."[10]

Almost immediately, the "virtual wall" stirred its own controversy. From the beginning the project ran behind schedule and cost much more than anticipated. Worse still, the technology did not work as expected. The ground sensors were set off by deer, rabbits, and other animals that stepped on them, as well as tumbleweeds and other blown-about brush. Wind and rain affected the quality of camera images to the point of rendering them useless, and there were other unanticipated software glitches.[11] In January 2011, after five years and roughly $1 billion spent, Homeland Security Secretary, Janet Napolitano, announced the cancellation of SBI-Net, admitting to its failures.

Despite such setbacks and criticisms, however, there are those who still laud the vision of a wall (real or virtual) at the U.S.-Mexican border. They believe firmly that it is the only reasonable solution to the "chaos" and "lawlessness" there. People like Jim Gilchrist, founder of the Minutemen Project, say it is absolutely necessary for our national security and our sense of integrity as a nation to construct a wall along the entire southern border.[12] "The southern border region is a loosely guarded, lawless wasteland, an open invitation to enter at will for illegal aliens, fugitives, terrorists, and criminal cartel members who want to avoid detection," he writes.[13] The only solution, he believes, is a physical barrier from San Diego to Brownsville. The wall cannot, however, be built in dribs and drabs, he says. To be effective, the barrier must "include dual concrete and steel reinforced walls 20 feet high and 10 feet deep into the ground. The two walls would run parallel with a 60-foot wide unpaved causeway between them. Stationary and mobile towers staffed with Border Patrol agents would provide a series of observation posts. High-tech video and sensory devices would be employed to detect any intrusion into the area between dual walls. Sonar devices would randomly check for tunneling activity." Gilchrist believes that such a complex fortification is "the last resort to survive as a sovereign nation, a nation's final attempt to preserve its heritage, independence, prosperity, and domestic tranquility."

The conservative politician, Pat Buchanan, agrees with Gilchrist's assessment. He writes, "Though the clock is running, America has one last chance to secure the borders and preserve the republic.... The first [step] is to build a permanent fence along the entire 2000-mile border with Mexico, defining, sealing, and securing it forever."[14] He advocates constructing the same twin fences and the same array of cutting-edge sensors and cameras. He says:

> Is this a Berlin Wall, as Mexican politicians wail? This is absurd. The Berlin Wall was a prison wall to lock a captive nation in. Like a fence around a school, a home, or the White House, a border fence is to keep unauthorized people out. Nor is it some

isolationist plot to cut us off from Mexico. There would be two hundred openings for rail and road traffic to facilitate trade, travel, and tourism. The lives of hundreds who perish in the desert and mountainous regions of our border every year would be spared.[15]

The Border Patrol too agree with Gilchrist and Buchanan. The wall built so far is an effective deterrent. Not only does such deterrence cut down on migrant deaths, but it also cuts down on illegal immigration and smuggling. Spokesmen for the Tucson sector Border Patrol are adamant in their belief that where walls have been constructed, illegal human traffic has dramatically decreased. "It won't stop everyone, but we believe most migrants will be deterred," says Jose Gonzalez of the Arizona Border Patrol.

Conservative politicians like Buchanan, anti-illegal immigration activists like Gilchrist, and Border Patrol spokesmen are not alone in their upbeat view of the wall. Recent opinion polls show that the majority of American citizens are actually in favor of it. Nonetheless, there are still many others who are vehemently opposed to it. To begin with, such opponents state that when fences and walls are erected along one segment of the border, migrants are simply redirected to other areas. This is what occurred in the wake of 1994's Operation Gatekeeper, when the Border Patrol's San Diego sector built fencing, increased the number of agents, and improved technology to deter border crossers. The result was that migrants simply attempted to enter elsewhere, leading to the "funnel effect."

Furthermore, even where there is a wall, people are still finding ways around it. Ladders are easily made out of scraps of wood or shoelaces, which are strung around steel pillars to form "steps." Metal fences are often cut through or dissolved in patches with blowtorches. There are also the elaborate tunnels, such as the one Border Patrol agents discovered in Nogales in June 2009. It was eighty-three-feet long and equipped with a ventilation system. It was just one of forty-seven tunnels found in Nogales since 1995.[16] There are even more astonishing means to circumvent the wall, ways that sometimes defy the imagination. Consider, for example, the recent increase in the use of ultralight planes, most often used in drug smuggling operations. While such attempts are rare, they nonetheless point to the extreme and creative lengths taken to cross over the wall.[17] On the humorous side, a *Los Angeles Times* article cited the arrest of a man who was smuggling drugs into the country by surfing onto one of the beaches near San Diego, and the *New York Times* published a short article entitled, "Smugglers Try Medieval Tech," reporting on drug smugglers' efforts to catapult marijuana over the border fence near Naco, Arizona.

Opponents of the wall also cite the environmental hazards. In particular, they stress how blockading the border also blockades the ability of certain species (some endangered) to migrate. They state that to build sections of the fence, the U.S. government, through the use of the Real ID Act of 2005, has been able to waive certain federal legislation, such as the Clean Air Act, the Endangered Species Act, the Native American Grave Protection and Repatriation Act, among other laws. They also stress the exorbitant cost of building and maintaining each mile of wall (estimates for construction costs vary and seem to average between $2 million and $3 million per mile) as well as the sheer logistical nightmare of trying to construct fencing (let alone the double fencing mandated in the Secure Fence Act) along some of the more difficult terrain, such as across deep canyons and dramatic mountain ranges. Moreover, in early 2011, several U.S. GAO reports concerning southwest border security stated that despite concerted efforts to secure the border, through infrastructure like fencing and increased personnel, "weaknesses remained," as did a range of uncertainties in terms of costs and effectiveness.[18] Despite spending $3 billion on southwest border security efforts in fiscal year 2010, U.S. Customs and Border Protection reported that while it had achieved some "operational control" in certain sectors, much of the southwest border remained extremely vulnerable to cross-border illegal activity.

But, above all, beyond the questions of cost and efficacy, what opponents dislike most about the wall is the overall message it sends to our neighbors. They say it is proof of America's exclusionary tendencies and xenophobic ways. Some mockingly refer to the wall as the "Great Wall of America," and to the United States as "Fortress America." Nor is there any shortage of disdain from Mexicans concerning construction of a wall along their northern border. Mexico's former president, Vicente Fox, called the construction of the wall "a disgraceful and shameful situation."[19] The current Mexican president, Felipe Calderón, called the barrier "a grave mistake," adding: "The fence doesn't resolve anything....Humanity committed a grave mistake in building the Berlin Wall. I'm sure the United States is committing a grave mistake in building this fence."[20]

It is no surprise that many faith-based activists, like the seventy-two-year-old Franciscan priest, Father Jerome Zawada, and the fifty-four-year-old Quaker, John Heid, have gotten into trouble with the law for protesting at the wall. Zawada and Heid were arrested while praying at a virtual-fence site twelve miles north of Sasabe. A private security guard alerted officials to their presence. Deputies rushed to the site, and when the two men refused to stop praying, they were arrested on suspicion of trespassing on government property. They chose the virtual-fence site "because it is symbolic of the federal government's militarization of the border, which they believe has led to the deaths of thousands of illegal immigrants in Arizona."[21]

It was not the first time that religious activists have been arrested at the wall. On several occasions, clergy and laity of various denominations have been arrested praying or giving communion along the Tijuana-San Diego segment of the wall—especially at Friendship Park, which overlooks the Pacific Ocean and where, over the years, family members separated by the border have come to meet and talk through the small gaps in the fencing. As part of the Secure Fence Act, Friendship Park was closed to the public (the claim was that contraband was being passed through the fence). Still, activists—religious and otherwise—continued to visit the site as a means of protesting the new law. The Reverend John Fanestil, an ordained elder in the United Methodist Church, told of how "the act of celebrating communion with people on both sides of the border at Friendship Park is now an act of civil disobedience."[22] He described almost being arrested on February 25, 2009, while trying to give communion to people on the Tijuana side of the border:

> All I was trying to do was serve communion. For the past eight months I have served communion weekly there, to people on both sides of the border. I have done so in solidarity with the thousands of people who have broken bread peacefully at this location across many years. On Saturday I offered communion to a group of 150 or so who had gathered in the U.S. I then turned to the south, intending to serve the crowd in Tijuana. A border patrol agent blocked my way, determined to make an impression. "You don't want to do this," he shouted at me, unsnapping the handcuffs of his uniform. I told him I just wanted to serve communion, but he stepped in front of me, holding out his hand. "If you bump into me," he shouted, "you'll be charged with assaulting an officer." "Okay, then," I replied. "I guess you'll have to arrest me, because I'm going to serve communion."[23]

Fanestil further described being led away by the officer and detained for thirty minutes before being released. He concluded:

> Of course Friendship Park is a symbol, one that points to a larger question: What is to become of our nation's southern border? Is this strip of land—more than 1,850 miles long—to be turned over to the Department of Homeland Security and reduced to a "zone of enforcement," straddled by walls? I cannot abide it because I know the border as an altogether different place. For millions of us whose relationships straddle the international boundary, the border is a place where human beings meet, a place of friendship, a place of communion. And that's why I'll be going back next Sunday afternoon, to try once more to serve communion at Friendship Park.[24]

As with so many aspects of the immigration debate, there seems very little middle ground concerning opinions of the wall. Regardless of what one believes—whether a border wall will help stop the deaths in the desert or actually increase them, whether it will make our nation safer, whether it is ethical—the larger question still remains: What does it mean to wall in a nation, or to wall out a neighboring one?

History teems with examples of walls; walls that today are the thrill of tourists, historians, and archaeologists who travel thousands of miles just to see them, and to imagine, speculate, and theorize about past invasions or grievances between tribes and nations. One might think of the Great Wall of China. Today, visitors flock in the hundreds of thousands to admire the sheer audacity of it as it snakes, marvelously visible from space, across the southern edge of inner Mongolia. Ultimately, though, like so many walls, the Great Wall of China did not keep its much-feared northern neighbors, the Mongols, from penetrating Chinese soil.

Or perhaps, one may think of Hadrian's wall, built from coast to coast across modern-day northern England, to prevent unsought southern migration. Now, it is a tumble of rocks, spreading across the rolling green highlands just a few miles south of Scotland. It is a UNESCO world Heritage Site and a reminder that the Roman Empire once claimed dominion over the territory. Like so many other walls and barriers—the Berlin Wall, the Maginot Line, the Israeli West Bank barrier—history mostly tells the tale: that in the end, the walls cannot contain the mass movements of people. Whether those migrations are forced, due to war, natural disaster, or the basic need to survive, or whether they are well strategized, due to the desire to overtake, possess, or occupy a neighboring territory, time seems to prove again and again that while walls may serve their purpose for a time, the course of history almost always renders them obsolete. Rather than formidable, they become "quaint," serving as magnificent reminders of the discordant nature of human relationships and the volatile essence of borderlines.

As for the U.S.-Mexican barrier wall, there is no telling how history will judge it. Where now there are steel pillars or metal mesh, might there someday be a gaggle of archaeologists, on their knees, unearthing the strange metal shards, speculating over what happened there? Clearly, as they examine the rusty fragments of helicopter pads or the fallen bollards at their feet, they will know that all was not well between neighboring territories. As Charles Bowden said, walls formalize an uneasy rapport: "We seem to love walls, but are embarrassed by them because they say something unpleasant about the neighbors—and us. They flow from two sources: fear and desire for control."

Existentially speaking, these two motivations—fear (ultimately of one's demise at the hands of an unknown entity) and the desire for control (over one's well-being)—are a large part of what makes us human and, more broadly speaking, animal. It is, on some level, an evolutionary trait, a way of overseeing our survival. We are, like the animals around us, territorial creatures. We set up fences around our houses, demarcate townships and states, establish culturally acceptable norms for how close one can come to our own bodies—the most intimate and fiercely guarded of "territories." We seem to live with a keen awareness of intrusion and an almost ineradicable sense of threat.

The question, then, becomes this: When does our instinct to demarcate and protect, to draw up lines and enforce them, go too far? Is it too much to fence in or fence out a nation? Does a wall such as the one between the United States and Mexico do more damage or more good? Does it enhance safety or put more lives in peril? Whose fear is quelled, and who gets slapped in the face?

Many times, as I visited different sections of the U.S.-Mexican barrier wall in southern Arizona, I was reminded of Robert Frost's poem, "Mending Wall." Although the setting of the poem is a bucolic northern New England township—far from the arid, harsh, highly contested reality of the southern borderlands—the verse nonetheless sheds remarkable light on the controversial nature of most any wall. The poem, on the surface, is about two neighbors who have come together to repair an old wall separating their two properties. As they do, a dialogue emerges between them—both whimsical and tense in tone—that reveals their differing opinions regarding the efficacy of such divisions. The poem commences with the author musing about walls:

> Something there is that doesn't love a wall,
> That sends the frozen-ground-swell under it,
> And spills the upper boulder in the sun,
> And makes gaps even two can pass abreast.
> The work of hunters is another thing:
> I have come after them and made repair
> Where they have left not one stone on a stone.[25]

The author makes his stance on walls clear: there is something displeasing about them, even if he cannot say exactly what. "Something there is," he says simply, that does not love them. That "something," in part, has to do with a wall's vulnerability to disrepair and erasure. In effect, he has come to mend the huge gaps in the wall, which are so large "even two can pass abreast." These gaps are the result of time and the elements, and the intervention of people—hunters in this case—who find the wall a nuisance to their endeavors and, as a result, have torn down the stones to keep the rabbits out of hiding and "to please the yelping dogs."[26] The point seems to be, from the beginning, that there is something quixotic—almost laughable—about building a wall, for it cannot withstand the test of time nor the desires of men who treat walls as mere impediments to their larger purposes.

The author informs his neighbor of the holes in the wall between their properties, and thus they "meet to walk the line" and replace "the boulders that have fallen to each." He says of the boulders and the wall:

> We wear our fingers rough with handling them.
> Oh, just another kind of out-door game,
> One on a side. It comes to little more:
> There where it is we do not need the wall:
> He is all pine and I am apple orchard.
> My apple tree will never get across
> And eat the cones under his pines, I tell him.
> He only says, "Good fences make good neighbors."[27]

In this simple exchange, the core discrepancies of opinion concerning fences and walls are made clear. While the author finds something absurd in walling off pine trees from apple trees, likening the whole endeavor to a game, his neighbor thinks quite differently. "Good fences make good neighbors," he says. With this statement, the reader is presented with the counterargument: Good fences make good neighbors. Perhaps there is something that actually *does* love a wall; perhaps the effort to demarcate what is "mine" from what is "yours" makes for more civilized and orderly relationships.

In response, the author wishes to challenge his neighbor's statement:

> ...I wonder
> If I could put a notion in his head:
> "Why do they make good neighbors? Isn't it
> Where there are cows?
> But here there are no cows.
> Before I built a wall I'd ask to know
> What I was walling in or walling out,
> And to whom I was to give offence.
> Something there is that doesn't love a wall,
> That wants it down." I could say "Elves" to him,
> But it's not elves exactly, and I'd rather
> He said it for himself. I see him there
> Bringing a stone grasped firmly by the top
> In each hand, like an old-stone savage armed.[28]

Here, the author grows playful in his musing. He wants to challenge his neighbor's statement by pointing out that "here there are no cows." There are just pine trees and apple orchard. He wants to say to his neighbor, "Before I built a wall I'd ask to know,/What I was walling in or walling out,/ And to whom I was to give offence." And then, he repeats, "Something there is that doesn't love a wall,/That wants it down."

Yet, he cannot say precisely what that *something* is. "It's not elves exactly," he jokes. And then, obliquely, he begins to make concessions to his neighbor's point of view. In his next observation, as he watches his neighbor reconstructing the wall, with stones in each hand, he likens him to "an old-stone savage armed." This analogy serves to answer the question. Suddenly, he sees his neighbor as a warrior, an armed savage, thus alluding to the primordially bellicose nature of mankind. In this vision, he sums up the unsettling raison d'être of most walls. They are, in the end, a manner of defending ourselves from our fellow human beings. The need for them speaks to the undeniable imperfectness of the human condition and the indissoluble dystopia that is our world: ours is no Garden of Eden but rather a contentious interplay of tribes, families, and neighbors. Perhaps certain walls are unnecessary; perhaps they do not contain strife at all but only heighten it; or perhaps they do make better neighbors. That depends on circumstance and opinion, but one thing is certain: the fact that we build them at all is a sad testimony to our inability to live together harmoniously. Thus, the author concludes:

> He moves in darkness as it seems to me,
> Not of woods only and the shade of trees.
> He will not go behind his father's saying,
> And he likes having thought of it so well
> He says again, "Good fences make good neighbors."[29]

In the end, neither man comes to agreement over the wall they have come together to mend. The first line of the poem sums up the author's stance: Something there is that doesn't love a wall. While the last line of the poem sums up that of his neighbor: Good fences make good neighbors. And there lies the ancient divide.

The argument is not unlike that going on every day in towns, cities, churches, schools, and dinner tables throughout Arizona. There are those who believe there is nothing to like about the growing physical barrier dividing Mexico from the United States. There are those, on the contrary, who believe it is the best solution to the chaos, violence, and death occurring along the southern border; that when push comes to shove, good fences make for better neighbors. And there are those in between, those who do not like the sight of the wall or who find it a sorry statement concerning two countries that cannot negotiate effective solutions concerning immigration, but who, at the same time, understand the reasons for the wall's ongoing construction. The wall inspires all manner of passionate debate and evokes a wide range of emotions: pride, rage, relief, repulsion, and sorrow. The one feeling it rarely elicits is indifference.

In the end, the fencing of Arizona and the continued construction of the wall is unprecedented in the history of the United States. How far it will span, how high it will go, how history will judge it all remain to be seen. What is clear is that the wall is the ultimate symbol of the ideological divide raging in the Tucson sector and throughout the country concerning illegal immigration.

CHAPTER 7

Invasions, Floods, and Barbarians: What's to Be Afraid of?

I am in Palominas, Arizona, on a sunny September morning to attend a gathering of the newly formed Patriots Coalition. The Patriots Coalition is a small civil patrol organization founded by Al Garza, former national executive of the Minuteman Civil Defense Corps (MCDC), Arizona's largest and most famous civil patrol group. The aim of the Patriots Coalition, similar to the aim of most civil patrol groups, including the MCDC, is to "monitor illegal activity along the border" as well as to lobby against "amnesty for those millions who are currently in our country illegally."[1]

Palominas, another dusty and dilapidated border town between Naco and the Coronado Mountains, is the place the Patriots Coalition has chosen for their three-week "muster." Musters are gatherings of private citizens who come together to "patrol" the border. They can last several days and nights, or even weeks. Most muster participants carry firearms, and many do so openly, which is permissible by law. They bring tents or RVs and camp out on private land near the border. Generally, the task of such civil patrol groups is to watch for undocumented migrants crossing the border. While they cannot arrest the migrants, they can call the Border Patrol to alert them to the migrants' whereabouts. When I asked members why they carried guns (if they could not use them to arrest migrants), answers ranged from "because this is America, it's our right" to "we must be able to defend ourselves at any minute against smugglers or enemies who could attack."

In Palominas, at "operation headquarters," the group gathers to discuss where to go in search of "illegals." It is a small group—less than two dozen members, only two of them women. They are sitting on fold-out lawn chairs, under the tattered awning of a rusty RV, eating donuts and talking about "the best places to find some illegals." Many are wearing T-shirts with the Patriots Coalition motto: "For God and Country." Al Garza, the group's founder, greets me with a hearty handshake and a big smile. He explains that "some of the guys" are already "up in the mountains." He says they spent the night up there "looking for aliens." He introduces me to everyone in the group, including two men who have traveled all the way from Kansas to participate in the muster. One of the men, Woody, says he's really hoping "to see some action." So far, he hasn't seen any. He is disappointed by this. "I wanna see some aliens," he says, his hand resting on the holster of his Colt 45.

"You gotta go up into the Coronado Mountains," Al Garza tells him. "Way up there, near Parker Canyon Lake. You might have to be patient, but you'll sure as hell see some action eventually."

"It's like bird watching," Woody jokes.

Everyone laughs.

That's when a man named Danny starts talking. Danny has been living on the border for years. He says he has watched the problem get worse, and, he says, he has watched the government do nothing about it. Wearing a dirty white T-shirt with the sleeves cut off and jeans riddled with holes, he is one of the few who is not carrying a firearm. He is sitting in a lawn chair, eating his third cream donut and petting a standard white poodle who is draped in a full-sized American flag.

"I could tell you *exactly* where to go up in those mountains to see more illegals than you bargained for," says Danny. "I'm up there all the time, fixing up my cameras." Then Danny explains what he means by his cameras. He has a website: borderinvasionpics.com.[2] For the past year, since November 2008, Danny has been hiking up into the Coronado Mountains to heavily traveled migrant trails. He knows the trails well. His project has been to place hidden cameras in the brush along these trails to capture images of migrants crossing into the United States through the Coronado Mountains. He has planted dozens of cameras. Many of them are equipped with thermal imaging to record nighttime crossings. "You won't believe what you'll see," he says. His recordings have made it onto shows like *Lou Dobbs Tonight* and have caught the attention of the Border Patrol who have tried, says Danny, to locate his cameras and dismantle them.

The idea, admittedly, is both creative and effective. A visitor to his website will see seemingly endless streams of migrants crossing into the United States. The homepage of his website catalogues, in chronological order, the dizzying array of "sightings" captured by the eyes of the cameras. It announces: "Thousands of individuals from foreign countries walk unchallenged across our southern border every day. We don't know who they are, where they come from, or their intentions. It is an invasion by definition."[3]

He attaches titles to many of his clips and adds commentary as well; as viewers watch the highlighted reel, they simultaneously read Danny's viewpoints on the matter. An example is the video he calls "Out of Control." This segment, from May 1, 2009 (shot at 8:17 P.M., using thermal imaging), shows twenty migrants being pursued by two Border Patrol agents. As we watch the twenty migrants running, one of Danny's captions pops onto the video: "With their inadequate numbers," it reads, "Border Patrol agents cannot control this vast area. This video illustrates that our southern border remains OUT OF CONTROL."

Another video goes by the title "Draggin' the Line." In this one, we see a line of migrants rushing down a trail, each one, unbeknown to them, passing the hidden camera. The last person in the line is dragging a large pine branch behind him as he goes, using it like a broom to sweep away the tracks. Danny's caption pops onto the video: "This is a group of 16—there are thousands more everyday.... We know absolutely nothing about them— EXCEPT that they walk into our country unchallenged ... and they are covering their tracks."

In an attempt at humor, a short film shows a drug smuggler wrestling with his oversized bundle. It is a one-minute, twenty-three-second clip, entitled "Drug Haulin' for Dummies." Before the drug smuggler enters the fixed space of the camera's view, words pop onto the screen: "Having trouble hauling your 60 lb. drug bundle? Experiencing lower back pain? Take some tips from this experienced drug runner... A self-explanatory tutorial." Then a man in jeans and a green sweatshirt appears among the brush. On the ground is an impressively large bundle of drugs. The man has stopped to take a jean jacket, fold it up, and tie it around his waist, so that it serves as a heavy-lifting belt. He looks up, as if he hears a sound or is making sure no one is around, then leans back completely onto the bundle. The bundle's length is from his waist to just above his head, its width larger than that of his torso. He braces himself, then straightens up, drug bundle attached to his back, puts on his hood and walks out of the camera's gaze. Words then appear on the screen, a sort of epilogue to the clip: "Filmed on location: Arizona/Mexico border, March, 2009.... Made possible by open borders advocates."

The viewer could spend all day on the website, watching film after film of migrants crossing the Coronado Mountains, kids straggling behind, mothers with babies on their hips, long lines of men and women weaving around the brush, water jugs dangling from their hands, drug smugglers, coyotes, small groups and larger groups. There is little denying that Danny makes his point: men, women, and children are entering the United States illegally, every day, in large numbers.

The platform of Danny's website is one of fear and outrage. He wants to show that the United States is being invaded. Many of the "invaders," he believes, are dangerous. At the very least, they are breaking the law. The border is largely unprotected, and meanwhile, the U.S. government is doing little to stop the lawlessness. The rhetoric of most civil patrol groups that have popped up along the border is similar.

The rise of civil patrol groups like the Patriots Coalition coincided, not incidentally, with the rise of border ministries.[4] As religiously inspired individuals, motivated by a set of biblical passages, scrambled to try to stop the death and suffering of migrants, those bound to a different mission, that of law and order, also rose to action. Groups of activists strongly opposed to illegal immigration began to form to express their outrage over the chaos at the southern border. The plight of ranchers, in particular, became the initial focal point of these patrol groups. One of the first groups to form was called Ranch Rescue. Its main goal, as its name suggests, was to provide support and assistance to ranchers along the borders whose lands and livestock were being harmed by rampant illegal immigration.[5]

Take the example of rancher, Roger Barnett. He was involved in a protracted court case that, like the "littering" and "harboring" trials of No More Deaths members, gained national attention. Since 1998, Barnett had been rounding up illegal immigrants who trespassed on his property and turning them over to the Border Patrol. He started doing this after migrants began "vandaliz[ing] his property, northeast of Douglas along Arizona Highway 80. He said immigrants tore up water pumps, killed calves, destroyed fences and gates, stole trucks and broke into his home. Some of his cattle died from ingesting plastic water bottles left behind by the immigrants.... Mr. Barnett said some of the ranch's established immigrant trails were littered with trash 10 inches deep, including human waste, used toilet paper, soiled diapers, cigarette packs, clothes, backpacks, empty 1-gallon water bottles, chewing gum wrappers and aluminum foil—which supposedly is used to pack the drugs the immigrant smugglers give their 'clients' to keep them running."[6]

The high-profile lawsuit against Barnett was "based on a March 7, 2004, incident in a dry wash on the 22,000-acre ranch, when he approached a group of illegal immigrants while carrying a gun and accompanied by a large dog."[7] There were sixteen migrants in all. Later, several of the migrants would file a suit, accusing Barnett of holding the group captive at gunpoint and threatening to shoot them or to command his dog to attack if they tried to escape before the Border Patrol arrived. Ultimately, Barnett was ordered by a U.S. federal jury to award approximately $70,000 to four of the women. It was not the first time that Barnett had rounded up migrants through such coercive measures. He admits to having spent $30,000 on electric sensors, which, when they go off, send him—with handgun, rifle, dog, high-powered binoculars and a walkie-talkie—in search of illegal immigrants. " 'This is my land. I'm a victim here,' Mr. Barnett said. 'When someone's home and loved ones are in jeopardy and the government seemingly can't do anything about it, I feel justified in taking matters into my own hands. And I always watch my back.' "[8]

Barnett's complaints are, unfortunately, not unique among ranchers living at the border. Many ranchers have felt ignored by the government who, they say, does not understand the toll illegal immigration and smuggling has had on their lives, livestock, land, and sense of security. In April 2011, highly respected fifth-generation Arizona rancher Jim Chilton testified before Congress about the hardships he had experienced as a cattleman at the border. "We have been burglarized twice. Many of our neighbors have suffered similar loss of security and property.... Ranchers cannot have peace of mind until the border is secured," he said in a plea for more effective enforcement measures, including completion of fencing in Arizona.

The sentiment that U.S. citizens are in jeopardy, as evidenced by the plight of ranchers, and the perception that the government is failing to adequately protect its people, has led to the advent and rise of civil patrol groups. The two largest groups—the Minuteman Project, and its Arizonan counterpart, the Minuteman Civil Defense Corps—coalesced behind these two complaints. Both groups made it their mission to have their complaints heard. They did so, in large part, by engaging media outlets, which happily covered their musters. The musters made for compelling news. Images of private citizens taking matters into their own hands began popping up on television and on Internet news sites. Minutemen members were shown building fences along the border where there were none; they were shown camping out in towns like Naco and Sasabe and searching for migrants at night, guns on hips, thermal binoculars in hand, "patrolling" the border themselves.

As former leader of the MCDC, Chris Simcox, said, these civil patrol groups never dreamed they would get so much attention. But they were thrilled to be in the spotlight.[9] The media ate up their events, bringing national attention to their cause. The border was shown for what it was: a chaotic, lawless, porous no-man's land, overrun with illegal drug and human smuggling. Their message came through clearly: Where was the government? It had abandoned its citizens!

Government inefficacy in matters of immigration and the fear of harm at the hands of illegal border crossers are the two reasons Al Garza cited for joining the civil patrol "movement." He told, with great earnestness, how he himself was Mexican American. His family had lived on the U.S. side of the border for generations. "Everything was civil, until just a few years back," he said. "That is when the invasion really started happening. I mean, I got land not far from here, you know, and suddenly all these illegals started showing up, trespassing on my land, stealing things from my property. But what really got me fired up, I mean, the reason I turned to this movement, is because of one day when a group of illegal Mexican men showed up and started making lewd gestures at my wife, grabbing their crotches and laughing. Then I called the police and Border Patrol. They showed up hours later. The men were long gone, and Border Patrol seemed to infer that they did not even believe my story. That's when I realized something was really wrong here. Our government doesn't care about its own citizens. That's when I joined up with the Minutemen."[10]

Later, when asked what he thought about the work of faith-based activists on the border, he answered, "Look, I'm a Christian too. I understand that a lot of those folks want to stop the suffering, and why shouldn't they? It's terrible. But they just help these illegals blindly. They don't care who they are, if they are criminals. And they don't care about the law. That's what really gets me. If you are so Christian, why are you breaking the laws? Or condoning people who do. It says in the Bible to follow the law. It's a Christian duty. That's why I chose the motto I did for the Patriots Coalition: *For God and Country*."[11]

This viewpoint is held by Jim Gilchrist, one of the Minuteman Project founders. In his book on the project, he stresses that even though he is Catholic, he does not believe the church should encourage illegal immigration, for to do so is to disregard federal law:

> The church is irresponsible to aid or encourage law breaking, including encouraging illegal aliens to think they can or should remain in the United States, or that they are owed full rights and benefits as citizens simply because they are here.... Moreover, civil disobedience by definition does not respect our rule of law. To deliberately tell us that because we are Catholics, we have a moral obligation to disobey the rule of law is itself problematic. According to our rule of law, there should be a distinction between church and state. Religion crosses the line when determining what laws should be cast aside and ignored and what laws are going to be respected.... We can all have sympathy for illegal aliens as human beings or as workers. However, the distinction between legal and illegal immigrants remains important.[12]

For folks like Garza, Gilchrist, and others, it is the rule of law that must come first. The distinction between legal and illegal is not, they say, meant to dehumanize immigrants. It is simply a necessary description that serves the rule of law.

It is not surprising that, for the most part, Border Patrol agents are thankful for the support of those like Garza and Gilchrist. On a "ride-along" with U.S. Border Patrol Agent Jorge Alejandro Gomez, I asked him what he thought of the Minutemen Project and the MCDC. "As long as they don't take the law into their own hands," Gomez said, "we pretty much appreciate their efforts."

By taking the law into their own hands, Gomez is referring to "incidents" such as the Barnett case. While they can carry firearms, civil patrol members are not allowed to use them, unless in self-defense. They cannot round up migrants, threaten them, or stop them. All they can do is call the Border Patrol when they have "sightings."

Nonetheless, broadly speaking, civil patrol groups and Border Patrol are aligned on the matter: it is in everyone's interest that the rule of law be obeyed when it comes to immigration. Gomez and other agents and representatives of the Border Patrol often cite statistics to defend their opposition to illegal immigration and to justify current operational tactics. "It is important for a country to be able to properly vet everyone coming across its borders," Gomez said further. "It's only fair. Last year, for example, 16% of the migrants we apprehended had criminal records in the United States. When we fingerprint them at processing centers, we see these records." He noted that offenses are sometimes severe: drug possession, gang-related violence, robbery, rape, assault and battery, child molestation, breaking and entering, even murder. "It's true that most of the people we arrest aren't out to hurt anybody. They don't have criminal records. But, unfortunately, you can never be sure."

Every day, agents like Gomez come across groups of undocumented men and women in remote areas of the desert. Sometimes agents are extremely outnumbered, Gomez says. While the vast majority of migrant groups are unarmed, this is not always the case. There are those who do carry arms, and more rarely, who use them. The majority of shootings are done by drug-related smugglers, as in the killing of Border Patrol Agent Robert W. Rosas Jr., who was fatally shot while patrolling alone near Campo, California, on the night of July 23, 2009. Rosas was killed in a desolate and rugged swath of terrain, approximately sixty miles east of San Diego, an area where drug and human smugglers frequently abound. Lured out of his vehicle by a group of smugglers who wanted to steal his night-vision goggles and other equipment, he was shot four times in the head and died soon after.[13]

Such killings are uncommon, but still, the possibility always exists (consider, more recently, the December 2010 killing of Agent Brian A. Terry, gunned down on duty in a remote canyon in southern Arizona). It is a possibility that lurks in the back of every agent's mind, said Agent Gomez. "Sometimes, we have to deal with a group of twenty, thirty, fifty migrants, and there is only two or three of us. We are totally outnumbered. You just can't know if any of them might try to pull something on you."[14]

But while Gomez stressed the imperative for everyone to respect immigration laws, he also expressed a lot of sadness and compassion for the people he apprehends. On our drive down to Nogales to see the main detention center and operational headquarters there, Gomez talked about his life.[15] He said that he was born in Mexico, just across the border, but he came as a child with his mother to Texas (*legally* he emphasized). He grew up in a small, impoverished border town in Texas and joined the marines in his early twenties. "I served this country before even being a citizen," he said. He met his wife, who is Maltese, while on a tour of duty in the Mediterranean. When he returned, he was naturalized as a U.S. citizen, and shortly after that, he decided to join the Border Patrol.

When I asked him what it was like to be Mexican-American and to have to arrest so many Mexican migrants, he sighed. "Honestly," he replied, "It can be hard sometimes. Most of them are just looking for a better life. Sometimes the stories they tell me just break my heart. And of course, I often get those who say to me, 'How can you arrest your own people? Don't you feel like a traitor?'"

When asked how it felt to be called a traitor, he answered, "I'm sort of used to it. And I feel okay in the end, because I really do believe that it is not good for anyone, this whole illegal immigration thing. I believe it's in everyone's best interest to follow the laws. They are there for good reason. It is dangerous for migrants to try to take such a journey in the first place, and it is unfair to the United States that they do not seek the right permission to come through a legal port of entry. All around, a bad idea."

Then Gomez spoke about the horror stories he hears on a nearly daily basis. "Just last week," he said, "We arrested this husband and wife. We couldn't get the wife to talk for the life of us. We tried everything, but she just kept silent, mute, you know? So then we took her aside, away from the husband, and she started talking. She said that she had been raped by their *coyote*. She was too ashamed to talk about it in front of her husband. We ended up sending her to a hospital in Tucson to be evaluated."

A few minutes later, Gomez spoke of his three children, one of whom was named after an orphaned migrant he met on duty. The orphan was one of two young children found by their mother's side. The mother was dead, and the girls were severely dehydrated. They were taken to the hospital for emergency evaluations, and Gomez was called in to watch over them as well as to try to contact a close relative, in the United States or Mexico, who could take the girls. "It's those kind of moments that just break your heart," he said, "Those two precious girls without a mother." He ended up naming his daughter after one of the girls.

These two stories—rape at the hands of a human smuggler, and two young girls found in the desert by their dead mother's side—are just two of hundreds that Gomez has heard over the years. Talking to Gomez, and other agents, one quickly realizes that most Border Patrol agents are deeply affected by the tragedies they witness firsthand. The majority are not callous individuals, as some of their opponents like to claim. Rather, most agents are simply doing their job, a job they believe is important and necessary. When asked what the most rewarding part of his job was, Gomez answered unequivocally, "It's knowing that I have saved lives. Sometimes you *know* you have saved a life. You come across dying migrants—women, children, old men, young men, toddlers even—in the desert, because you just happen to be there, or because you get an emergency call and you are first on the scene. Then there are those who we apprehend, who are not necessarily close to death but who are so far out in the desert or mountains, you start wondering if they ever would have made it out alive. In a way, even though it is sad for the migrants when they are caught, it is a good thing, because we know at least that they are not wandering around lost. They can't die, you know?"

Another Border Patrol agent I met while photographing the wall said, "Before I joined the Patrol, I saw things in a much more black and white sort of way. I had some really strong opinions—I'll just say that. But the daily encounter with migrants, it changes you. You feel a lot more sympathy. You realize most are coming from really sad situations. But still, you know, we've got to do our job."

Comments like this point to the fact that many Border Patrol agents find themselves straddling an uneasy divide, between a sense of compassion for migrants *and* a strong sense of duty to "protect and serve." As the Reverend Robin Hoover of Humane Borders said: "Many United States Border Patrol agents working in southern Arizona...perceive themselves first as peace officers and secondly as front line defenders of the homeland. This observation is particularly true of those agents with longer tenures in southern Arizona."[16]

It is crucial to underscore this more compassionate side of individual Border Patrol agents, since their image is often tarnished by the vociferous complaints of their opponents, many of whom include the faith-based activists highlighted earlier. Such is the case with No More Deaths' two reports, *Crossing the Line: Human Rights Abuses of Migrants in Short-Term Custody on the Arizona/Sonora Border*, and the follow-up report, *A Culture of Cruelty: Abuse and Impunity in Short-term U.S. Border Patrol Custody*. Both reports are damning critiques of Border Patrol practices and of agents, many of whom are portrayed in both reports as acting disrespectfully at best, and abusively at worst. As *A Culture of Cruelty* states, "It is clear that instances of mistreatment and abuse in Border Patrol custody are not aberrational. Rather, they reflect common practice that is part of the largest federal law enforcement body in the country."[17]

Border Patrol agents like Gomez express dismay over such criticisms. They are made from a distance, he says. "While their hearts may be in the right places," Gomez stressed, such critics fail to see the total reality of the situation. "They don't have to walk into a group of twenty, thirty migrants, who may or may not be armed. They don't have to experience the fear of being outnumbered like that. Sometimes even if they aren't armed, migrants will throw rocks. A fair few agents have wound up in the hospital from being hit by rocks."

Gomez's comments point to a certain lack of moral imagination on the part of Border Patrol critics. While many faith-based activists seem able "to put themselves in the shoes of migrants," they seem much less inclined to imagine the challenges, fears, and emotional hardships facing many agents. "Sometimes I think of my family when I'm out there," Gomez added. "You want to return home in one piece."

Instead of acknowledging the courage it must take for agents to enter such situations, critics are quick to denounce the strategies employed by the Border Patrol. They accuse current Border Patrol methods as being useless at best. At worst, they are immoral and inhumane, driven by xenophobia and unnecessary fear, and resulting in the deaths of hundreds every year in the desert. Moreover, certain critics say, many migrants in short-term custody are the victims of cruel treatment, which is a reflection of a systemic culture of Border Patrol abuse.

To what extent current border strategies and short-term custody standards are effective and humane is arguable. What is true, though, is that fear is a major motivating factor behind border enforcement policy. As one reads in most Customs and Border Protection literature, there is reason for U.S. citizens to fear "illegal activity" at the border, whether it concerns terrorism, narcotics, weapons, or human cargo. This "fear factor" has been further compounded by the tragic events of 9/11, which are often seamlessly conflated into the immigration debate. As stated in one U.S. Customs and Border Protection summary concerning its strategy:

> In the wake of the terrorist attacks of September 11, 2001, the Border Patrol has experienced a tremendous change in its mission. With the formation of a new parent agency, U.S. Customs and Border Protection (CBP), the Border Patrol has as its priority mission preventing terrorists and terrorist weapons from entering the United States. The Border Patrol will continue to advance its traditional mission by preventing illegal aliens, smugglers, narcotics, and other contraband from entering the United States as these measures directly impact the safety and security of the United States.[18]

Fear is a core justification for current immigration strategies. In order to guarantee "the safety and security of the United States," everyone entering the country must be properly vetted. Thus, the Border Patrol motto is to "gain, maintain and expand operational control" of the border.[19] During a ride-along with Tucson's Border Patrol, I saw many of these "security and safety measures" up close. I saw it in the central command room of the Nogales headquarters, where dozens of operators sat, meticulously monitoring their camera screens, which projected images of anyone moving suspiciously just over the border (at the moment of my visit, operators had homed in on what seemed to be a few trash pickers on the hillside in Nogales, Sonora, near the Mariposa port of entry). Just down the hall from the central command room was the "arms checkout counter," where agents came to pick up their weapons, their bandoliers, ammunition, and the "radiation detectors" they have been required to wear on their shoulders since September 11, 2001.[20] On the wall behind the weapons cache, large posters of "wanted illegal aliens" were hung and a television screen alerted agents about any dangerous activity in the area. On the same floor was the detention center, where apprehended migrants were fingerprinted and criminal background checks conducted. I was allowed into the detention center. Inside, there were two large holding cells—one for women, the other for men—behind which a dozen migrants stood, some wrapped in thin wool blankets, most staring through the glass of the cell, looking immeasurably sad and tired.

Later that day, I was given access to the I-19 checkpoint, where every vehicle heading north must stop to be sniffed by German shepherds from the K9 unit. The dogs sniff for any trace of narcotics, while agents speak to drivers and passengers, asking if they are American citizens. The I-19 checkpoint underscores the complex confluence of fears behind illegal immigration. Agents and dogs are searching for one of several things: drugs, weapons, terrorists, or undocumented passengers. It is an example of how the issue of illegal immigration bleeds into other issues, making it difficult to separate one fear from another. It is a complicated web. Often, one "problem" is connected to another problem.

The I-19 checkpoint is a case in point. At our stop at the checkpoint, during the ride-along, I was allowed to sit on the side of the road and watch how it worked. While German shepherds sniffed intensely around stopped vehicles (the rims of tires, underneath floor mats, inside engines, just about everywhere), agents peered into unrolled windows to verify who was traveling inside.

"Those dogs are incredible," I said to one of the agents, marveling at the olfactory prowess of the German shepherds. The dogs didn't seem to miss a thing.

"Yeah," answered one of the on-duty agents. "We got one guy here a few days ago in this van. The dog smelled something and went mad. But we couldn't find anything. Most likely, the guy had been smoking drugs or something a few days earlier, and the smell had lodged into the upholstery of the van. So we had to let him go."

"If dogs don't smell anything, how do you decide to pull someone over?" I asked.

Another agent tried to explain the criteria. "It's a picture. We're trained to see the picture."

"You look for certain things," agent Gomez added. "Like certain sneakers, or brands of clothes. Or, you are careful to watch for body language. If they look away, or tell a story and then change it, it looks suspicious."

As we stood on the side of the road at the checkpoint, I watched as several vehicles were pulled over, some because the dogs had detected a smell, others because the drivers seemed "edgy." I was taken over to an air-conditioned tent where I watched agents interrogate a driver who had been pulled over. It was true: the driver seemed nervous. He kept changing his story. When asked if the car he was driving was his, the man said yes, then no, then yes again.

"Which one is it?" an agent asked.

"No. Well, I just bought it," the man answered, staring at the ground.

"From who?" the agent asked.

"Brother-in-law."

"The dogs smelled something in your car," the agent said.

"Well, I don't know what my brother-in-law was doing with it before I bought it."

The conversation goes on, in Spanish, while Gomez and other agents offered me their commentary on the situation.

"There's something not right about this guy," Gomez said.

I agreed. The man was jittery, and his answers were not consistent.

In an effort to find something, the man's car was X-rayed by a large truck that ran up and down beside it (at which point I was advised to step aside to avoid radiation). In the end, the man was let go. But as we left the checkpoint, a van from Nogales with several passengers was pulled over.

"Yeah, we got a van the other day with this kid in it. A van just like that one. The kid was young, and he was loaded with drugs," said Gomez.

As Gomez pulled away from the checkpoint, I wondered: What *exactly* is everyone so afraid of? Why the radiation detectors, the checkpoints, the weapons caches, the cameras, the wall, the blackhawks, the K9 units, the civil patrol musters, and everything else? Did the level of fear equal the level of threat?

One thing was clear: such measures reflect the fear that the United States is in real peril and must be protected. Common terminology points to this sense of threat. Illegal immigration across the U.S.-Mexican border is often referred to as a "flood" or an "invasion," while those crossing are frequently called "aliens," or even "barbarians." In his *State of Emergency: The Third World Invasion and Conquest of America*, conservative politician Pat Buchanan asks the rhetorical question: "Who are the invaders?" His response is, "They are strangers, millions and millions of strangers in our midst."[21]

It is this fear of the stranger, the millions and millions of them, that lies at the heart of anti-illegal immigration arguments. Generally speaking, the fear falls into three broad categories.[22] The first category involves the fear of criminal elements: terrorists and other nefarious characters (rapists, murderers, drug dealers, and other criminals) who come to this country illegally. Either such people are here to hurt U.S. citizens intentionally or they have the potential to do so. The second fear concerns more domestic worries: even if they are not criminals, illegal immigrants will take our jobs, deplete taxpayer-run institutions (hospitals, schools, etc.), and drain public funds meant for deserving American citizens. The third and more abstract fear concerns the idea that the current trend of illegal immigration is a threat to some perceived "American way of life." This argument promotes the idea that, unlike the waves of European immigration in the late 1800s and early 1900s, current immigrants (primarily Spanish speaking) are not assimilating properly. Such immigrants are not making the effort to learn English or partake in American culture. As a result, they lack patriotism, which strengthens a nation. Furthermore, goes the argument, such lack of pride and loyalty dilutes the overall strength of American character. Such a dilution is contributing to the current collapse of American civilization and power.

Concerning the criminal and terrorist element, one need only turn, for example, to the hair-raising book, *Invasion,* by popular conservative commentator and author, Michelle Malkin. The first sentence of the book is an evocation of 9/11. She writes: "The nineteen hijackers who invaded America on September 11, 2001, couldn't have done it without help from the United States government. We unlocked our doors, spread out the welcome mat, and allowed these foreign visitors to plot death and destruction in the comfort of our own home."[23]

Malkin, like many other anti-illegal immigration advocates, argues that the U.S. government's lax and/or overly generous immigration policies are essentially at fault for the catastrophic events of September 11. The only way to fix the problem, she believes, and to stop "foreign menaces" from entering America, is to seal up the border and come down hard on illegal immigrants currently living here. This hard-line stance, which opposes any path to legalization for those illegal immigrants already living in the United States, stresses the idea that among the "good" illegal immigrants, who come looking for work, there will always be some "bad" ones too. Whether terrorists, drug dealers, or other criminals does not matter. Malkin's approach sees that "it only takes one apple to sour the bunch." Everyone entering the United States must be properly vetted, for the safety and well-being of all Americans.

Moreover, people like Malkin argue, if immigrants come illegally, then their first act on U.S. soil was, by its very definition, unlawful. Even if the crime seems petty, in comparison with terrorism or drug trafficking, not entering the United States at an official port of entry is still a crime, making the offender a criminal. Such an act should disqualify anyone from amnesty. Why reward someone who has disrespected the law and the sovereign borders of the United States? Malkin's stance is a common one, and it is behind the controversial raids, long-term incarcerations, and deportations of hundreds of thousands of undocumented immigrants over the past decade. In fact, in 2009, under the Obama administration, such deportations reached an all-time high, with approximately 400,000 immigrants removed from the country.[24]

Malkin and others like her believe that although America's tradition of hospitality to immigrants has been well intentioned, it is, at this point in history, reckless and naïve. Such hospitality, including U.S. refugee policies, is putting the country at risk. As she writes:

> Our most generous historic offer to the world's politically oppressed—shelter from tyranny—is routinely used against us by our enemies. . . . Among the foreign America-haters who invoked asylum: convicted murderers Mir Aimal Kansi and World Trade Center bomb plotters Ramzi Yousef and Sheik Omar Abdel Rahman. . . . Could Emma Lazarus, who wrote the famous sonnet affixed to the Statue of Liberty, ever have imagined our nation embracing the likes of terrorist travelers when she beckoned the poor "wretched refuse" of foreign shores?[25]

As a result of this abuse of America's generosity, terrorists and other criminals have been able to infiltrate, destroy, and threaten the United States. As Malkin argues further: "Those who oppose post-September 11 efforts to crack down on illegal immigration perpetuate a perilous myth. They believe we can continue to ignore the "good" illegal immigrants streaming across the borders (e.g., Mexican workers) without compromising our ability to screen out the "bad" illegal immigrants (e.g., Middle Eastern terrorists)."[26]

Making matters worse, Malkin says, terrorists are not the only ones to worry about. There are also the hundreds of thousands of undocumented immigrants who are also criminals—and not just petty ones. Malkin addresses this "criminal element" in several graphic and hair-raising chapters in her book. She highlights certain infamous (illegal Latin American) criminals, such as Angel Maturino Resendiz who became known as the "Railway Killer." Malkin dedicates an entire chapter of her book to detailing the twelve American citizens "who lost their lives because the INS [Immigration and Naturalization Service] failed to do its job and keep dangerous aliens [like Resendiz] out of the country," she says. "No, they were not among the thousands who died in the September 11 terrorist attacks. They are the little-known victims of an illegal alien from Mexico whose criminal career made a bloody mockery of our borders and our immigration laws."[27]

In a section called "Portraits of Grief," she gives the names of each of the twelve victims, provides a small description of the productive lives they were leading before being murdered by Resendiz, then writes of each crime in shocking detail. She tells, for example, how a young man named Christopher Maier and his girlfriend went for a late-night stroll along some railroad tracks near a college campus. "Resendiz accosted the couple and demanded money....He dragged Maier into some weeds ten feet from the train tracks, and then tied up and gagged the couple using belts, torn clothing, and straps from a fanny pack....Using a fifty-two-pound rock, Resendiz bludgeoned the six-foot, five-inch tall Maier to death....While Maier lay hogtied and dying, choking on his own blood, Resendiz raped his girlfriend and beat her unconscious."[28]

These sorts of horrific descriptions fill the pages of Malkin's book. Inevitably, they appeal to the human instinct of fear, transmitting the sense that one is never safe, even less so because of all the strangers living among us. We are also less safe, Malkin says, because the U.S. government is failing to adequately protect its citizens from such criminals as Resendiz. In the section called "Before Killing a Dozen Americans: Resendiz's Brushes with the Law," Malkin documents the many times Resendiz was arrested in the United States for other crimes. She details his sentences, his paroles, his deportations and voluntary returns, and yet still, he managed to slip through the cracks of the INS (now ICE, Immigration and Customs Enforcement) and law enforcement. Malkin's point is to demonstrate the shameful inefficacies of current federal immigration and border policies and to show how such shortcomings translate into real and present danger for American citizens. Malkin is one of many who would say that yes, the level of fear does equal the level of true threat.

As a result, Malkin believes, citizens have a right to be outraged at the U.S. government for not adequately protecting its people. Her book goes on to discuss "Foreign Cop-Killers on the Loose," the "Torturers Next Door" (more stories of illegal alien criminals), and the egregious incompetence of current U.S. immigration policy. She concludes that the U.S. government must "militarize the border," that is, "guard the front door" and "lock the back door." I linger on Malkin's book, not because it is unique but quite the contrary. Her book is one of many others like it, all of which pitch the same message (the dangers of illegal immigration) through a similar tactic of storytelling regarding a few illegal immigrants who have acted barbarically.[29]

Absent from Malkin's narratives are, of course, the contributions made by the "good" illegal immigrants, or how the cheap labor they provide helps the U.S. economy. In part, this is because many like Malkin believe that even if they come with good intentions, illegal immigrants still do harm in terms of more mundane domestic concerns. These domestic concerns fall within the second "fear category" espoused by many anti-illegal immigration advocates. One need only look to the arguments of the Minuteman Project's founder, Jim Gilchrist, to see this. He writes: "The illegal alien crisis is misconstrued by many as only 'one' issue. But that seemingly sole issue harbors a wealth of major issues having a dramatic effect on the lives of all Americans and the future health and prosperity of the United States."[30] Among these negative effects, Gilchrist mentions the "terrorist and criminal" elements addressed earlier, but he goes much further in providing examples of more mundane concerns. These concerns range from the diseases immigrants are bringing into the United States ("the thousands of undetected cases of communicable and deadly tuberculosis," for example) to the ways illegal immigrants are draining taxpayer funded institutions, such as schools or hospitals:

> Our emergency clinics and hospitals are closing their doors under the immense financial pressure of providing free medical services to...large numbers of illegal aliens....Public schools are seriously overcrowded and financially overburdened....Except for life-saving medical treatment, under what legal authority is the United States required to medicate, educate, shelter, feed, or otherwise provide for the welfare and sustenance of foreign nationals who have already broken our laws to come here?[31]

The opinion here is that American citizens are being unfairly burdened by the millions of illegal immigrants living in the United States. Such viewpoints are bolstered by organizations like the Center for Immigration Studies (CIS), a non-profit research organization that promotes reduction in immigration numbers. The paper by Steven Camarota, director of research at the Center for Immigration Studies, entitled "The High Cost of Cheap Labor: Illegal Immigration and the Federal Government," speaks to the belief that illegal immigration creates a fiscal net loss to the U.S. government. Using Census Bureau data, Camarota concluded, "when all taxes paid (direct and indirect) and all costs are considered, illegal households created a net fiscal deficit at the federal level of more than $10 billion in 2002. We also estimate that, if there was an amnesty for illegal aliens, the net fiscal deficit would grow to nearly $29 billion."[32] The largest costs, Camarota concluded, came from Medicaid, treatment for the uninsured, food assistance programs, the federal prison and court systems, and federal aid to schools.

The discontent behind such argumentation is not limited to the perceived dollar cost to the U.S. government. It also involves the idea that such large numbers of illegal immigrants are taking away jobs from Americans and/or keeping wages too low. Many individuals and groups, however, disagree with this opinion. As with so many aspects of the immigration debate, there is always a strong counterpunch. In this case, one may look, for example, to Immigration Works USA, an organization of business coalitions working to advance their belief, based upon their own experience as small business owners, that immigrant workers help, rather than hurt, the economy. "Even with today's high unemployment, employers in many sectors—agriculture, high-tech, the seasonal economy—who have made every effort to hire qualified American workers continue to need immigrants to keep their businesses open and contributing to the economy," says the organization.[33]

In a humorous attempt at making a similar point, farmworkers teamed up with comedian Stephen Colbert to launch a campaign called "Take Our Jobs." The campaign invited unemployed Americans to apply for one of many agricultural jobs posted as the 2010 harvesting season approached. On the homepage for the "application form," it explained: "There are two issues facing our nation—high unemployment and undocumented people in the workforce—that many Americans believe are related. Missing from the debate on both issues is an honest recognition that the food we all eat—at home, in restaurants and workplace cafeterias (including those in the Capitol)—comes to us from the labor of undocumented farm workers.... Farm workers are ready to welcome citizens and legal residents who wish to replace them in the field. We will use our knowledge and staff to help connect the unemployed with farm employers. Just fill out the form to the right and continue on to the request for job application." Making the point that such agricultural work is grueling, there is a (farcical) disclaimer at the bottom of the application, which reads: "Job may include using hand tools such as knives, hoes, shovels, etc. Duties may include tilling the soil, transplanting, weeding, thinning, picking, cutting, sorting & packing of harvested produce. May set up & operate irrigation equip. Work is performed outside in all weather conditions (Summertime 90 + degree weather) & is physically demanding requiring workers to bend, stoop, lift & carry up to 50 lbs on a regular basis."[34] With or without humor, the cost versus benefit argument concerning undocumented and "less-skilled" immigrants continues to be one of the most controversial questions in the immigration debate.[35]

Last, a third source of fear concerning illegal immigration is that it is diluting and endangering the "American way of life." This argument is addressed by conservative politician Pat Buchanan and by former Harvard professor of international studies Samuel P. Huntington. Buchanan, for example, begins his book, *State of Emergency: The Third World Invasion and Conquest of America*, with a reflection titled "How Civilizations Perish." He compares the collapse of the Roman Empire with the imminent collapse of American civilization. He blames the unprecedented influx of illegal (Latin American) immigration on this gathering demise. Drawing from Arnold Toynbee, he concludes that the three "mortal perils" of great civilizations are "dying populations, disintegrating cultures, and invasions unresisted."[36]

Due to the radical shift in immigration patterns in recent decades (i.e., the large numbers of Mexican and other Spanish-speaking immigrants), Buchanan avers that America is suffering from all three mortal perils: fertility rates among (mostly Anglo-Saxon) American citizens is drastically down, while that of recent immigrants is on the rise (add into that "the anchor baby" phenomenon—the child born in the United States who is automatically a citizen);[37] the American culture is disintegrating due to the newer wave of Spanish-speaking immigrants who are not assimilating as did Europeans in the early twentieth century; and this "invasion" has gone largely unchecked by the U.S. government and its liberal elites. "This is not immigration as America knew it, when men and women made a conscious choice to turn their backs on their native lands and cross the ocean to become Americans. This is an invasion, the greatest invasion in history," writes Buchanan.[38]

Moreover, the newest immigrants, Buchanan argues, show little to no patriotism for America. "Patriotism is the soul of a nation," he writes. "It is what keeps a nation alive. When patriotism dies, when a nation loses the love and loyalty of its people, the nation dies and begins to decompose."[39] Samuel P. Huntington, in a more measured and less apocalyptic tone, picks up on Buchanan's themes of patriotism and nationalism and the detrimental effects mass immigration is having on American identity and power. In his controversial book, *Who Are We? The Challenges to America's National Identity*, Huntington argues, in a similar vein, that the salience and substance of "American national identity" are eroding. By salience he means the importance Americans attribute to their national identity, and by substance he means that which distinguishes Americans from other peoples.[40] The substance of which Huntington speaks is Anglo-Protestant culture. As he writes:

> Key elements of that culture include: the English language; Christianity; religious commitment; English concepts of the rule of law, the responsibility of rulers, and the rights

of individuals; and dissenting Protestant values of individualism, the work ethic, and the belief that humans have the ability and the duty to try to create a heaven on earth, "a city on the hill." Historically, millions of immigrants were attracted to America because of this culture and the economic opportunities it helped to make possible.... In the late twentieth century, however, the salience and substance of this culture were challenged by a new wave of immigrants from Latin America.[41]

This new wave of immigrants has led, he argues further, to the spread of Spanish as the second language of the United States as well as "Hispanization trends in American society." Such trends, alongside the popularity of "creeds of multiculturalism" and "the assertion of group identities based on race, ethnicity and gender, are effectively diluting the salience and substance of America's formative Anglo-Protestant culture."[42] As a result of this cultural dilution, Huntington believes, much like Buchanan, that American civilization is under some sort of mortal threat:

> All societies face recurring threats to their existence, to which they eventually succumb. Yet some societies, even when so threatened, are also capable of postponing their demise by halting and reversing the processes of decline and renewing their vitality and identity. I believe that America can do that and that Americans should recommit themselves to the Anglo-Protestant culture, traditions, and values that for three and a half centuries have been embraced by Americans of all races, ethnicities, and religions and that have been the source of their liberty, unity, power, prosperity, and moral leadership as a force for good in the world.[43]

The questions that arise in arguments such as Huntington's are these: When does pride of country and heritage cross the line into ethnocentrism and racism? Is the call to "recommit to the Anglo-Protestant culture, traditions, and values" ultimately xenophobic? Or is it purely the expression of a proud patriot? Is there something being lost in the newest trends of immigration, something essential to America?[44] Most who oppose such argumentation believe firmly that calls like these, for immigrants to better assimilate to "American values," are inherently racist. Critics of civil patrol groups, for example, accuse such groups of being bigoted at the core. In fact, for this reason, Jim Gilchrist refers to his organization as "the multiethnic Minuteman Project." He makes a point to emphasize in his book that "the Minuteman Project's non-white volunteers, who comprise 20 percent of the Project's membership, drop their jaws in awe at the abysmal, mean-spirited" accusations of individuals and groups who call them racist.[45] Gilchrist defends his group further against "the faulty logic of its critics," emphasizing that just because the organization opposes illegal immigration does not mean it is racist. He writes, "This could not be further from the truth. The multiethnic

Minuteman Project has an African-American on its board of directors and professes allegiance to the United States of America. We abhor racism and we welcome all peoples to America, as long as they arrive legally, with the determination to become law-abiding citizens."[46]

Nonetheless, folks like Buchanan, Gilchrist, Huntington, and their many followers stress the absolute necessity of proper assimilation of immigrants. "Multiculturalism and diversity are commendable goals," says Gilchrist. "But they are selfish and aimless agendas of blind social engineers when not accompanied with 'assimilation' into the host country. If we are to be a unified nation, then we should strive to be an 'assimilated' nation."[47] In short, the argument goes, without true assimilation, there is no unity; and without unity, there is disintegration; the center cannot hold. If immigration continues as it is, in the same chaotic, lawless, and unassimilated fashion, the next generation of Americans "will inherit a tangle of rancorous, unassimilated, squabbling cultures with no cohesive bond, and a certain guarantee of the death of this nation as a harmonious 'melting pot.' "[48]

Huntington argues that, unlike earlier patterns of immigration, the latest population of immigrants to the United States (primarily Mexicans and Central Americans) has demonstrated a unique resistance to the kind of assimilation that keeps America robust and powerful. By assimilation, Huntington means that new immigrants "be accepted into American society [by] embracing English as the national language, [taking] pride in their American identity, [believing] in the principles of the American Creed, and [living] by the Protestant ethic (to be self-reliant, hardworking, and morally upright)."[49] He believes that while America has been in part an immigrant nation, "much more importantly, it has been a nation that assimilated immigrants and their descendants into its society and culture."[50] Huntington is referring to the "Americanization of millions of immigrants until the 1960s," mostly, although not entirely, of European descent.

It is the new pattern of Latin American immigration, Huntington says, that makes proper assimilation difficult.[51] Mexican immigration, he argues, is completely different from previous patterns of immigration. "Contiguity, numbers, illegality, regional concentration, persistence, and an historical presence combine to make Mexican immigration different from other immigration and to pose problems for the assimilation of people of Mexican origin into American society," he concludes.[52]

By contiguity, he is referring to the inherent proximity of Mexico to the United States; the nearly 2,000 miles of border—that long, thin, porous line in the sand—between the two countries. By numbers, he is referring to the unprecedented numbers of men, women, and children who are crossing that line. Because there are such high numbers (of mostly illegal Mexicans and Central Americans), "regional concentration" is occurring: whole neighborhoods and towns, large sections of cities, do not properly integrate into the American way of life. For example, there is often little need to learn English, as most transactions in such regionally concentrated areas can be conducted in Spanish, keeping Hispanic communities too insular. And there is no indication that these trends will let up any time soon.

These factors, Huntington and others argue, dissuade the newest Latin American immigrants from feeling a proper sense of patriotism for the United States. As Huntington says, "the ultimate criterion of assimilation is the extent to which immigrants identify with the United States as a country, believe in its Creed, espouse its culture, and correspondingly reject loyalty to other countries and their values and cultures."[53] In other words, patriotism is one of the strongest unifying forces of a nation. For a nation to be healthy, it must share a sense of common destiny, a common pride of history, and a single, uniform language.

Similarly, when he likens the fall of America to the fall of Rome, Buchanan states that creeds of multiculturalism and lack of proper patriotism are much to blame for America's current loss of power on the world stage. He writes, "Rome became a polyglot city of all creeds and cultures of the empire. But these alien peoples [immigrants from the North] brought with them no reverence for Roman gods, no respect for Roman tradition, no love of Roman culture. And so, as Rome conquered the barbarians, the barbarians conquered Rome."[54] Likewise, due to current immigration trends, Buchanan and others aver, the United States is turning into a polyglot nation, a tower of Babel that is destined to fall.

There are many who believe it is worthless to read the arguments of politicians and commentators like Malkin, Gilchrist, Buchanan, or Huntington. Their opponents may tag them as xenophobic, simplistic, conservative, or racist. Many would not dare to read their books, finding their ideas too offensive. But the reality is that such argumentation exists, and it is not marginal. Their viewpoints represent entrenched anti-illegal immigration sentiment. They represent real fears, and real discontent, of real people. No matter what side one takes, it is important that these fears, aroused by illegal immigration, be acknowledged as they are the motivations for organizations like the Minuteman Project, the MCDC, the Patriots Coalition, the Border Patrol, and for millions of individual citizens, lobbyists, and lawmakers opposed to illegal immigration.

Inarguably, illegal immigration brings with it many challenges and difficulties, high emotions, and strong opinions. Fear is a natural part of the debate. But the core question that remains is this: Does the level of fear equal the level of threat? Many, such as those involved in the border ministries highlighted earlier, would say no. They claim that the level of fear is excessive, and hence immoral. Folks like Malkin, Gilchrist, Buchanan, and Huntington are demonizing immigrants. Worse still, Border Patrol strategies, motivated by too much fear, have resulted in a death trap for hundreds of men, women, and children every year.

Many such critics argue that the post-9/11 climate has only exacerbated this unnecessary rhetoric of fear. As Zbigniew Brzezinski, former aide to Jimmy Carter, says:

> The "war on terror" has created a culture of fear in America. The Bush administration's elevation of these three words into a national mantra since the horrific events of 9/11 has had a pernicious impact on American democracy, on America's psyche and on U.S. standing in the world.... The record is even more troubling in the general area of civil rights. The culture of fear has bred intolerance, suspicion of foreigners and the adoption of legal processes that undermine fundamental notions of justice.[55]

The way in which 9/11 has been conflated into larger debates regarding immigration, Brzezinksi and many like him argue, has damaged the ethical fabric of the United States. "The culture of fear" has exploded into intolerance and suspicion of foreigners, and, Brzezinski concludes, "Someday Americans will be ashamed of this record [of fear and persecution] as they now have become of the earlier instances in U.S. history of panic by the many prompting intolerance against the few."[56]

In her book on the phenomenon of civil patrol groups in Arizona, Roxanne Lynn Doty writes:

> Individuals such as Simcox, Gilchrist, and the many others who are part of the anti-immigrant movement—both private citizens and policy makers—are merely the bearers of sentiments and ideologies whose force and significance is to be located at the collective level. Individual names and faces may be unknown and/or quickly forgotten, but the phenomenon itself lives on, feeding off powerful sentiments that lurk beneath the surface of our professed values of equality and respect for individual human beings and their rights.[57]

Fear is perhaps the most powerful sentiment lurking beneath the surface of our collective fabric. In few places does it seem quite as strong as in current anti-illegal immigration rhetoric. But how can we measure when such fear is an acceptable form of self-preservation, and when it morphs into collective paranoia? When is the fear healthy, and when does it turn deadly? Most recently, these questions have been asked in response to Arizona's controversial immigration law, Senate Bill 1070, to which I turn now.

CHAPTER 8

Senate Bill 1070: Wagers of Love and Fear at the Border

O n the night of March 27, 2010, highly respected Arizona rancher, Robert N. Krentz Jr. was found shot to death in a remote part of his 35,000-acre ranch, a few miles north of the border.[1] He was found dead on his ATV about 1,000 feet from where the shooting took place. The motor of the ATV was still running, its lights were on, and there were spin-out marks in the dirt, indicating, according to Cochise County Sheriff Larry Dever, that Krentz was trying to escape whoever shot him.[2] Krentz's last known communication was to his brother whom he radioed while he was out checking water lines and fencing on the ranch. He was said to have told his brother that there was an "illegal alien" nearby.[3] That communication and the fact that the ranch was located along a highly trafficked drug corridor led many to assume that Krentz was gunned down by an illegal Mexican smuggler.

The reaction in the community to Krentz's murder was one of fear, outrage, and suspicion. Many quickly pointed the finger at the federal government, accusing it of improperly securing the border. Ranchers vowed to be more cautious, to offer less or no hospitality to migrants in distress. "Usually if somebody needs help, you walk up to them and help them," said Wendy Glenn, a friend and neighbor of Robert Krentz who reported having heard Mr. Krentz's radio transmission. "We won't just walk up and offer help any more."[4] While ranchers like Glenn vowed to offer less hospitality to migrants in the wake of Krentz's murder, law enforcement officials tried to piece together a credible story explaining the tragedy. Investigators surmised that retaliation might have been a motive for the killing. The day before the shooting, Phil Krentz, Robert Krentz's brother, reported drug smuggling activity on the ranch to the Border Patrol. "Agents found 290 pounds of marijuana on the ranch and followed tracks to where they found and arrested eight illegal immigrants."[5] Investigators wondered whether these arrests were connected to the murder.

The death of Krentz became the tipping point in the immigration debate, not just in Arizona, but across the United States. It was a major impetus behind the drafting and signing of the controversial immigration law known as SB 1070. In the weeks following Krentz's murder, "the killing became symbolic of Arizona's porous and violent border, setting off a flurry of demands from residents, politicians and law enforcement leaders for more troops and resources at the border."[6] One of these resources became Senate Bill 1070, which was signed into law on April 23, 2010, less than a month after Krentz's death.

Originally called Support Our Law Enforcement and Safe Neighborhoods Act, SB 1070 became the strictest immigration law in the nation. In a strategy of "attrition by enforcement," the law was aimed at "discourag[ing] and deter[ring] the unlawful entry and presence of aliens and economic activity by persons unlawfully present in the United States" through several measures.[7] The law officially made it a crime for undocumented migrants to set foot in Arizona and made it unlawful for employers to knowingly hire undocumented workers or for anyone to knowingly transport illegal immigrants. The most controversial aspect of the law, however, granted law enforcement agents broad new powers to interrogate and arrest anyone they *suspected* of being in the United States illegally. The law stated these two provisions: "Where reasonable suspicion exists that the person is an alien who is unlawfully present in the United States, a reasonable attempt shall be made, when practicable, to determine the immigration status of the person," and "A law enforcement officer, without a warrant, may arrest a person if the officer has probable cause to believe that the person has committed any public offense that makes the person removable from the United States."[8]

As soon as the law was signed by Arizona governor, Jan Brewer, criticisms began flying. Detractors called the law racist and a serious violation of basic civil rights, while those in favor called it "a measured, reasonable step" in the effort to secure the border, "giving Arizona police officers another tool when [coming] into contact with illegal aliens during their normal law enforcement duties."[9]

Once again, the new law underscored the highly polarizing nature of the immigration debate and the seeming lack of any middle ground. Unlike many of the daily dramas going on in southern Arizona, the passing of SB 1070 immediately grabbed national attention. Overnight, people across the country, on all sides of the debate, were stirred up and weighing in, arguing over the new law as well as over how to effectively secure the border and enact proper immigration reform.

Proponents of the law like Kris Kobach, who was Attorney General Ashcroft's chief advisor and is currently secretary of state of Kansas, expressed confidence in the new measure. In a *New York Times* op-ed, he wrote:

> Arizona law didn't invent the concept [of reasonable suspicion]: Precedents list the factors that can contribute to reasonable suspicion; when several are combined, the "totality of circumstances" that results may create reasonable suspicion that a crime has been committed. For example, the Arizona law is most likely to come into play after a traffic stop. A police officer pulls a minivan over for speeding. A dozen passengers are crammed in. None has identification. The highway is a known alien-smuggling corridor. The driver is acting evasively. Those factors combine to create reasonable suspicion that the occupants are not in the country legally.[10]

Kobach's opinion attempts to refute the major complaint of SB 1070—that it leads to racial profiling. Kobach and others say that skin color or accent would not be criteria for reasonable suspicion. Rather, reasonable suspicion is born from a totality of circumstances. Nor does it violate the Fourth Amendment guarantee against unreasonable searches or seizures. There must be proper probable cause, such as Kobach describes. A picture must emerge, after, for example, a legitimate traffic stop: too many people in a car, no identification, along a highway like I-19, driver and passengers acting strangely.

How skin color or accent do not count as "factors" in this picture, Kobach does not say. But he does mention that Section 2 of the bill states that law enforcement officials "may not solely consider race, color or national origin" in making stops or determining immigration status. "Arizona is the ground zero of illegal immigration," says Kobach. In the void created by the federal government's inability to effectively handle immigration, folks like Kobach believe Arizonans deserve to take matters into their own hands, and they did so through the passage of SB 1070.

In a statement given before signing the bill into law, Governor Jan Brewer expressed her confidence in the fairness of SB 1070. After having "listened patiently to both sides" and praying "long into the night" before deciding to sign it, she concluded that the law would ultimately act as "another tool for our state to use as we work to solve a crisis we did not create and the federal government refused to fix."[11] The bill, she said in a statement, "strengthens the laws of our state and protects all of us, every Arizona citizen and everyone here in our state lawfully. And it does so while ensuring that the constitutional rights of ALL in Arizona remain solid."[12] Like so many in

support of the law, Governor Brewer claimed that the measure would protect citizens from the border violence that every day "creeps its way north."
In her closing remarks, Brewer reiterated the law's fairness, saying:

> I believe Arizona, like America, is governed by laws. Good laws…well-intentioned
> laws…laws that confer respect and that demand respect in return. In his third State of
> the Union address, President Theodore Roosevelt said, "No man is above the law and
> no man is below it; nor do we ask any man's permission when we require him to obey
> it. Obedience to the law is demanded as a right; not asked as a favor." So, let us move
> forward—ever mindful of our rights—ever faithful to the law.[13]

While those like Brewer and Kobach expressed their belief in the logic,
necessity, and constitutionality of the bill, millions of others lamented it as
shameful and racist. Within hours of its signing, protests and boycotts
erupted, not just in Arizona but across the nation. Opponents took to the
streets in dozens of U.S. cities. Neighboring cities, counties, and states
called for businesses to withdraw investments from Arizona. Even the
National Basketball Association team, the Phoenix Suns, protested by
changing their team jersey to "Los Suns." The law, opponents argued, did
not protect Arizonans or U.S. citizens, as Governor Brewer declared. Instead,
it was a breach of cherished American civil liberties. Some likened it to the
Jim Crow South, others to Nazi Germany, and still others to the Japanese
internment camps. Cardinal Roger Mahoney, one of the country's most
outspoken clergy in favor of immigrant rights, wrote:

> The law is wrongly assuming that Arizona residents, including local law enforcement per-
> sonnel, will now shift their total attention to guessing which Latino-looking or foreign-
> looking person may or may not have proper documents. That's also nonsense. American
> people are fair-minded and respectful. I can't imagine Arizonans now reverting to German
> Nazi and Russian Communist techniques whereby people are required to turn one another
> in to the authorities on any suspicion of documentation. Are children supposed to call 911
> because one parent does not have proper papers? Are family members and neighbors now
> supposed to spy on one another, create total distrust across neighborhoods and commu-
> nities, and report people because of suspicions based upon appearance?[14]

Critics like Cardinal Mahoney remained unconvinced by the law, believing
that it would enable rampant racial profiling, despite the clause in section 2,
cited by Kobach. People wanted to know, What were the criteria for determining reasonable suspicion, and how would law enforcement officials *not*
consider ethnicity, accent, or skin color as factors? Ultimately, critics of the
bill said it violated the Fourteenth Amendment, which guarantees equal
protection under the law.

On April 29, just days after the bill was signed by Governor Brewer, two lawsuits were filed against it. The first was filed by Tucson police officer, Martin Escobar, who argued that there was no "race neutral" criteria for discerning if someone was here illegally. Escobar, who became a U.S. citizen as an adult and works for the Tucson Southside Police Division, said that over 50 percent of the residents he encounters are Latino. Moreover, Escobar cited the statistic that in 2007–2008, approximately 24 million Mexicans visited Arizona legally. Escobar believed there was no way to assess reasonable suspicion without succumbing to racial profiling. His lawsuit claimed that SB 1070 violated the First, Fourth, Fifth, and Fourteenth Amendments of the U.S. Constitution, as well as the Supremacy Clause. Even without such constitutional breaches, the law would jeopardize the hard-won trust between law enforcement and citizens. Women who were abused by their husbands, for example, would not seek police intervention for fear of being deported; families would not bring their sick children to the hospital; those with information regarding gang or criminal activity would no longer contact police departments.

The second lawsuit was filed by the National Coalition of Latino Clergy and Christian Leaders, who claimed, like Escobar, that it violated the Supremacy Clause of the constitution. The Supremacy Clause, part of Article VI, declares that federal law trumps state law and that state officials must always respect higher federal law. A few months after the National Coalition of Latino Clergy and Christian Leaders filed suit on these grounds, so did the U.S. Department of Justice. On July 6, 2010, in an attempt to prevent the bill from going into effect (ninety days after its signing), the Obama administration filed its suit, claiming SB 1070 violated the "preeminent authority" of the federal government and that the state of Arizona was interfering in what should be a federal matter.

A few weeks earlier, in a speech delivered during a naturalization ceremony for two dozen foreign-born members of the U.S. military, Obama himself called SB 1070 "misguided." He questioned "the civil rights implications" of the legislation and expressed concern that it would "threaten to undermine basic notions of fairness that we cherish as Americans." Meanwhile, a majority of faith leaders came together to condemn SB 1070 and to appeal for comprehensive immigration reform. Jim Wallis, one of the most strident evangelical voices in favor of immigration reform, called the new law "a social and racial sin." Not only was it "mean-spirited" and "ineffective, ... cross[ing] many moral and legal laws," Wallis wrote in his *God's Politics* blog, but furthermore, it went against one's "Christian conscience":

> We all want to live in a nation of laws, and the immigration system in the U.S. is so broken that it is serving no one well. But enforcement without reform of the system is merely

cruel. Enforcement without compassion is immoral. Enforcement that breaks up families is unacceptable. And enforcement of this law would force us to violate our Christian conscience, which we simply will not do. It makes it illegal to love your neighbor in Arizona.... Jesus...instructed his disciples to "welcome the stranger," and said that whatever we do to "the least of these, who are members of my family" we do to him. I think that means that to obey Jesus and his gospel will mean to disobey SB 1070.... Many Christians in Arizona won't comply with this law because the people they will target will be members of our "family" in the body of Christ. And any attack against them is an attack against us, and the One we follow.[15]

Across most theological lines, clergy and laity denounced what they saw as an inhumane anti-immigrant law. It was not universal condemnation, however. Some religious groups were divided by it, feeling conflicted yet again over how to strike a proper balance between love of stranger and respect of law, both of which, according to popular biblical interpretations, are divinely mandated. One such example involves members of the Church of Jesus Christ of Latter-day Saints. The denomination's thirteen "Articles of Faith" offer contradictory mandates.[16] The 13th article states, "We believe in being honest, true, chaste, benevolent, virtuous, and in doing good to all men," while the 12th article, reminiscent of Romans 13, asserts: "We believe in being subject to kings, presidents, rulers, and magistrates, in obeying, honoring and sustaining the law."[17] This call to do good to all men while being subject to the rule of law is the challenge facing many Christians and non-Christians alike in matters of immigration.

Despite this tension, however, people like Wallis believe SB 1070 is a clear sin:

[It] should be denounced as [a sin] by people of faith and conscience across the nation. This is not just about Arizona, but about all of us, and about what kind of country we want to be. It's time to stand up to this new strategy of "deportation by attrition." It is a policy of deliberate political cruelty, and it should be remembered that "attrition" is a term of war. Arizona is deciding whether to wage war on the body of Christ. We should say that if you come after one part of the body, you come after all of us.[18]

Christians like Wallis see SB 1070 (as well as current raids and deportations) as an outright attack against their faith. Furthermore, Wallis asserts that the law is "not just about Arizona. It is about all of us, and the kind of country we want to be." His statement points to the battering the state of Arizona has taken in the wake of Governor Brewer's signing the law into effect. "Today, Arizona stands as the state with the most xenophobic and nativist laws in the country," declared the Reverend Samuel Rodriguez, president of the National Hispanic Christian Leadership Conference.[19]

But as a *New York Times* article said, "Arizona is well accustomed to the derision of its countrymen. The state resisted adopting Martin Luther King's birthday as a holiday years after most other states embraced it. The sheriff in its largest county forces inmates to wear pink underwear, apparently to assault their masculinity. Residents may take their guns almost anywhere.... But while Arizona may have become a cartoon of intolerance to much of America, the reality is much more complex."[20]

Indeed, the reality *is* much more complex. Many Arizonans are angered at what they see as an unfair portrayal of their state. Some feel they are being scapegoated and caricatured. Arizona is just one part of the body, they say, and the whole body is sick. It is easy to point the finger from afar, but the problem of immigration is much more complex. Ultimately, the blame should not be placed on Arizona but on the federal government. *The Arizona Republic* released an editorial expressing its dismay over SB 1070, but it also laid the blame squarely on the U.S. government's inability to effectively deal with immigration reform and border security. Such incompetency has left Arizona to fend for itself. The editorial called the law "ugly and indefensible" but stressed that it is simply symptomatic of a larger problem. Arizona is no different from the rest of the country except that it also happens to be a major corridor of drug trafficking and human smuggling: "We are a state of racial, intellectual, and cultural diversity. In many ways a microcosm of the country—no better, no worse. But unlike other states, Arizona has an illegal-immigration superhighway running north from the border into our biggest metropolitan areas."[21]

The violence and chaos that have resulted from this superhighway and from the federal government's inability to properly handle it—including its inability to foresee how "hardening the borders in Texas and California" could lead to the massive funneling of migrants and smugglers through the harsh desert and remote wilderness of Arizona—have resulted in a "frightening stew":

> The feds did nothing while Arizona saw a running gun battle on its main interstate highways. The feds did nothing while drophouses festered by the hundreds in our neighborhoods. The feds did nothing while Phoenix became the kidnapping capital of the country. The feds did nothing as rancher Robert Krentz was murdered on his border-area ranch. Feeling cornered and anxious, Arizona lashed out with a nasty immigration bill.... But those in other states who defame Arizona need to look in the mirror. This is your problem, too. This is America's problem.... It is a fantasy to believe that Arizona is an island, a racist backwater isolated from the other 49. We are you. We are what happens when the brunt of a national problem is [borne] by one state. Rather than make Arizona the scapegoat, we can all make it the catalyst to finally fix our national immigration system.[22]

The point is well made: This frightening stew is America's problem, not just Arizona's. The volatility in the Sonoran desert and the volatility of people's emotions around the issue are indicative of a much larger problem. Ranchers like Robert Krentz become the symbols; and laws like SB 1070 become the result.

The day before SB 1070 was meant to take effect, federal judge Susan Bolton blocked the most controversial aspects of the law. Bolton ruled that, based upon precedent, many of the statutory provisions of SB 1070 were preempted by the United States government.[23] Bolton did not cite racism per se. Nor did she cite the Equal Protection Clause of the Fourteenth Amendment. Rather, in her ruling she stated, "the mandatory requirement that Arizona law enforcement officials and agencies check the immigration status of any person arrested," would both "burden legally-present aliens" as well as "divert federal resources from the federal government's other responsibilities and priorities."[24] Moreover, the provision to check the immigration status of all arrestees puts undue pressure on local law enforcement agencies, while at the same time burdening lawfully present aliens (and citizens) with "the possibility of intrusive police practices that might affect international relations and generate disloyalty."[25]

Ultimately, Bolton's reasoning went back to the Supremacy Clause invoked by the Obama administration, from Article VI of the U.S. Constitution: "This Constitution, and the Laws of the United States which shall be made in Pursuance thereof; and all Treaties made, or which shall be made, under the Authority of the United States, shall be the supreme Law of the Land; and the Judges in every State shall be bound thereby, any Thing in the Constitution or Laws of any State to the Contrary notwithstanding." Hence, when federal law and state law come into conflict, federal law reigns supreme. Bolton reasserted that matters of immigration, in particular, are federal matters and must be regulated by the U.S. government rather than by individual states. Bolton drew from precedent established in *Hines v. Davidowitz*, a 1941 ruling, concluding that the purpose of the Alien Registration Act (also known as the Smith Act) was to provide a single national immigration system that was "integrated" and "all-embracing."[26] The goal of a federally regulated immigration system is "to make a harmonious whole," and to facilitate amicable relations between nations. As such, any attempt by Arizona to create or enforce its own immigration laws is preempted by U.S. federal law.

At the end of her injunction order, Bolton made sure to stress that in blocking certain provisions of SB1070, "the Court by no means disregards Arizona's interests in controlling illegal immigration and addressing the concurrent problems with crime including the trafficking of humans, drugs, guns, and money." Nonetheless, "even though Arizona's interests may be consistent with those of the federal government, it is not in the public interest for Arizona to enforce preempted laws."[27]

Many Arizonans were angered over Bolton's ruling. What recourse did they have if the "supreme Law of the Land" was ineffectual and outmoded, as in the case of federal immigration laws? In the absence of a functional national immigration system, what is Arizona to do? In an opinion piece for the *New York Times*, Arizona's Cochise County sheriff, Larry Dever, wrote: "The people of Cochise County support the state's immigration law [SB 1070] because we want this violence to end. Understandably, we get frustrated and disheartened when the White House, which has failed to secure the border for generations, sues us for trying to fill the legal vacuum."[28]

Sheriff Dever, who is responsible for patrolling eighty-three miles of the U.S.-Mexican border, makes the point that because of "the legal vacuum" at the federal level, nobody is winning in Arizona. "At best," he wrote, "illegal aliens and smugglers trespass, damage ranchers' land, steal water and food and start fires. At worst, people who have come here hoping for freedom and opportunity are raped and abandoned by smugglers and left to die in the desert. Nor are the migrants the only victims. Just over a year ago, while officials of the Department of Homeland Security were declaring they had secured 'operational control' of most of the southern Arizona border, my friend Robert N. Krentz Jr., a local rancher, was murdered, most likely by drug smugglers."[29]

The fate of SB 1070 lies in the future of legal proceedings. Bolton's ruling was immediately appealed, and a year later, the fight over the law carries on. What seems clear is that SB 1070 will not go softly into the night; much talk is being made of its eventual appearance in the Supreme Court. Meanwhile, in the absence of any federal immigration legislation, dozens of other states have been drafting immigration-related laws, many mirroring Arizona's tough enforcement measures. So far, though, most states have not succeeded in passing such laws, either because they have been set aside due to more pressing matters such as state budget debates, or because pro-immigrant groups, including many business owners, have been lobbying against such harsh legal actions.

Whatever the eventual outcome, it seems clear that one constructive purpose of SB 1070 lies in its pointing to the moral imperative for immigration reform at the congressional level. During the height of the SB 1070 controversy, President Obama delivered a speech at American University's School of International Service calling for bipartisan cooperation in the effort to overhaul what he called America's "fundamentally broken" immigration system, admitting that the current system reflects "years of patchwork fixes and ill-conceived revisions," which have led to paralyzing "backlogs and bureaucracy."[30] He blamed the "creakiness" of the system on a combination of nasty political posturing, intransigent partisanship, and a certain moral laziness of everyone: on the part of government, on the part of businesses, and on the part of individuals. Immigration reform, he said, was "not only a political issue, not just an economic issue, but a moral imperative as well."

Whether Congress can break through its political stalemates and bipartisan paralysis is another question. Federal immigration reform, like most matters involving immigration, is a messy and complex subject. There is no shortage of voices weighing in on how to fix the system, but many of these voices tend to oversimplify the issue. Part of this oversimplification arises because many politicians, law makers, lobbyists, and other parties with opinions concerning reform have little awareness of the true realities of immigration on the ground. Few have spent significant time at the U.S.-Mexican border to really comprehend the painful complexity facing those living there (ranchers, migrants, Border Patrol agents, activists, Tohono O'odham tribal members, etc.); nor have they spent ample time with families separated by deportation, or undocumented workers who have lived in the shadows of the United States for years or even decades.

Another part of the oversimplification problem is also related to the multidimensional reality of what real immigration reform would require. Often, people take up only one side of the issue, such as, What do we do about the estimated 11 million undocumented immigrants living in the United States today? This argument often gets watered down to the question of amnesty versus mass deportation. Does the government provide a path to legalization for those living here already, or does it continue its policy of deportation? In his July 1, 2011, speech on the matter, President Obama suggested that the solution lies neither in blanket amnesty nor in mass deportations. Rather, it must be something in between. On the one hand, illegal immigrants living in the United States should be held accountable for entering illegally or overstaying their visas, he said, so as not to make a mockery of those lawfully waiting in line to enter the country. At the same time, the government must also find ways to help those already here forge a path toward legal status so as not to break apart families or violently uproot those who have made this country their home. It is a tricky balance: to appropriately honor established laws while also honoring the dignity, struggles, and dreams of those who are already living here.

Still, even if one desires to find a middle ground between amnesty and deportation, finding this involves simultaneously resolving dozens of other issues. For example, the United States must also confront its current visa system. Many believe that the country must drastically change the annual numbers and types of visas it gives out and consider implementing a proper worker visa program that takes into account U.S. labor needs and the role of immigrant workers in sustaining the U.S. economy. Those who believe in the need for such worker visa programs, which would radically increase the number of visas to low-skilled workers, fundamentally believe in the benefit of immigrant labor. Meanwhile, there are those who believe that such labor is ultimately a drain on the U.S. government, that more immigrants mean more cost to public welfare systems.[31]

Further complicating the question of worker visas is the problem of implementing effective systems of verification and identification so that workers coming here are both properly vetted by their home countries and accurately tracked by U.S. authorities on a regular basis. This would require the governments of sending nations to invest time and money in conducting the necessary background checks required by receiving nations; and in the United States, government funds would have to be allocated to further develop effective identification strategies, such as the E-verify program (which is not short of critics) or biometric identification techniques (also heavily criticized).

Such issues, moreover, only deal with more short-term aspects of immigration reform. There is no lack of long-term questions either. These longer-term questions are even more complicated and less clear-cut. They involve conflicting opinions and analyses concerning current international trade and labor practices. Some believe, for example, that trade agreements such as the North American Free Trade Agreement (NAFTA) have destroyed the livelihoods of small subsistence farmers: U.S. subsidies to large agricultural enterprises have allowed them to charge less for their products. This has hurt Mexican farmers who could not compete. Many of them, as a result, have been uprooted. Some of these farmers have migrated illegally to the United States. Critics of such trade practices also point to the inhumane working conditions and destructive environmental effects of factories like *maquiladoras*, foreign-owned assembly plants, most in northern Mexican border towns, which import duty-free materials and employ cheap labor to create low-cost products. These critics also believe the rise of multinational corporations has only widened the gap between the poor and the wealthy, ultimately engendering lower standards of living, poorer health, urban violence, and the impossibility of upward mobility. Conversely, proponents of current economic policies like NAFTA point to the ways in which reduced tariffs and big factories have both enabled a larger trade flow and created jobs for millions.

Another long-term issue, which is steeped in ideological division, involves U.S. drug enforcement policies. Everyone agrees that the ways in which drug trafficking and human smuggling have become increasingly linked has had tragic effects on migrants, in both the United States and Mexico. Many blame the "War on Drugs" for the escalation in violence.

U.S. policies—making drugs illegal, offering military and intervention aid to other countries to curb the flow of drugs—has not worked; rather than stop the illegal drug trade, these policies have only fueled the violent underground networks that respond to U.S. demand and consumption. Critics say that instead of being illegal, drugs should be regulated; prevention, not punishment, should be the course of action. Those behind U.S. drug enforcement policies, however, say the War on Drugs is not to blame for the lawlessness and violence of Mexican narcotraffickers; rather, these intervention efforts are a logical and necessary strategy to combat the devastating effects of drug use on families, individuals, and entire communities in the United States.

Even a cursory look at the manifold difficulties plaguing immigration reform shows that while everyone can agree on the need for reform, it is not something that will happen quickly. It will require fierce political will, patience to hear and consider different viewpoints, money, time, heated yet humane dialogue, and the willingness to go beyond the oversimplified refrains and political posturing that have so far mired the debate.

The sobering reality is that, so far, most proposed federal legislation that seeks some sort of middle ground—for example, between amnesty and deportation—has failed. The DREAM Act (The Development, Relief and Education for Alien Minors Act) is an example of this failure. The bill proposed ways of providing illegal non-citizen minors with a path toward earning permanent residency. This path was not without certain conditions. The minor had to be of "good moral character," to have graduated from a U.S. high school, to have come to the country before the age of sixteen, and to have lived here for at least five years. The DREAM Act attempted to address those who were most "guiltless" in the immigration equation: the children who came illegally with their parents, and who, being minors, never made the choice to break the law. Moreover, they are children who have been raised in American society and attended American public schools but who have no way of acquiring legal residency.

Versions of the DREAM Act have been bouncing around in Congress for nearly a decade, but so far without success. In December 2010, the House of Representatives passed a version of the bill, but it then failed to pass in the Senate by only a handful of votes. If national will is unable to come to some resolution regarding the lowest common denominator in the immigration equation—children—then it is hard to see any bright horizon for effective reform.

Even more bleak, behind all the talk surrounding Senate Bill 1070 and the need for immigration reform, there was little mention of the ongoing migrant deaths in the Sonoran desert. "The southern border is more secure today than at any time in the past 20 years," President Obama said in his "immigration speech" on July 1, 2010. But he did not mention at what moral cost: the ever increasing deaths of men, women, and children desperate enough to risk their lives to come here for new and better beginnings. In fact, July 2010 proved to be one of the most deadly months to date for migrants in southern Arizona. While accusations flew over SB 1070, injunctions were issued, and speeches were delivered, fifty-nine more bodies turned up in the Pima County Medical Examiner's office. There was such an overflow that the examiner's office was forced to use a refrigerated trailer to store the surfeit of bodies.

Equally as surprising, despite the president's rebuke of SB 1070; the condemnation of clergy; the rallies, boycotts, lawsuits against Arizona, and accusations of racism, according to all major opinion polls, the majority of Arizonans and Americans polled were in favor of SB 1070.[32] Such support is made more confusing by the 2007 survey by the Pew Forum on Religion and Public Life, which concluded that 78.4% of Americans consider themselves Christian. If so many Americans consider themselves Christian, and if the majority of Christian groups express support for immigration reform, condemnation of migrant deaths, and the priority of neighborly love and hospitality, why are so many Americans in favor of SB 1070? Nor are such calls for love and compassion of strangers limited to the Christian tradition. In the Hebrew Bible there are thirty-six commands to "love the stranger," and many similar fiats to love those who are most vulnerable, such as widows and orphans.[33] This imperative to act with loving-kindness toward the most vulnerable is also prominent in Muslim scriptures and commentary, in Buddhist texts, in much humanist philosophy, and in the majority of many of the world's other prominent religious traditions.

The popularity of SB 1070 points to a dissonance between moral and religious calls to love neighbor as self and the, perhaps ineradicable, existential realities of human fear and threat that others elicit in us. Beyond all the political noise at the border and the nuances of conflicting ideologies concerning reform, there are still many core existential quandaries when it comes to the immigration equation. These existential questions concern the experience of alterity, that is, of one's encounters with "the other" or others who are strangers.

In his book *Civilization and Its Discontents*, Sigmund Freud problematized the commandment "to love neighbor as self" and elucidated why it is so difficult. Freud concluded that to love neighbor as self is, in fact, quite unnatural. The injunction, Freud wrote, "is known throughout the world and is undoubtedly older than Christianity."[34] However, although we consider it a natural claim now—to love neighbor as self—Freud believed that such "unconditional love" went against our most basic instincts of self-preservation. At an earlier point in human history, before the advent of civilization, he argued, the notion of valuing others as much as oneself "was still strange to mankind." But as individuals suppressed their own desires to conform to the norms of society, the idea of "loving neighbor" came into being. What was once a shocking and new concept was put forth as normal. Freud wrote:

> Let us adopt a naïve attitude towards it [the command to love neighbor], as though we were hearing it for the first time; we shall be unable then to suppress a feeling of surprise and bewilderment. Why should we do it? What good will it do us? But, above all, how shall we achieve it? How can it be possible? My love is something valuable to me which I ought not to throw away without reflection. It imposes duties on me for whose fulfillment I must be ready to make sacrifices. If I love someone, he must deserve it in some way.[35]

Let us, like Freud, briefly adopt a naïve attitude toward the concept and ask the questions within the context of the U.S.-Mexican border: Why *should* we love our southern neighbors who come here without papers? What good will it do us? Why should I love, for example, the Honduran man I met at El Comedor, the one with the wounded leg? Perhaps in the soup kitchen, with others around, I can trust him not to hurt me. But what if he and I were elsewhere, alone, on a dark street? Most likely, we would pass each other in the street and nothing would come of it. But there is always the possibility that, in different circumstances, with a different power dynamic, the encounter could turn violent, or at least feel threatening. The question may seem dramatic, but it is fair to ask. Why must I love this man who might otherwise pose a threat to me, especially if such love, as Freud believed, entails inherent sacrifice and is not something to throw away without reflection?

It is easy to love others, Freud said further, when others resemble us in some way, when they are part of our family, of our citizenry, our royalty, our tribe, our gender, our race. The more my neighbor resembles me, the easier it is to love him or her, since in certain ways, I am loving myself and reinforcing my own value systems and interests:

> He [my neighbor] deserves it [my love] if he is so like me in important ways that I can love myself in him; and he deserves it if he is so much more perfect than myself that I can love my ideal of my own self in him....But if he is a stranger to me and if he cannot attract me by any worth of his own or any significance that he may already have acquired for my emotional life, it will be hard for me to love him. Indeed, I should be wrong to do so, for my love is valued by all my own people as a sign of my preferring them, and it is an injustice to them if I put a stranger on par with them. But if I am to love him (with this universal love) merely because he, too, is an inhabitant of this earth, I fear that only a small modicum of my love will fall to his share....What is the

point of a precept enunciated with so much solemnity if its fulfillment cannot be recommended as reasonable?[36]

As Freud believed, loving our neighbor is easier when we *know* our neighbor, which is to say, when we are *familiar* with him or her; this sort of love can work to our advantage, allowing us to vicariously love, or affirm, our way of being in the world. But to *love* a stranger unequivocally, "merely because he is an inhabitant of the earth" is impossible at best, reckless at worst. Reckless, because in many ways such universal love of an absolute foreigner can prove harmful to self and tribe. By "putting a stranger on par" with oneself, one risks a shift in power. "If it will do him [the stranger] any good he has no hesitation in injuring me.... [He may] show his superior power; and the more secure he feels and the more helpless I am, the more certainly I can expect him to behave like this to me."[37]

Freud's view of humanity is, admittedly, pessimistic. For Freud, humankind is largely, at its core, driven by base instincts. That is why he said that the stranger "has more claim to my hostility and even my hatred," because "the original nature of man" is one of self-interest. In order to survive and thrive, one must rely on a certain innate and implacable aggression that allows one to get ahead, or merely survive, at the expense of others. If one's own child is hungry and one has little food, one would give the food to one's child. Not to do so, Freud would say, is unnatural, ridiculous even; and to believe one would do otherwise is simply grandiose.

Hence, Freud concluded that loving neighbor as self was a "grandiose commandment." Such a conclusion is interesting within the context of the U.S.-Mexican border, since many faith-based humanitarian aid groups there are often accused by their detractors as being both naïve and grandiose: They naïvely aid criminals and lawbreakers while sanctimoniously claiming a higher moral law—that of universal neighborly love—rather than acknowledging the base elements of human nature and the consequent need for strict and punishable legal codes.

Concerning the violent and selfish nature of humankind, Freud wrote further:

The element of truth behind all this, which people are so ready to disavow, is that men are not gentle creatures who want to be loved, and who at the most can defend themselves if they are attacked; they are, on the contrary, creatures among whose instinctual endowments is to be reckoned a powerful share of aggressiveness. As a result, their neighbor is for them not only a potential helper or sexual object, but also someone who tempts them to satisfy their own aggressiveness on him, to exploit his capacity for work without compensation, to use him sexually without his consent, to seize his possessions, to humiliate him, to cause him pain, to torture and kill him.

Homo homini lupus. Who, in the face of all this experience of life and history, will have the courage to dispute this assertion?[38]

Freud cited a laundry list of historical atrocities as undeniable proof of this aggressive nature, from the invasions of the Huns to the horrors of World War I. Freud himself lived through World War I and wrote *Civilization and Its Discontents* on the brink of World War II, in an environment of rising anti-Semitism (the Nazis would come to full power in Germany just months after the publication of *Civilization and Its Discontents*). Freud was clearly influenced by this atmosphere of war, destruction, and ethnic hatred. As a Jew forced to flee from Austria to England, he would die in exile, thus corroborating his view that *homo homini lupus*, man is a wolf to man: "Aggression is an original, self-subsisting instinctual disposition in man," he wrote, an evolutionarily gainful tool of survival.[39]

Freud challenged his readers to come to terms with these brutal and inherent parts of humanity. Inevitably, "the time comes when each one of us has to give up as illusions the expectations which, in his youth, he pinned upon his fellow-men, and when he may learn how much difficulty and pain has been added to his life by their ill-will."[40] That is why, he concluded, "nothing else runs so strongly counter to the original nature of man" as the commandment, "Love thy neighbor as thyself." In short, this commandment of love, Freud posited, was an unhealthy defense mechanism that arose through humanity's attempt to mute its aggressive, self-indulgent tendencies. It was an unreasonable, naïve, and simply impossible moral injunction.

Yet, while universal love was no answer for Freud, neither was the law. The law, Freud believed, was simply a communal expression of aggression or dominance, a tool of control that advanced the interests of an entire group or society. In a famous correspondence between Einstein and Freud, dated 1931–1932, in which Einstein asked Freud if and how mankind would ever rid itself of "the war menace," Freud described the role of law in the creation of civilization:

> Thus, under primitive conditions, it is superior force—brute violence, or violence backed by arms—that lords it everywhere. We know that in the course of evolution this state of things was modified, a path was traced that led away from violence to law. But what was this path? Surely it issued from a single verity: that the superiority of one strong man can be overborne by an alliance of many weaklings, that *l'union fait la force*. Brute force is overcome by union; the allied might of scattered units makes good its right against the isolated giant.... Thus we may define "right" (i.e., law) as the might of a community. Yet it, too, is nothing else than violence, quick to attack whatever individual stands in its path, and it employs the selfsame methods, follows like ends, with but one difference: it is the communal, not individual, violence that has its way.[41]

Laws were enacted to stifle the brute violence that reigned before the advent of civilization. The path from anarchy and brute violence to law and order, however, still did not eradicate human aggression. Rather, it simply masked it behind the notion of "right," or the might of the group. This comment suggests that Freud saw the law as a form of institutionalized violence. Instead of one person acting alone in the pursuit of pleasure, attaining what he or she desired, often at the expense of others, it became the group, acquiring what was advantageous to its communal well-being, through justification by the law.

Freud's psychological and philosophical analyses, concerning love and law, are particularly illuminating when considered in light of the current dilemmas and dramas playing out at the U.S.-Mexican border. Freud speaks to the inherent tensions in the self-other encounter; the difficulties, even the folly, of attempting to love one's neighbor as self. Because of the natural threat that others will always pose, offering love and hospitality to strangers is risky. One risks losing one's place and power. One risks being taken advantage of, supplanted, disparaged, hurt in some way, even murdered. And for what? What is gained from throwing one's love about so freely, aside from a sense of self-importance? To love the undocumented migrant who stumbles into one's territory, to provide him or her with amnesty, to open the border, or tear down the fences that separate self from other, nation from nation, is, by Freud's measure, simply unrealistic. Yet, turning to the law, Freud would say, is not much better, for it too is simply another form of human aggression; a systematic and coercive mechanism that serves the interests of the group in power. Thus, enforcing immigration laws, the act of sealing in and out, of delineating who belongs and who does not, of punishment for the crime of illegal entry, belies a sort of communal favoritism that, while perhaps more realistic in terms of human nature, can be seen as exclusionary at best, and violent and unethical at worst.

Existentially speaking, Freud's viewpoint touches on what philosopher Jean-Paul Sartre meant by his famous refrain, *"l'enfer c'est les Autres,"* hell is other people. In his tome, *Being and Nothingness: A Phenomenological Essay on Ontology*, Sartre meticulously examined what he saw as the "problem of others." Other people, Sartre wrote, force us out of a labyrinth of solipsism. "My original fall is the existence of the Other," he declared.[42] To say that the existence of the Other is our primordial downfall is a strong statement. Why such a damning assessment of the self-other relationship? Because, for Sartre, the mere presence of an Other is an assault on our freedom. The Other interrupts our ability to self-define and self-determine. By his very nature, the Other will always have the capacity to chisel away at our autonomy. The moment the Other's gaze lands upon us, we are no longer masters of ourselves; we are judged and defined, and hence "made alien" to ourselves. Symbolically speaking, the gaze of another person equals an inexorable loss of freedom: subject becomes object; the judge becomes the judged. This loss of freedom is the primordial problem posed by the Other:

> The Other is the hidden death of my possibilities.... Thus in the shock which seizes me when I apprehend the Other's look, this happens—that suddenly I experience a subtle alienation of all my possibilities.... I *am no longer master of the situation*.[43]

It is this inherent loss of mastery over our situation that can make others seem so threatening. The Other will always impose limits upon us. These limits can vary in nature and scope. At one extreme, the Other has the capacity to strip us of life, that is, of all our freedom, through murder. Or the Other may strip away degrees of our freedom through an endless range of mechanisms, from the severe to the benign: imprisonment, torture, impoverishment, taxation, judgment—the ways in which the Other acts as the death of the individual's possibilities are almost limitless. "The Other has made [the world] alien to me," Sartre wrote further.[44] Such alienation, of the self from the self, through the imposition of the Other, can lead to a sense of perpetual danger, "a danger [which] is not an accident but the permanent structure of my being-for-others."[45]

Alongside making us alien to ourselves, the Other will also remain alien to us. It is a devastating and reciprocal alienation. As William James expressed the problem:

> We are practical beings, each of us with limited functions and duties to perform. Each is bound to feel intensely the importance of his own duties and the significance of situations that call these forth. But this feeling is in each of us a vital secret, for sympathy with which we vainly look to others. The others are too much absorbed in their own vital secrets to take an interest in ours. Hence the stupidity and injustice of our opinions, so far as they deal with the significance of alien lives. Hence the falsity of our judgments, so far as they presume to decide in an absolute way on the value of other persons' conditions.[46]

What James's comment brings to light is the tragic impossibility of ever *truly* understanding an Other. We are too steeped in our own experiences of the world, and others in theirs, to ever fully grasp opinions and ideas beyond our own. There exists a core alienation between self and other. We are grossly limited by our intensely subjective experiences of the world, the result of which is a sort of empathic blindness. Others' lives will, on some level, always remain impenetrable to us, as our lives—and our vital secrets—will remain to others.

The assessments of Freud, Sartre, and James concerning the self-other encounter are, inarguably, quite grim. They stress some of the inherent tensions and fears that arise in this encounter. There are those, however, who would disagree with such pessimistic notions of the self-other relationship. Philosopher Emmanuel Levinas, for example, believed quite differently. Instead of emphasizing the problem posed by the existence of others, he emphasized the opportunity in the self-other encounter. The existence of others, he said, serves as the birth, not the death, of our possibilities. For Levinas, others are not our original downfall but rather the genesis of our self-awareness. The Other is an invitation. The symbol of this invitation was, for Levinas, the human face. Levinas might agree with Sartre that the human face, or gaze, forces us out of our "reef of solipsism." It demands a response from us. In this sense, the face of the Other is still a disturbance. It is "the disturbance of the Same by the Other."[47] But, Levinas argued, it is a disturbance that can lead us to "an awakening."

Part of this awakening is, Levinas said, a sense of responsibility for the Other:

The relation to the face is straightaway ethical.... The first word of the face is the "Thou shalt not kill." It is an order. There is a commandment in the appearance of the face, as if a master spoke to me. However, at the same time, the face of the Other is destitute; it is the poor for whom I can do all and to whom I owe all.... I am he who finds the resources to respond to the call.[48]

In essence, Levinas argued, the face of the Other is a summons. It asks us to assume responsibility, by going beyond ourselves, and responding to and serving the Other:

The subjectivity that says *I* takes on meaning in this responsibility of the first-come, of the first person torn from the comfortable place that he or she occupied as a protected individual in the concept of the *I in general* of the philosophies of self-consciousness. The question of the Other turns back into responsibility for another.[49]

The original ethics, or "first philosophy," Levinas argued, has always been the face-to-face encounter. The face of the Other reminds us that we are not alone, and that, as a result, we are wholly and undeniably responsible for the well-being of the Other who stands before us. Unlike Freud or Sartre, Levinas emphasized the opportunity that exists in the meeting between self and stranger. He did not speak of what can be lost, but rather of the merits of assuming responsibility for others. In this sense, his "first philosophy" corresponds to the biblical injunction to offer radical hospitality to strangers.

Contemporary philosopher Richard Kearney described the event of encountering strangers as "a wager." Using scriptures as an example, he wrote, "[In] Exodus and Kings and Deutoronomy and the Prophets, and further still, through Christian and Islamic Scriptures, [one sees how] the decision for hospitality over hostility is never made once and for all; it is a wager that needs to be renewed again and again."[50] In turning to the stories of Judeo-Christian and Islamic scripture, Kearney wrote of how "inaugural moments of faith often begin with someone replying to an uninvited visitor—Abraham under the Mamre tree, Mary at the instant of annunciation, Muhammad in his cave." Kearney asked, "Are we meant to respond to this 'advent of alterity'... by waging war or peace? By caring for the orphan, the widow and the stranger, or by hating and smiting one's enemies?"

Kearney's point is that there is no blueprint for how to respond to strangers. Herein lies the tension in Arizona, and, in large part, at the heart of the immigration reform debate: Do we see the uninvited stranger as a threat to our freedom and well-being or as an invitation to a deeper moral awakening? There is no right or wrong answer to the question. It is a matter of interpretation. How we answer the question depends largely on how we understand what it means to be human, the significance and responsibility of others to oneself, and of oneself to others.

These questions point to why, perhaps, the issue of illegal immigration is both so incendiary and so hard to resolve, because it digs down deep to the core of what it means to be human. In southern Arizona, these existential dilemmas are always at play, because, by its nature, the border is a place of constant encounters between self and other. These encounters force individuals and groups to consider and evaluate different responses to others. In this case, the others are undocumented migrants, and SB 1070 is one response. It is a response that has come after years of frustration and high emotions, in which Arizona has served as the busiest illegal smuggling corridor in the nation, resulting in a "frightening stew" of migrant deaths and chaos, and culminating in the murder of rancher Robert Krentz.

Some believe SB 1070 was drafted in a spirit of fear, hatred, and bigotry. Others claim it was drafted out of necessity, in a spirit of protection and patriotism. Is SB 1070 a "social and racial sin" or "a measured and reasonable step"? Is it an echo "of German Nazi and Russian Communist techniques" or is it a "good and well intentioned law"?

Whatever one believes about SB 1070, there are few who would disagree that the law points to the dire need for federal movement concerning immigration reform. How such reform will be negotiated and drafted is unclear. But what is clear is that until that day, Arizona's "frightening stew" will continue to simmer and boil over.

CHAPTER 9

Postscript: What *Would* Jesus Do?

Imagine Jesus standing in the desert—not one of the many deserts in Judea or Galilee, but the Sonoran desert on a steamy summer July evening in the year 2010. Let him wear what you want—white robes, or shorts and a T-shirt—and let him look however you imagine: hirsute or clean shaven, dark-skinned or light-skinned. Perhaps he is out for an evening stroll, to empty his mind, or to consider the majesty of the saguaro cactus and the light of the low sun on the red land.

Now imagine that Jesus sees a small group of illegal immigrants stumbling toward him from afar. They look thirsty and confused. He is not uninformed. He knows of the thousands of migrant deaths that have occurred in the Sonoran desert over the past decade. He knows, too, that they have crossed the border illegally, violating federal laws. He knows that U.S. immigration policies are outmoded and inefficient, and that, in the void of any sort of visionary reform, people are going to extremes: migrants are risking their lives and dying, while the U.S. government is trying to wall up the border.

Now we ask, What would Jesus preach in the hills and valleys of southern Arizona? Would he take an ax to the border fence? Would he tell supporters of Senate Bill 1070, "Let him who is without sin cast the first stone"; or ask the Minutemen, "How can you take the speck from your neighbor's eye but still not notice the log in your own eye?"; or instruct Border Patrol agents, "Forgive those who have trespassed against you"? Would he stand in the desert and tell the migrants he comes across to return home, since the last shall be first, and the poor shall inherit the earth? Might he echo Paul's words and declare, as there is no Jew or gentile, no slave or free man, no male or female, neither is there Mexican or American, citizen or alien, legal or illegal?

While it is an entertaining exercise to ask what Jesus would do about the current immigration mess, the question is in no way frivolous. In a country in which 78 percent of Americans consider themselves Christian, according to a 2007 survey by the Pew Forum on Religion and Public Life, ideas about Jesus carry political import.

Talk to Christians at the border and you will see this firsthand: the name of Jesus is invoked to support a range of opinions, from eradicating the border to walling it up entirely.

For example, a member of the faith-based aid organization, No More Deaths, was clear on his answer of what Jesus would do. "He would welcome them, no doubt," he said at a pro-immigrant rally in front of the De Concini courthouse in Tucson. "It's all over the Bible: love your neighbor, help the stranger, treat the least of these with utmost compassion. Folks like the Minutemen have no biblical grounds to argue their case."

But talk to Al Garza, former national executive of the Minuteman Civil Defense Corps, and he will tell you a different story. "Sure, you gotta be nice to your neighbor, but that doesn't mean ignoring the rule of law." Echoing Romans 13, Garza said, "The law is a gift from God. We are called as good Christians to follow the law. Jesus would understand that."

Conversely, a Catholic nun I spoke to in Mexico said, "Jesus knows: There are no borders. There is only the kingdom of God." She has spent the last decade working at migrant shelters throughout Mexico and says she has no qualms about trying to help migrants enter the United States illegally.

It seems that a lot of folks are certain of what Jesus would do. But how is one to know, especially because what Jesus would do depends on *which* Jesus one is talking about. The Jesus of history or the Jesus of faith? And if of faith, which version of faith? Protestant, Catholic, Mormon, Orthodox? The Jesus according to Luke, or the Jesus according to John? The Pauline Jesus or the Jesus of one of the early church fathers?

Ideas about Jesus are like the five loaves and the two fishes that fed the 5,000: they are ever multiplying.

Even Richard Dawkins, whose 2006 best-seller *The God Delusion* referred to religions as mind viruses and the idea of a personal god as insanity, calls himself an "atheist for Jesus." According to the Oxford biologist, Jesus was an icon of radical super niceness, exhibiting a form of compassion that Dawkins calls "just plain dumb." It was a flavor of compassion that managed to subvert all the Darwinian nastiness required for the survival of the fittest. If only Jesus' radical ethics could catch on, says Dawkins, then it might "lead society away from the nether regions of its Darwinian origins into [the] kinder and more compassionate uplands of post-singularity enlightenment."

What would Dawkins' "super nice Jesus" do when confronted with a group of migrants in the desert? Certainly he would provide immediate first aid (water, food, bandages), but what about his ethic of radical super niceness? Would it translate into a message of universal welcome to migrants who come illegally? For to draw a line in the sand is to promote a sort of nasty evolutionary segregation required to survive and thrive. It is to divide *us* from *them*, the bigger from the smaller, the fitter from the weaker, the citizen from the non-citizen. To let everyone in the door is simply stupid, evolutionarily speaking. There are not enough resources to go around. But the un-Darwinian, super nice Jesus would not balk at such existential threats.

Take the Lukan story of the Good Samaritan. It is a story that is often quoted by faith-based immigrant rights groups like No More Deaths and Humane Borders to justify their humanitarian work in the desert and to protest border enforcement policies. The Samaritan transgressed the social and religious norms of the day by providing aid and refuge to an ethnic foe, a Judean. The unexpected hospitality of the Samaritan exemplifies Jesus' idea of neighborliness. It is an idea that can be traced back to the calls in Leviticus (19:18, 19:34) to love one's neighbor as oneself, and to treat aliens with unyielding compassion.

In the Babylonian Talmud (*Shabbat* 31a), we read of the teachings of the famous rabbi Hillel, a contemporary of Jesus. When asked by a student to sum up the whole Torah while the student stood on one foot, Hillel answered: "What you find hateful do not do to another. This is the whole of the Law. Everything else is commentary. Now go learn that!"

Many folks, Christians and non-Christians alike, concur that the core of Jesus's message was rooted in this conception of compassion. In order to live it out, Jesus preached unconventional egalitarianism in the shadow of Roman tyranny, and he paid for it with his life.

While many Christian leaders in the United States have been divided on other hot-button issues, such as abortion and gay marriage, many have discovered a united front on the subject of immigration. Christian groups— from liberal UCC congregations to the more conservative National Association of Evangelicals—have turned to Jesus's radical ethic of compassion as reason to promote federal immigration reform that both favors amnesty and enables more humane border policies.

Of course, there is no way to know what Jesus would do. Since Jesus made his appearance on the stage of humanity, his name, words, and story have been invoked to support innumerable causes and principles, some of which could not be more different. "Beware of finding a Jesus entirely convenient to you," warn the scholars of the Jesus Seminar in their book, *The Five Gospels: The Search for the Authentic Words of Jesus.*

In the end, maybe Jesus would do something that we cannot even envision. If there is one thing that most people agree on, it is that the figure of Jesus had a knack for the unexpected. Many of his most memorable sayings advocated reversals of social logic meant to shock his audience: love your enemies; if someone takes your coat, give him your cloak too; offer the other cheek if someone hits you; it is the poor who are lucky; it is the grieving who shall inherit the earth; it is the wide and smooth road that leads to death; those who find life will lose it.

In this sense, maybe the *very* thing Jesus would do to stop migrant deaths in the desert, or to overhaul America's broken immigration policies, or to undo the partisan divide that paralyzes Washington is the very thing we cannot imagine.

To know what Jesus might do is, perhaps, to travel to the edge of knowledge, to some lonely and untapped outpost of the mind, beyond the stark divides that haunt us, beyond our tired notions of good over evil, of law versus compassion, of amnesty versus deportation, of legal or illegal. It would mean harnessing the originality and vision that defines the figure of Jesus, his revolutionary and egalitarian spirit, and ending up somewhere wholly new.

Above all, that is what the immigration debate needs more than anything: Radical Vision.

As Jesus says of his disciples, "Seeing they do not perceive, and hearing they do not listen, nor do they understand."

Perhaps it is the same for us.

Conclusion.
And the Deaths Go On...

When the United States began cracking down on illegal immigration in popular urban crossing areas in the 1990s, the common belief was that most migrants would not try to enter through the vast scorching wilderness of the Sonoran desert. Through Operation Gatekeeper in California, Operation Hold the Line in Texas, and Operation Safeguard in Arizona, a massive increase in border infrastructure and personnel was executed. Ground sensors, surveillance cameras, fencing, and agents were deployed at pivotal crossing zones along the U.S.-Mexican border. It was a deliberate policy of deterrence and an unprecedented attempt to "gain operational control of the border." But rather than keeping migrants out, it simply redirected them to more dangerous and remote areas in southern Arizona. This shift in migration turned swaths of the Sonoran desert into corridors of death.

While there is no way to know exactly how many have perished in southern Arizona, the remains of over 2,000 migrants have been officially recovered between 2000 and 2010.[1] This number, however, still does not account for the hundreds of bodies that go missing, presumed destroyed by the harsh desert elements or the wild animals, never to be recovered. Now, in southern Arizona, the month of May is known as the beginning of "the season of death," when the temperature starts its merciless climb into the triple-digit heat and more migrants begin perishing.

There is a lot of finger pointing over these deaths. The Border Patrol blames unscrupulous *coyotes* for leading migrants into such remote and dangerous areas, leaving them to suffer and die if they become sick or too tired to continue the journey. Many of southern Arizona's most active humanitarian groups, interfaith and otherwise, blame the U.S. government for enacting such a lethal border enforcement strategy and for lacking the foresight to see how increased infrastructure at core urban crossing zones would only push migrants into the desert. Many such activists believe this "militarization" strategy, of forcing migrants into the Arizona wilderness was deliberate; others claim it was unforeseen, a blend of hubris and naivety but nonetheless unforgivable. Meanwhile, some ranchers, as well as most anti-illegal immigration activists, blame the government too, for *not* clamping down sufficiently; for *not* properly sealing up the border. They believe that the effort at border security has been conducted in a partial, inconsistent, and whimsical fashion, leaving gaping swaths of certain sectors, like the Tucson sector, vulnerable to uncontrolled illegal activity. One tragic result of this, they say, is the migrant deaths.

While some migrants do not know the extent of danger facing them when they take their first steps into the Arizona desert, most are aware that they are putting their lives on the line. And still, they take that first step. And a second. And thousands after that. They do it, not because they want to, but because whatever they are leaving behind is so hopeless that to risk death, for a shot at a more promising future, is worth it.

Of course, not everyone crossing the borders comes earnestly in search of better days. One cannot deny that among the vast majority of well-intentioned migrants there are drug smugglers, unprincipled *coyotes*, criminals, and some who simply lack good intentions. Still, the majority of those crossing the desert are not dangerous or malicious. They are the mothers who want to provide for their children; the teenagers searching for their parents who have gone north; children and the elderly; families escaping violence or squalor, trying to move, step by step, toward a better life.

Even with the economic downturn in the United States, southern Arizona saw 252 migrant deaths in fiscal year 2010.[2] During the research and writing of this project, I estimate that approximately 550 migrants died in Arizona; and those are only the ones whose remains were found.

There are two hard cold facts that everyone—from Walt Staton to Al Garza, the Reverend Hoover to Jim Gilchrist, Sister Robles to Pat Buchanan, Cardinal Mahoney to Governor Brewer, Maryada Vallet to Agent Gomez— can agree on: the deaths are an utter tragedy, and they reflect a broken system.

The problem is that there is little agreement on *exactly how* to remedy the system so that deaths can be removed from the immigration equation. The lack of agreement—not only in Arizona, but also across the nation—can be blamed, in part, on the breathless complexity of the issue. At a very basic level, attempting to solve migrant deaths begins with asking questions about what the border means to us. How should such a sweeping international border be humanely yet effectively maintained? How might respect for basic human rights be balanced with respect for the rights of the state to secure and protect? But before we even tackle these questions about rights and security, we must ask an even simpler question: How are we currently conceptualizing and interpreting the border?

Most international borders are, by their nature, "erratic convergence zones." They invite a certain testing of the limits of the laws. They are places where citizens of neighboring nations merge and mingle through trade and commerce, often taking advantage of certain incongruities between the codes and rules of one country and those of another. These sometimes morally foggy intersections, which can produce such phenomena as sweatshops or dental and pharmaceutical tourism, can quickly morph into more lethal and dangerous enterprises. The U.S.-Mexican border is no exception to these realities. The drug trade, the weapons trade, and the human smuggling trade have, in recent decades, become part of the fabric of the U.S.-Mexican border. As a result, the border has come to be interpreted, in large part, as a gateway of nefarious operations and bad characters.

But perhaps we need to rethink this interpretation, or at least think more deeply about it, because, in light of migrant deaths, how we choose to interpret the border, to make sense of its history and complexity, has become an intensely moral project. It is too simplistic to only interpret the border as a national security imperative. While the fears and frustrations of many are justified in reality, by reducing the issue to one of lawless people and of the need for 2,000 miles of double-layered fencing, we risk understanding only a slice of the problem.

We would benefit from a more humane and nuanced interpretation of the border. By nature, we tend to see conflict with a sort of myopia, pointing to the more attention-grabbing aspects of a dilemma. But often, those sensational aspects are actually symptoms of a larger, more multidimensional, more historically intricate problem. In terms of the U.S.-Mexican border, we need to push our minds to see each problem occurring there as one part of an interconnected web. For example, the decision to risk one's life walking through the Arizona desert is rooted in certain systematic socioeconomic failures: to egregious poverty, social inequality, a lack of a means of upward mobility. Poverty, violence, disenfranchisement, and despair: these are the factors that lead to migration. When you ask migrants at the border, or even undocumented workers across the nation, if they wanted to leave their homeland, most say, *no*. Most will speak of how they miss the food back home, the music, their loved ones, their church, their favorite park, songs, and customs. But most will also say that they felt like they had little or no choice but to leave; their lives felt untenable back home.

Furthermore, while there are no excuses for the greed, corruption, and violence of smugglers (whether of drugs, weapons, or humans), one must at least ask the question, What factors, particularly socioeconomic factors, drove them to make such horrible choices? While we need not necessarily have sympathy for these smugglers, we must consider the communal motivations that impel them, particularly the lack of economic opportunities, and the toll such lack can take. Moreover, at this point, the migrant death spiral can no longer be isolated from elements of organized crime. Today, many *coyotes* are linked into drug smuggling rings. This was not always the case. "Ten years ago, the [human] smuggling business was mostly just a mom and pop business affair, local folks charging a little bit of money to help migrants make the crossing," said Cecile Dumer, director of the migrant shelter in Naco, Sonora. "Now, it's become a deadly affair, with so many *coyotes* involved with larger criminal groups."

The U.S.-Mexican border *is* a place of extreme behavior, a place where social and economic ills are being played out with terrifying and tragic outcomes. Still, though, it is important to define the border, not just in terms of national security issues and unsavory characters but also in terms of justice, equity, compassion, and a healthy global economy. We must consider the failings of the global economy, to examine how certain trade policies have affected migration and crime, so that we can see the border as a symptom of larger problems that affect us all. In this sense, our well-being is at stake in what happens to migrants crossing the Sonoran desert. Their deaths are linked, in some part, to the unhealthy systems of labor and trade that we, as a human community, have designed and that we partake in.

That is why the border must be seen as a political, economic, social, and moral issue, not just a security headache. Part of this more holistic interpretation would allow us to see more clearly how migrant deaths at the border are also linked to our need to reexamine national immigration policies, which have not been overhauled in decades. So far, all such legislative attempts at reform have utterly failed, such as the Comprehensive Immigration Reform Act of 2006, led by a bipartisan group of senators, as well as the DREAM Act, which in 2010 passed the House but not the Senate. The only major legislative actions on immigration in the last decade have focused on border control enforcement strategies, like the Secure Fence Act.

Part of the reason for this lack of legislative movement is that, like the border, immigration is a complicated issue that calls for reexamination. It involves the highly charged questions of how to deal with the millions of undocumented immigrants already here, of how to hold people accountable for coming or staying illegally while also considering their contributions to the United States, of how to consider the factors that drove them to migrate in the first place, and of how to respect current laws without fracturing family unity. Each of these are deeply moral questions with no clear-cut answers.

Making matters worse, all of these questions are connected to even larger, and sometimes more abstract, historical and psychological forces: our various understandings of multiculturalism, diversity, patriotism, hospitality, capitalism, neighborliness, global terrorism, and the self-other encounter. It is difficult to see matters clearly with so much going on. Trying to solve the migrant death tragedy is like opening a Russian nesting doll, only to find another one underneath it, and another one after that, and another and another, seemingly ad infinitum. One can quickly feel overwhelmed or hopeless.

This is another reason that common ground is so elusive in southern Arizona: because emotions are running so high. How could they not? Confronted with such a morally muddy issue, without simple answers, people become reactive. In the void of real solutions, they feel helpless and anxious. They lash out. They lose the ability to think and act clearly. As English philosopher Edmund Burke commented: "No passion so effectively robs the mind of all its powers of acting and reasoning as fear." It is not only fear that inhibits rational discussion. Anger and despair are part of the mix. These emotions often push people to take sides, to act in extreme manners, to grow more opinionated and less able to hear different views, to think superficially, to get trapped within small dark ideological boxes.

If there is any hope in taking death out of the immigration equation, it must be found through rational and patient debate. This dialogue must actively involve not just politicians but everyone affected: migrants, ranchers, law enforcement personnel, activists, human rights groups, lawyers, religious coalitions, policy makers, academics, economists, Mexican officials, and ordinary citizens in Arizona and across the nation. It must also occur on multiple levels: internationally, between Mexican and U.S. government officials; at the domestic level, not just in Washington but also in towns and cities across the nation; and at the local level, in border communities such as in the Tucson sector. Realistically, it will require a boggling amount of time, money, cooperation, political will, and intense imagination.

Unfortunately, at the moment, the U.S. economy is struggling to regain momentum. Unemployment remains high. U.S. debt levels continue to grow. People are rightly concerned about how they will survive in this new humbled America. There are few sectors of the workforce that are not being affected by the tumultuous and grim economic landscape. Thus, we may be tempted to think that trying to reconceptualize the border or trying to reimagine immigration reform simply cannot be a priority at this time. This is, in some ways, quite understandable. Yet it also reflects the short-sightedness that has plagued the immigration debate from the start, limited our conceptions of the border, and led to migrant deaths. After all, ours is a global economy. For better or worse, the economic crisis in the United States is not isolated from matters of immigration, from organized crime, from migration patterns, and border politics; they are all interconnected. The economic upheaval in the United States points to certain core systemic flaws in the ways we have chosen to conduct international trade, seek out labor, cut costs, build businesses. Many of these practices have influenced migration patterns and increased tensions at international border zones. This is why addressing border and immigration issues in the United States must be a priority, not only because it is our moral imperative to seek ways to end migrant deaths and suffering but also because to do so is to get involved in the work of trying to imagine a healthier global economy.

Meanwhile, right now, a Border Patrol agent is putting on his uniform for another shift. There is a nun cutting green beans for hungry migrants. There is an aid worker leaving out jugs of water under a mesquite tree. There is a woman and her child sleeping in a shelter in Nogales. There is an old man in a Border Patrol-chartered bus being deported to a dark dusty border town. There is a rancher locking his door in fear. There is a villager in Chiapas who is packing his bags for the journey north. There is a drug smuggler hauling his bundle through the Coronado Mountains. There is someone putting her money into the hand of a *coyote*, taking her first steps into the Sonoran desert. And there is you, reading this, asking yourself, what should we do?

ACKNOWLEDGMENTS

This project could not have happened without the generous help and participation of key members of various organizations involved in matters of immigration in the Tucson area. It is true that these groups do not always see eye to eye on such matters, and perhaps some would be dismayed to see their names in the same list as those with whose views they are in such opposition. I hope I do not offend anyone in trying to include as many pivotal voices as possible. My aim in these pages has been, in large part, to make space for conflicting beliefs to be heard. With this in mind, I would like to give thanks to Noel Andersen, Lilli Mann, and Delle McCormick at Borderlinks; the Reverend John Fife; Sister María Engracia Robles, Sister Alma Delia Isaías, and Sister Imelda Ruiz, of the soup kitchen and women's shelter in Nogales; Father Martin McCintosh and Father Sean Carroll of the Jesuit Refugee Service; the many migrants at El Comedor in Nogales who shared their experiences with me; a very special thanks to Maryada Vallet, Walt Staton, Sarah Roberts, and Jim Walsh of No More Deaths; Doug Roupp and the Reverend Robin Hoover of Humane Borders; Cecile Dumer at the migrant shelter in Naco; Bruce Parks of the medical examiner's office in Tucson; Mike Wilson of the Tohono O'odham Nation; Walt Collins of the Samaritans; Shura Wallin of the Green Valley Samaritans; Al Garza of the Patriots Coalition; Jim Gilchrist of the Minuteman Project; and a very warm thanks to Border Patrol Agent Jorge Alejandro Gomez for taking me around Nogales, and to Border Patrol Agent Mario Escalante for making it happen. Thanks also to Michael D. Jackson, Stephanie Paulsell, and Amy Hollywood of Harvard University; to Patrick Jordan of *Commonweal Magazine*; to Cynthia Read at Oxford University Press as well as Lisbeth Redfield, Marc Schneider, Nick Mafi, Deborah Reade, Patterson Lamb, Gunabala Saladi, all of whom have made this process so smooth; Melissa, for her unbeatable child care; and to my parents, Duncan, and Jasper, for their patience, love, and support.

NOTES

INTRODUCTION

1. *Coalición de Derechos Humanos,* "Arizona Recovered Remains," http://www.derechoshumanosaz.net/index.php?option=com_content&task=view&id=20&Itemid=34.
2. The southern border is divided by the Border Patrol into nine sectors: the San Diego sector; the El Centro sector; the Yuma sector; the Tucson sector; the El Paso sector; the Marfa sector; the Del Rio sector; the Laredo sector; and the McAllen sector.
3. Border Patrol Agent Jorge Alejandro Gomez, e-mail message to author, September 29, 2009. Furthermore, as Gomez wrote, for the previous fiscal year, 2007–2008, "48% of marijuana seizures were here in Arizona and 56% of arrests were also here in Arizona compared to the whole southwest border." Interestingly, as will be addressed later, apprehensions for illegal entry dropped significantly for fiscal year 2009–2010, to approximately 212,000 apprehensions in the Tucson sector. This drop can be explained by a number of factors, including the economic downturn and more effective border security measures, although, inarguably, these are still high numbers and do not, of course, include those who successfully cross into the United States illegally through the Tucson sector.
4. Border Patrol Agent Jorge Alejandro Gomez, e-mail message to author, September 29, 2009. "They could be anyone from a child molester, murderer, robber, gang member, rapist, etc.," Gomez said further.
5. Robin Hoover, "Remarks of Reverend Hoover" (paper presented at the World Council of Churches Fourth Annual United Nations Advocacy Week, New York City, November 17, 2008).
6. Ibid.
7. *Naomi Shihab Nye Varieties of Gazelle* (New York: Greenwillow Books, 2002).

CHAPTER 1

1. The fact that only roughly10 percent of migrants are brought to trial has caused much uproar in humanitarian circles. There is, to date, no systematic process by which certain migrants are brought to trial while others are not. Many humanitarian groups claim that the randomness of such selection is part of a larger "scare tactic," and is, as a result, unethical. Until there is a uniform policy, it seems that such criticisms will continue. Added to these criticisms are questions of whether migrants are receiving due process as intended by the Fifth Amendment of the U.S. Constitution.

CHAPTER 2

1. *Time,* "Nation: Deathtrap (Thirteen Aliens Die in Desert)," July 21, 1980, http://www. time.com/time/magazine/article/0,9171,924300,00.html.
2. Ibid.
3. Ann Crittenden, *Sanctuary: A Story of American Conscience and the Law in Collision* (New York: Weidenfeld & Nicolson, 1988), 4–12.
4. Ibid., 5.
5. Ibid., 13–24. As Crittenden writes, "The Salvadorans could not have picked a worse time to test the quality of mercy in American immigration policy." She is referring to the flood of refugees from other countries who were also seeking political asylum in the United States, in particular, Iranian students and Cuban dissidents. Due to Cold War politics, most refugees from El Salvador were considered communists; they were on the wrong side of the political divide, and hence, generally unwelcome under Reagan's policies.
6. UNHCR, Convention and Protocol Relating to the Status of Refugees (Article 1, A [1]), http://www.unhcr.org/protect/PROTECTION/3b66c2aa10.pdf.
7. President, statement, "Refugee Act of 1980 Statement on Signing S. 643 into Law," March 18, 1980.
8. UNHCR, Convention and Protocol Relating to the Status of Refugees (Article 1, F [a]).
9. Crittenden, *Sanctuary,* 20.
10. Pierrette Hondagneu-Sotelo, *God's Heart Has No Borders: How Religious Activists Are Working for Immigrant Rights* (Berkeley: University of California Press, 2008), 144.
11. Ibid.
12. Crittenden, *Sanctuary,* 32.
13. Ibid., 63.
14. Ibid.
15. John Fife, "Civil Initiative," in *Trails of Hope and Terror: Testimonies on Immigration,* ed. Miguel A. de la Torre (Maryknoll, NY: Orbis Books, 2009).
16. In Crittenden, *Sanctuary,* 74.
17. The Reverend John Fife, interview with the author, January 24, 2009.
18. Fife, "Civil Initiative."
19. *The New Oxford Annotated Bible,* ed. Bruce M. Metzger and Roland E. Murphy (New York: Oxford University Press, 1991), 214 OT.
20. David Van Biema, "Does the Bible Support Sanctuary?" *Time,* July 20, 2007, http:// www.time.com/time/world/article/0,8599,1645646,00.html (accessed September 2009).
21. Crittenden, *Sanctuary,* 62.
22. Alexia Salvatierra, "Sacred Refuge," *Sojourners* 36, no. 9 (September/October 2007): 12–17.
23. Ibid.
24. Hondagneu-Sotelo, *God's Heart Has No Borders,* 146.
25. *The New Oxford Annotated Bible,* 150 OT.
26. National Association of Evangelicals, "Resolution on Immigration," http://www.nae.net/ resolutions/347-immigration-2009" (accessed June 2010).
27. Ibid.
28. Ibid.
29. In part, the Sanctuary movement was influenced by liberation theology, which rose to prominence in the1960s and 1970s, primarily in the Catholic church throughout Latin America. Liberation theology strove to interpret the Bible in a manner that promoted socioeconomic freedom for "the least of these." Religiously minded thinkers and writers,

such as Gustavo Gutiérrez, Leonardo Boff, and Juan Luis Segundo, challenged the Catholic church to reexamine the connections between theology and social justice, faith, and ethics. Their approach to the scriptures placed less emphasis on otherwordly aspects of Christian faith, such as the pursuit and joys of heaven, and stressed, rather, the realities of the present world, the suffering of the here and now, and the privileged place of the poor and oppressed in the eyes of God. In a letter by Sanctuary founder, Jim Corbett, to his supporters, Corbett spoke of liberation theology and how it had energized much of Central America. He wrote that "a new religious awareness has been spreading through Latin America, a revolutionary religious consciousness taking root in basic communities that are determined to live the freedom, peace, and justice of the Kingdom in actuality" (in Crittenden, *Sanctuary,* 40). Many Sanctuary activists, like Corbett, were deeply influenced by this "revolutionary religious consciousness," taking inspiration from such key figures as Bishop Oscar Romero who was assassinated, in part, for living out some of the ideas of liberation theology. The first words of Romero's last sermon speak to this: "Let no one be offended because we use the divine words read at our mass to shed light on the social, political and economic situation of our people. Not to do so would be unchristian....I know many are shocked by this preaching and want to accuse us of forsaking the gospel for politics. But I reject this accusation."

30. Robin Hoover, "Remarks of Reverend Hoover" (paper presented at the World Council of Churches Fourth Annual United Nations Advocacy Week), New York City, November 17, 2008.
31. Donald Senior, "Beloved Aliens and Exiles: New Testament Perspectives on Migration," in *A Promised Land, A Perilous Journey: Theological Perspectives on Migration,* ed. Daniel G. Groody and Gioacchino Campese (Notre Dame, IN: University of Notre Dame Press, 2008), 21.
32. Ibid., 22.
33. Ibid., 23, 24.
34. National Association of Evangelicals, "Resolution on Immigration."
35. *The New Oxford Annotated Bible,* 97 NT.
36. Ibid., 98 NT.
37. Ibid.
38. In Crittenden, *Sanctuary,* 56.
39. Ibid., 151.
40. John Fife, interview with the author, January 24, 2009.
41. John Fife is the founder of the Tucson group No More Deaths that will be highlighted in Chapter 4.
42. Salvatierra, "Sacred Refuge."
43. Ibid.
44. Ibid.
45. Joseph H. Carens, "The Case for Amnesty: Time Erodes the State's Right to Deport," *Boston Review,* May/June 2009, http://bostonreview.net/BR34.3/carens.php (accessed September 2009).
46. The counterargument is, of course, that we are breaking laws all the time: from jaywalking to riding our bikes on the sidewalk, to surpassing the speed limit.
47. Van Biema, "Does the Bible Support Sanctuary?"
48. Ibid.
49. Ibid.
50. *The New Oxford Annotated Bible,* 224 NT.
51. National Association of Evangelicals, "Resolution on Immigration."

52. Mark Galli, "Blessed Is the Law—Up to a Point," *Christianity Today,* http://www.christianitytoday.com/ct/2006/aprilweb-only/114-53.0.html, April 7, 2006. Furthermore, he points out, it is difficult to understand how any American can consider law-and-order "supreme" when one of this nation's most celebrated moments was the hooliganism we call the Boston Tea Party, and when this nation itself was founded on overthrowing not just a law but an entire government. Our Declaration of Independence is nothing but an explanation to the world for this law-defying act, Galli says.

53. See, for example, Laurie Goodstein, "Obama Wins Unlikely Allies in Immigration," *New York Times,* www.nytimes.com/2010/07/19/us/politics/19evangelicals.html, July 18, 2010.

54. Galli, "Blessed Is the Law." Moreover, New Sanctuary advocates have used the language of the more conservative branches of American public life, claiming that immigration reform is a "family values" issue: deporting men and women who have been in the United States for many years, they argue, and who have married American citizens and had children with them, violates the sanctity of the family. "Living with one's family is a fundamental human interest. The right to family life is considered a basic human right...and concern for family values has played a central role in American political rhetoric in recent decades," says Joseph Carens.

55. Michael Luo, "A Closer Look at the 'Sanctuary City' Argument," *New York Times,* http://www.nytimes.com/2007/11/29/us/politics/29truth.html, November 29, 2007.

56. Cambridge City Council, "Policy Order Resolution," www.cambridgema.gov/cityClerk/PolicyOrder.cfm?item_id=13247, May 8 2006.

57. Ibid.

58. Cinnamon Stillwell, "San Francisco: Sanctuary City Gone Awry," *San Francisco Chronicle,* http://articles.sfgate.com/2008-07-16/opinion/17120431_1_sanctuary-city-immigration-status-illegal-immigrants, July 16, 2008.

59. Ibid.

60. Jesse McKinley, "San Francisco at Crossroads over Immigration," *New York Times,* http://www.nytimes.com/2009/06/13/us/13sanctuary.html, June 13, 2009.

61. Ibid.

62. Stillwell, "San Francisco."

63. United States Conference of Catholic Bishops, Inc. and Conferencia del Episcopado Mexicano, "Strangers No Longer: Together on the Journey of Hope," http://www.usccb.org/mrs/stranger.html, January 22, 2003.

64. National Association of Evangelicals, "Resolution on Immigration."

65. Ibid.

66. Hoover, "Remarks of Reverend Hoover."

67. Crittenden, *Sanctuary,* xviii.

CHAPTER 3

1. The Tohono O'odham reservation is the second largest Native American reservation in the United States (it is roughly the size of Connecticut). Due to its remoteness, many migrants try to pass through it on their way north. As a result, it is the place where a disproportionate number of migrant deaths have occurred in recent years. Mike Wilson is a tribal member who has four water stations of his own on O'odham land (he has named the water stations after the four gospels: Matthew, Mark, Luke, and John); in a recent phone interview he said that of the 253 migrants who died in southern Arizona during 2009–2010, 107 of those migrants were found on O'odham land (phone interview, April 8, 2011).

2. Robin Hoover, *Desert Fountain Newsletter*, July–September 2009.

3. Ken Ellingwood, *Hard Line: Life and Death on the U.S.-Mexico Border* (New York: Pantheon Books, 2004), 137.

4. Humane Borders/*Fronteras Compasivas*, "Humane Borders Fact Sheet" (accessed January 2008).

5. Humane Borders, "Humane Borders Essays and Opinion Pieces: The Story of Humane Borders," http://www.humaneborders.org/news/news_storymarch05.html, March 2005.

6. Ellingwood, *Hard Line*, 144.

7. Ibid., 145.

8. Ibid., 144.

9. Humane Borders, "Humane Borders Essays and Opinion Pieces."

10. Ibid.

11. *The New Oxford Annotated Bible*, ed. Bruce M. Metzger and Roland E. Murphy (New York: Oxford University Press, 1991), 934 OT.

12. Humane Borders, "Humane Borders Essays and Opinion Pieces."

13. Ibid.

14. Robin Hoover, *Desert Fountain Newsletter*, July–September 2009.

15. Humane Borders/*Fronteras Compasivas*, http://www.humaneborders.org (accessed June 2009).

16. Humane Borders/*Fronteras Compasivas*; *Desert Fountain Newsletter*, January–March 2009.

17. According to the Arizona State Land Department annual report from 2009–2010, only 17.5 percent of Arizona land is privately owned. As for the rest, 12.7 percent is state owned, 42.2 percent is owned by the federal government, and the remaining 27.6 percent is in Indian trust. The status of land in Indian trust is complex. Technically, the federal government still holds legal title to the land, but for the exclusive benefit of an Indian tribe or Nation (see http://www.land.state.az.us/report/report2010_full.pdf, p. 19).

18. Humane Borders, "Humane Borders Essays and Opinion Pieces."

19. Mike Wilson, phone interview with author, February 2011. In two recent interviews (April 2011), with Mike Wilson and John Fife, there was talk of the Nation reconsidering the idea of allowing Humane Borders to put water tanks on its land.

20. Hoover, *Desert Fountain Newsletter*, July–September 2009.

21. Ibid.

22. Ellingwood, *Hard Line*, 148.

23. Humane Borders/*Fronteras Compasivas*, "Humane Borders Fact Sheet," January 2008.

24. The Reverend Robin Hoover, interview with the author, January 2009.

25. Humane Borders, "Humane Borders Essays and Opinion Pieces."

26. Ibid.

27. The Reverend Robin Hoover, interview with the author, January 2009.

28. As part of their mission, Humane Borders has worked on attracting the attention of major media sources. At the Humane Borders headquarters there is a media room with filing cabinets filled with more than 1,500 articles featuring Humane Borders. Hoover believes that "getting the news out" about the crisis will raise awareness and help bring about change.

29. Humane Borders, "Humane Borders Essays and Opinion Pieces."

30. To learn more about Project Find Me and Hoover's latest thoughts and undertakings, see www.robinhoover.com.

31. *The New Oxford Annotated Bible*, 91 OT.

CHAPTER 4

1. One does not always think immediately of the trauma suffered by many of those actively engaged in humanitarian work along the border. Maryada Vallet, one of No More Deaths' most dedicated members, would tell me later that night, after the meeting, how she had been suffering from increased nightmares since working with No More Deaths. "It can really take a toll on you psychologically," she said. "You just can't prepare sometimes for the things you see."

2. No More Deaths, http://www.nomoredeaths.org/index.php/Information/faithbased. html. The majority of No More Deaths members identify as Christians. Not everyone, however, is overtly Christian; hence the group uses the inclusive term "people of faith and conscience" to include those who are not moved by a particular theology but rather by a sense of moral duty.

3. No More Deaths states its mission to migrants as this: "Direct aid that extends the right to provide humanitarian assistance; witnessing and responding; consciousness raising; global movement building; encouraging humane immigration policy" (http://www.nomoredeaths. org/index.php/Information/history-and-mission-of-no-more-deaths.html).

4. No More Deaths, *Crossing the Line: Human Rights Abuses of Migrants in Short-term Custody on the Arizona/Sonora Border*, September 2008, 6.

5. Sarah Roberts, interview with the author, January 2009.

6. No More Deaths, www.nomoredeaths.org.

7. Bonnie Henry, "Desert Druid Writes On," *Arizona Daily Star*, http://azstarnet.com/lifestyles/article_44bb6c9b-de27-5a91-b402-259727e10e17.html, May 17, 2009.

8. Bonnie Henry, "Byrd Is 'Model of Hospitality' to Border Crossers' Helpers," *Arizona Daily Star*, http://azstarnet.com/lifestyles/article_ed1e40a9-bd7b-588a-8ea0-923de1fd0b96. html, May 17, 2009.

9. United States Code, Title 8, "Aliens and Nationality," http://www.law.cornell.edu/uscode/8/usc_sup_01_8.html.

10. Henry, "Byrd Is 'Model.'"

11. Amnesty International USA, "Humanitarian Aid Is Never a Crime: Background on Prosecution of Daniel Strauss and Shanti Sellz," http:www.amnestyusa.org/us/humanitarian_aid.html., 2007.

12. Tim Vanderpool, "The Activist Question," *Tucson Weekly*, July 9, 2009.

13. Ibid.

14. It is worth mentioning that most Border Patrol agents also see their job as a humanitarian endeavor, not just because they are serving their country and keeping U.S. borders more secure, but also because they believe that they are there to help migrants in distress. And indeed, they do. Agent Jorge Alejandro Gomez, for example, when asked what was the most rewarding part of his job, responded: "Knowing that I am saving lives. I cannot tell you how many migrants I have come across in the desert. If I hadn't been there, they would have died."

15. Vanderpool, "The Activist Question."

16. Brian J. Pederson, "Conviction Has Crossers' Water Supplier Defiant," *Arizona Daily Star*, http://azstarnet.com/news/local/crime/article_1ff7961c-bf46-5d61-8452-a760cb298709.html, June 4, 2009.

17. Walt Staton, interview with the author, March 2009.

18. Vanderpool, "The Activist Question."

19. Dan Millis, "Guilty, but No Punishment," www.nomoredeaths.org/Volunteer-Reflections/dan-millis-guilty-but-no-punishment.html.

20. No More Deaths, "No More Deaths Volunteer Found Guilty of Littering," http://nomoredeaths.org/index.php/Press-Releases/nmd-volunteer-bound-guilty-of-littering. html, June 3, 2009.

21. No More Deaths, "Litter or Life? Letters of Support and Media Hits," http://nomoredeaths.org/index.php/Updates-and-Announcements/litter-or-life-letters-of-support-and-media-hits.html, June 16, 2009.

22. No More Deaths, "NMD to Put Water on Refuge," http://nomoredeaths.org/index.php/Updates-and-Announcements/nmd-to-put-water-on-refuge.html, July 2009.

23. No More Deaths, "Feds Hand Out 13 Littering Tickets," http://www.nomoredeaths.org/index.php/Press-Releases/feds-hand-out-13-littering-tickets.html, July 9, 2009.

24. Ashley Powers, "Arizona Immigration Debate at Heart of Littering Case," *LA Times*, http://articles.latimes.com/2009/aug/13/nation/na-water-immigrants13, August 13, 2009.

25. *Arizona Daily Star*, "Accord Needed on Water Bottles Left in Desert," editorial, http://azstarnet.com/news/opinion/editorial/article_f95bb356-0cbf-5f23-9b29-2c78af905d38.html, July 13, 2009.

26. Ibid.

27. Powers, "Arizona Immigration Debate."

28. Ibid.

29. Ibid.

30. No More Deaths, "Humanitarian Convicted of 'Littering' Sentenced to Community Service, Banned from Refuge," http://www.nomoredeaths.org/index.php/Press-Releases/humanitarian-co ... of-littering-sentenced-to-community-service-banned-from-refuge.html, August 12, 2009.

31. Ibid.

32. "Water in the Desert," editorial, *New York Times*, August 16, 2009.

33. No More Deaths, *Crossing The Line:* 7.

34. Ibid., 4.

35. Ibid.

36. Ibid.

37. Ibid., 41.

38. Ibid., 42.

39. Ibid., 46.

40. Ibid., 9.

41. Jim Walsh, "Abuse Documentation Update," http://www.nomoredeaths.org/Updates-and-Announcements/abuse-documentation-update.html.

42. No More Deaths, "No More Deaths Releases Recommendations for Border Patrol Short-Term Custody Standards," http://www.nomoredeaths.org.

43. No More Deaths, *No Más Muertes, 2011, A Culture of Cruelty: Abuse and Impunity in Short-term U.S. Border Patrol Custody*, http://www.cultureofcruelty.org/wp-content/uploads/2011/09/CultureofCrueltyFinal.pdf, 4.

44. Ibid., 5.

45. Border Patrol Agent Mario Escalante, interview with the author, June 2009.

46. No More Deaths, http://www.nomoredeaths.org/index.php/Information/faithbased.html.

47. John Fife, "Civil Initiative," in *Trails of Tears and Hope*, ed. Miguel de la Torre (Maryknoll, NY: Orbis Books, 2009).

48. Ibid.

49. Chris Simcox, interview with the author, February 2009.

50. No More Deaths, http://www.nomoredeaths.org/index.php/Information/faithbased.html.

51. Ibid.

52. John Fife, interview with author, April 11, 2011.

53. Ibid.
54. Douglass S. Massey, Jorge Durand, and Nolan J. Malone, *Beyond Smoke and Mirrors: Mexican Immigration in an Era of Economic Integration* (New York: Russell Sage Foundation, 2002), 7.
55. Ibid., 9.
56. Ibid., 73.
57. Fife, "Civil Initiative."

CHAPTER 5

1. Samaritans, www.samaritanpatrol.org (accessed July 2009). For the Tucson Samaritans' most current website, see http://www.tucsonsamaritans.org/index.html. For the Green Valley Samaritans' most current information, see http://www.gvsamaritans.org/Green_ Valley-Sahuarita_Samaritans/Home.html.
2. Olivia Ruiz Marrujo, "The Gender of Risk: Sexual Violence against Undocumented Women," in *A Promised Land, A Perilous Journey: Theological Perspectives in Migration*, ed. Gioacchinno Campese and Daniel G. Groody (Notre Dame, IN: University of Notre Dame Press, 2008), 225.
3. Samaritans, http://samaritanpatrol.org (accessed July 2009).
4. Whatever the reasons for bringing Maricela to a safe house, the Samaritans have not gone unnoticed by law enforcement, as evidenced by what happened to Kathryn Ferguson, one of the group's members. On January 11, 2008, in one of the strangest cases involving humanitarian activists, Ferguson—who was out on a regular Samaritans' run with her son and another volunteer—was handcuffed by Bob Ruiz, a special agent of the U.S. Bureau of Land Management. When she asked why she was handcuffed, Ruiz said she was being a nuisance. Ferguson reports that she was handled roughly and searched inappropriately. When she showed up in court for the hearing, the charges (of "being a nuisance") were dropped as mysteriously as they were made. See Tim Vanderpool, "Requiem for an Arrest: Charges against a Samaritans Activist Are Mysteriously Dropped," *Tucson Weekly*, http:// www.tucsonweekly.com/tucson/requiem-for-an-arrest/Content?oid=1092883, October 9, 2008.
5. Bruce Parks, interview with the author, February 25, 2009.
6. Robin Hoover, "Remarks of Reverend Hoover" (paper presented at the World Council of Churches Fourth Annual United Nations Advocacy Week, New York City, November 17, 2008).
7. Ibid.

CHAPTER 6

1. Sasabe, like Nogales and Naco, has its counterpart in Mexico. There is Sasabe, Arizona, and Sásabe, Sonora. The two towns with the same name are contiguous, cut in half by the border. The shared name says something about the towns' shared histories: one name, one town, divided by the border.
2. Duncan Kennedy, "Divided View as U.S. Fence Goes Up," *BBC News*, January 31, 2008.
3. Ibid.
4. One Hundred Ninth Congress of the United States of America (Second Session), "Secure Fence Act of 2006," January 3, 2006.
5. Ibid.
6. See United States Government Accountability Office, "Border Security: Preliminary Observations on Border Control Measures for the Southwest Border," February 15, 2011.
7. Charles Bowden, "Our Wall: The U.S.-Mexico Border," *National Geographic*, http://ngm. nationalgeographic.com/2007/05/us-mexican-border/bowden-text, May 2007.

8. President of the United States, "Gadsden Purchase Treaty, December 30, 1853," Article I, Avalon Project, http://avalon.law.yale.edu/19th_century/mx1853.asp.

9. Of particular interest in Nogales is the stunning artwork that hangs along the wall on the Mexican side (it was prohibited on the American side). There are crosses to honor dead migrants, beautiful murals depicting the hardships of the journey, and larger than life *milagros* (religious folk charms that are traditionally used as votive offerings). The wall has proven to be an outlet of creative protest and inspiration at different locations, from San Diego to Brownsville.

10. United States Customs and Border Protection, "Tucson Sector Project," http://www.cbp. gov/xp/cgov/border_security/sbi/projects/project_descrip/tucson_project.xml, November 10, 2008.

11. Daniel B. Wood, "Arizona's 'Virtual' Border Wall Gets a Reality Check," *Christian Science Monitor*, http://www.csmonitor.com/USA/2008/0402/p12s01-usgn.html, April 2, 2008.

12. Jim Gilchrist, interview with the author, August 3, 2009.

13. Jim Gilchrist, "An Essay by Jim Gilchrist," http://www.minutemanproject.com/essay.php, September 2008.

14. Patrick J. Buchanan, *State of Emergency: The Third World Invasion and Conquest of America* (New York: St. Martin's Press, 2006), 254.

15. Ibid.

16. Brady McCombs, "Agents Find 16th Tunnel in Nogales since October 1," *Arizona Daily Star*, June 12, 2009.

17. See, for example, Customs and Border Protection, "Ultralight Plane Crashes in Arizona, Smugglers Apprehended," http://www.cbp.gov/xp/cgov/newsroom/news_releases/may_2009/05302009.xml, May 30, 2009. Or in the catalogue of deaths recorded by Coalición de Derechos Humanos, you will see, as one of the many causes of death, "plane crash." This is the case, for example, of a thirty-four-year-old man named Juan Gabriel Torres Hernandez who died when his ultralight plane crashed trying to fly over the wall (Coalición de Derechos Humanos, "Arizona Recovered Remains," http://www. derechoshumanosaz.net/index.php?option=com_content&task=view&id=20&Itemid=34).

18. See United States Government Accountability Office, "Border Security: Preliminary Observations on Border Control Measures for the Southwest Border (Testimony Before the Subcommittee on Border and Maritime Security, Committee on Homeland Security, House of Representatives)," February 15, 2011; and United States Government Accountability Office, "Border Security: DHS Progress and Challenges in Securing the U.S. Southwest and Northern Borders," March 30, 2011.

19. Associated Press, "Mexican President Criticizes U.S. Border Wall," December 15, 2005.

20. BBC News, "Mexico Anger over U.S. Border Fence," October 27, 2009.

21. Brady McCombs, "Two Men Praying at Virtual-Fence Site Are Arrested," *Arizona Daily Star*, http://azstarnet.com/news/local/border/article_c997c5a0-0fc0-54a4-b8be-ea4ab7c3735a.html, August 7, 2009.

22. John Fanestil, "Friendship across Fences: Communion and Civil Disobedience on the U.S.-Mexico Border," *God's Politics*, http://blog.sojo.net/2009/02/11/friendship-across-fences-communion-and-civil-disobedience-on-the-us-mexico-border/, February 11, 2009.

23. John Fanestil, "'Good Guys and Bad Guys' on the Border," *God's Politics*, http://blog.sojo. net/2009/02/27/good-guys-and-bad-guys-on-the-border/, February 27, 2009.

24. Ibid.

25. Robert Frost, "Mending Wall," *Collected Poems of Robert Frost* (New York: Halcyon House, 1931), 47.

26. Ibid.
27. Ibid.
28. Ibid., 47–48.
29. Ibid., 48.

CHAPTER 7

1. Patriots Coalition, www.patriotscoalition.com (last accessed June 2010; the site is no longer active).
2. Danny did not want to give his last name to anyone, since his cameras have been so controversial. As a result, I can only refer to his website (www.borderinvasionpics.com). The website is, without a doubt, one of the most fascinating pieces of material I happened upon during my research. There are, of course, hundreds of anti-illegal immigration websites, as well as dozens of websites connected to a variety of civil patrol groups dedicated to patrolling the border, but this one is quite unique in its content and presentation.
3. Ibid.
4. Since it is not my aim to provide an extensive history of the phenomenon of civil patrol groups, I will point the reader to two helpful sources documenting the matter from very different perspectives: Roxanne Lynn Doty's recent book, *The Law into Their Own Hands* (Tucson: University of Arizona Press, 2009), and Jim Gilchrist and Jerome Corsi's book, *Minutemen: The Battle to Secure America's Borders* (Los Angeles, CA: World Ahead Publishing, 2006). While Doty's book provides a more academic and critical voice concerning these groups, the Gilchrist and Corsi book gives an insider's view, as Jim Gilchrist is the founder of the Minuteman Project.
5. Doty, *The Law into Their Own Hands*, 30.
6. Jerry Seper, "16 Illegals Sue Arizona Rancher," *Washington Times*, http://www.washingtontimes.com/news/2009/feb/09/16-illegals-sue-arizona-rancher/?page=all, February 9, 2009.
7. Ibid.
8. Ibid.
9. Chris Simcox, interview with the author, February 2009.
10. Al Garza, interview with the author, September 19, 2009.
11. Ibid.
12. Gilchrist and Corsi, *Minutemen*, 277.
13. Richard Marosi, "Mexican Teen Admits Killing U.S. Border Patrol Agent," *Los Angeles Times*, http://articles.latimes.com/2009/nov/21/local/la-me-border-agent21-2009nov21, November 21, 2009.
14. Border Patrol Agent Jorge Alejandro Gomez, interview with the author, September 18, 2009.
15. While I have not come across an official statistic documenting the percentage of Border Patrol agents who are Mexican American or Latino, in my experience it seemed that those numbers must be very high. Over 50 percent of the agents I met while conducting research had Spanish surnames, were born in Mexico, and were later naturalized as U.S. citizens, or came from families that were of Mexican descent. Many had grown up along the border and spoke Spanish fluently. Moreover, recent Border Patrol policy has changed to include, as a prerequisite of becoming an agent, fluency or near-fluency in Spanish. Those who do not know Spanish must now, as part of their extensive training, undergo several months of intensive language courses in Spanish.
16. Robin Hoover, "Humane Borders Essays and Opinion Pieces: The Story of Humane Borders," http://www.humaneborders.org/news/news_storymarch05.html, March 2005.

17. No More Deaths, *No Más Muertes*, 2011, *A Culture of Cruelty: Abuse and Impunity in Short-term U.S. Border Patrol Custody*, http://www.cultureofcruelty.org/wp-content/uploads/2011/09/CultureofCrueltyFinal.pdf, 5.

18. United States Customs and Border Protection, *National Border Patrol Strategy* (Washington, DC: U.S. Customs and Border Protection, 2004), 2.

19. Ibid., 9.

20. I asked a few agents whether their "radiation detectors" had ever gone off. They all said, "Sure, but not because anyone was carrying materials for weapons of mass destruction." It turns out that the detector often goes off with trace amounts of things like radioactive iodine, a substance used, for example, in the treatment of certain diseases such as cancer or thyroid disease.

21. Patrick J. Buchanan, *State of Emergency: The Third World Invasion and Conquest of America* (New York: St. Martin's Press, 2006), 13.

22. These three categories are my own. There may be others, but these are the three that seemed most central.

23. Michelle Malkin, *Invasion: How America Still Welcomes Terrorists, Criminals, and Other Foreign Menaces to Our Shores* (Washington, DC: Regnery, 2002), ix. Interestingly, Malkin herself is the daughter of two Filipino immigrants.

24. See, for example, Peter Slevin, "Deportations of Illegal Immigrants Increase under Obama Administration," *Washington Post*, http://www.washingtonpost.com/wp-dyn/content/article/2010/07/25/AR9780199890934.html, July 26, 2010.

25. Malkin, *Invasion*, 11.

26. Ibid., 29. It is worth mentioning that, to date, no terrorists or terrorist suspects have actually been known to come through the U.S.-Mexican border. That does not mean that they could not, or have not, but it is something that Malkin fails to mention.

27. Ibid., 87.

28. Ibid., 91.

29. Moreover, simply browse the Internet and you will find a seemingly endless array of sites, blogs, and chat rooms that highlight similar themes—for example, groups like Desert Invasion—U.S.; Get My Country Back; Illegal Aliens U.S.; Deportaliens.com; Noinvaders.org; Let's Take Back America; 9/11 Families for a Secure America; National Security Whistleblowers Coalition; NoAmnesty.com; Predatory Aliens; Escaping Justice; Citizens for a Secure Border; Wake Up America Foundation; We Need a Fence.

30. Jim Gilchrist, "An Essay by Jim Gilchrist," *Georgetown University Law Journal*, September 2008, 3.

31. Ibid., 5.

32. Steven A. Camarota, "The High Cost of Cheap Labor: Illegal Immigration and the Federal Government," *Center for Immigration Studies*, http://www.cis.org/articles/2004/fiscal.pdf, August 2004.

33. Immigration Works USA, "Principles," http://www.immigrationworksusa.org/index.php?p = 50.

34. See, www.TakeOurJobs.org.

35. See, for example, Harry J. Holzer, "Immigration Policy and Less-Skilled Workers in the United States: Reflection on Future Directions for Reform," *Migration Policy Institute*, http://www.migrationpolicy.org/pubs/Holzer-January2011.pdf, January 2011.

36. Buchanan, *State of Emergency*, 2.

37. A recent study estimated that 8 percent of babies born in the United States in 2008 were born to unauthorized immigrants, and all were granted automatic citizenship under the Citizenship Clause of the Fourteenth Amendment. See Alice Brice, "Report: 8 Percent of U.S. Newborns Have Undocumented Parents," CNN, August 12, 2010, http://www.cnn.com/2010/US/08/11/hispanic.study/?hpt = T2.

38. Buchanan, *State of Emergency*, 5.

39. Ibid., 139.

40. Samuel P. Huntington, *Who Are We? The Challenges to America's National Identity* (New York: Simon and Schuster, 2004), xv.

41. Ibid., xvi.

42. Ibid.

43. Ibid., xvii.

44. Interestingly, these are the same highly charged back-and-forth arguments occurring in European countries such as France, the United Kingdom, and Germany. While the topic cannot be addressed here, it is informative to see that such strikingly similar questions are being asked in European parliaments, such questions as, for example, Is there a "French essence" that is being lost to current North African immigration patterns? How should "French values" be instilled into immigrant populations? How important is it that new immigrants properly assimilate to a French "way of life," revere French history, speak French fluently? These questions arose again with Germany's Angela Merkel pronouncing the "utter failure of multiculturalism" and, a few months later, England's David Cameron making similar critiques of multiculturalism. They are also implicitly present in France's ongoing secularization campaigns that have banned Muslim headscarves in schools and more recently banned burqas and public prayer.

45. Gilchrist and Corsi, *Minutemen*, 14. Also, in every conversation I had with Gilchrist over the phone, he referred to his organization numerous times as "the multiethnic Minuteman Project."

46. Ibid.

47. Jim Gilchrist, "An Essay by Jim Gilchrist," *Georgetown University Law Journal*, September 2008, 12.

48. Ibid.

49. Huntington, *Who Are We?*

50. Ibid., 182.

51. Ibid., 183.

52. Ibid., 230

53. Ibid., 241.

54. Buchanan, *State of Emergency*, 2.

55. Zbigniew Brzezinski, "Terrorized by 'War on Terror': How a Three-Word Mantra Has Undermined America," *Washington Post*, http://www.washingtonpost.com/wp-dyn/content/article/2007/03/23/AR9780199890934.html, March 25, 2007.

56. Ibid.

57. Doty, *The Law into Their Own Hands*, 104.

CHAPTER 8

1. Randal C. Archibold, "Ranchers Alarmed by Killing Near Border," *New York Times*, www.nytimes.com/2010/04/05/us/05arizona.html, April 4, 2010.

2. Brady McCombs, "Cochise Ranch Area Outraged by Killing," *Arizona Daily Star*, http://azstarnet.com/news/local/border/article_32642381-6314-53b4-aff1-570dbd1d6834.html, March 30, 2010.

3. Ibid.

4. Archibold, "Ranchers Alarmed."

5. McCombs, "Cochise Ranch Area Outraged."

6. Brady McCombs, "Focus in Krentz Killing on Suspect in U.S.," *Arizona Daily Star*, http://azstarnet.com/news/local/border/article_35ef6e3a-5632-5e58-abe7-e7697ee2f0d5.html, May 3, 2010. In an ironic twist, shortly after SB 1070 was passed, it was announced that the leading suspect in the Robert Krentz murder was not, in fact, a

Mexican but rather an American citizen. At the time of writing, the case remains unresolved.

7. State of Arizona Senate, "Senate Bill 1070," Forty-ninth Legislature, Second Regular Session, 2010, http://www.azleg.gov/legtext/49leg/2r/bills/sb1070s.pdf (Section One, 8–10).

8. Ibid. Section Two, 22–24 and 37–39.

9. Kris W. Kobach, "Why Arizona Drew a Line," *New York Times*, www.nytimes.com/2010/04/29/opinion/29kobach.html, April 29, 2010.

10. Ibid.

11. Jan Brewer, "Arizona Immigration Law: Gov. Brewer's Statement," *azcentral.com*, http://www.azcentral.com/news/articles/2010/04/23/20100423arizona-immigration-law-brewer-statements-CR.html, April 23, 2010.

12. Ibid.

13. Ibid.

14. Cardinal Roger Mahoney, "Arizona's Dreadful Anti-immigrant Law," Cardinal Roger Mahoney Blogs L.A., http://cardinalrogermahonyblogsla.blogspot.com/2010/04/arizonas-new-anti-immigrant-law.html, April 18, 2010.

15. Jim Wallis, "Arizona's Immigration Bill Is a Social and Racial Sin," *God's Politics*. http://blog.sojo.net/2010/04/21/arizonas-immigration-bill-is-a-social-and-racial-sin, April 21, 2010.

16. Andrew Adams, "Religion Becomes a Topic of Discussion in Immigration Debate," *ksl.com*, http://www.ksl.com/?nid=148&sid=10598741, April 30, 2010.

17. The Church of Jesus Christ of Latter-day Saints, "The Articles of Faith," *The Official Scriptures of the Church of Latter-day Saints*, http://scriptures.lds.org/en/a_of_f/1/.

18. Wallis, "Arizona's Immigration Bill is a Social and Racial Sin."

19. Steven Martin, "On Arizona's Draconian Immigration Law: Major Religious Groups Condemn Inhumane Anti-immigrant Law in Arizona," *New Evangelical Partnership for the Common Good*, http://www.newevangelicalpartnership.org/?q=node/38, April 23, 2010.

20. Randal C. Archibold and Jennifer Steinhauer, "Welcome to Arizona, Outpost of Contradictions," *New York Times*, www.nytimes.com/2010/04/29/us/29arizona.html, April 28, 2010.

21. *The Arizona Republic*, "Law Is a Plea for U.S. Action," http://www.azcentral.com/arizonarepublic/opinions/articles/2010/04/28/20100428wed1-28.html, April 28, 2010.

22. Ibid.

23. The following are the portions of the law that Bolton blocked: Portion of Section 2, "requiring that an officer make a reasonable attempt to determine the immigration status of a person stopped, detained or arrested if there is a reasonable suspicion that the person is unlawfully present in the United States, and requiring verification of the immigration status of any person arrested prior to releasing that person"; Portion of Section 3, making it "a crime for the failure to apply for or carry alien registration papers;" Portion of Section 5, making it "a crime for an unauthorized alien to solicit, apply for, or perform work"; and portion of Section 6, "authorizing the warrantless arrest of a person where there is probable cause to believe the person has committed a public offense that makes the person removable from the United States."

24. Susan R. Bolton, injunction order, *The United States of America v. The State of Arizona*, Case 2:10-cv-01413-SRB, Document 87, July 28, 2010.

25. Ibid. Bolton emphasized that the requirement to check immigration status of arrestees is exacerbated by certain factors, including the fact that there are many "very minor, non-criminal violations of state law, including jaywalking, failure to have a dog on a leash, or

riding a bicycle on the sidewalk" (ibid.). Bolton concluded that allowing such simple violations to end in immigration checks would unfairly burden everyone involved.

26. The Act, passed in 1940, was a national security measure, which made it illegal for anyone to advocate overthrowing the United States. The same act also required non-citizens, aged fourteen and over, to register with the U.S. government. The following year, Pennsylvania passed a law requiring non-citizens to register with the state. The opinion of the Court was that the federal government should be in charge of immigration matters, not individual states. As Justice Hugo L. Black wrote: "The supremacy of the national power in the general field of foreign affairs, including power over immigration, naturalization and deportation, is made clear by the Constitution, [and] was pointed out by the authors of The Federalist in 1787, and has since been given continuous recognition by the Court."

27. Ibid.

28. Larry A. Dever, "Abandoned on the Border," *New York Times,* www.nytimes.com/2011/05/13/opinion/13Dever.html, May 12, 2011.

29. Ibid.

30. President, speech, "Remarks by the President on Comprehensive Immigration Reform," American University School of International Service, July 1, 2010.

31. A related issue is the question of providing more visas to high-skilled workers as well. As many have pointed out, the United States so often trains foreigners at its universities, some of the best universities in the world, but then does not provide them a means of staying in the country and contributing to cutting-edge research and innovation.

32. Daniel B. Wood, "Opinion Polls Show Broad Support for Tough Arizona Immigration Law," *Christian Science Monitor,* http://www.csmonitor.com/USA/Society/2010/0430/Opinion-polls-show-broad-support-for-tough-Arizona-immigration-law, April 30, 2010.

33. Richard Kearney, *Anatheism: Returning to God after God* (New York: Columbia University Press, 2010), 21.

34. Sigmund Freud, *Civilization and Its Discontents,* translated by James Strachey (New York: W.W. Norton, 1961), 65.

35. Ibid., 66.

36. Ibid.

37. Ibid., 67.

38. Ibid., 68.

39. Ibid., 81.

40. Ibid., 70.

41. Sigmund Freud, *Why War? A Correspondence between Albert Einstein and Sigmund Freud* (Chicago: Chicago Institute for Psychoanalysis, 1978).

42. Jean-Paul Sartre, *Being and Nothingness,* translated by Hazel E. Barnes (New York: Washington Square Press, 1992), 352.

43. Ibid., 354, 355, 358.

44. Ibid., 350.

45. Ibid, 358.

46. William James, *On Some of Life's Ideals: On a Certain Blindness in Human Beings. What Makes a Life Significant* (Folcroft, PA: Folcroft Library Editions, 1974).

47. Emmanuel Levinas, *Ethics and Infinity: Conversations with Philippe Nemo,* translated by Richard Cohen (Pittsburg: Duquesne University Press, 1985), 121.

48. Ibid., 87, 89.

49. Ibid., 120.

50. Richard Kearney, *Anatheism: Returning to God after God.*

CONCLUSION

1. See http://derechoshumanosaz.net/projects/arizona-recovered-bodies-project/
2. Brady McCombs, "AZ Border Saw Record 252 Deaths in Fiscal '10," *Arizona Daily Star*, http://azstarnet.com/news/local/border/article_c50f048f-acf9-52a9-8863-6e5969360091.html, October 5, 2010.

BIBLIOGRAPHY

Adams, Andrew. "Religion Becomes a Topic of Discussion in Immigration Debate." *ksl.com*.
   http://www.ksl.com/?nid=148&sid=10598741. April 30, 2010.
Adler, Rudy, Victoria Criado, and Brett Huneycutt. *Border Film Project: Photos by Migrants and
   Minutemen on the U.S.-Mexico Border*. New York: Harry N. Abrams, 2007.
Amnesty International, USA. "Humanitarian Aid Is Not a Crime: Background on Prosecution
   of Daniel Strauss and Shanti Sellz." http://www.amnestyusa.org/us/humanitarian_aid.
   html (accessed April 2009).
Andreas, Peter. *Border Games: Policing the U.S.-Mexico Divide*. Ithaca, NY: Cornell University
   Press, 2009.
Archibold, Randal C. "Ranchers Alarmed by Killing Near Border." *New York Times*. www.
   nytimes.com/2010/04/05/us/05arizona.html. April 4, 2010.
———, and Jennifer Steinhauer. "Welcome to Arizona, Outpost of Contradictions." *New York
   Times*. www.nytimes.com/2010/04/29/us/29arizona.html. April 28, 2010.
———. "Judge Blocks Arizona's Immigration Law." *New York Times*. www.nytimes.
   com/2010/07/29/us/29arizona.html. July 28, 2010.
Arizona Daily Star. "Accord Needed on Water Bottles Left in Desert." Editorial. http://azstar-
   net.com/news/opinion/editorial/article_f95bb356-0cbf-5f23-9b29-2c78af905d38.
   html. July 13, 2009.
Arizona Republic. "Law Is a Plea for U.S. Action." Editorial. http://www.azcentral.com/
   arizonarepublic/opinions/articles/2010/04/28/20100428wed1-28.html.
   April 28, 2010.
Associated Press. "Mexican President Criticizes U.S. Border Wall." Fox News. http://www.fox-
   news.com/story/0,2933,178772,00.html. December 15, 2005.
Banerjee, Neela. "New Coalition of Christians Seeks Changes at Borders." *New York Times*.
   http://www.nytimes.com/2007/05/08/washington/08immigration.html.
   May 8, 2007.
BBC News. "Mexico Anger over U.S. Border Fence." October 27, 2006.
Susan R. Bolton, injunction order, *The United States of America v. The State of Arizona*, Case
   2:10-cv-01413-SRB, Document 87, July 28, 2010.
Border Invasion Pics. http://www.borderinvasionpics.com.
Bowden, Charles. "Our Wall: The U.S.-Mexico Border." *National Geographic*. http://ngm.
   nationalgeographic.com/2007/05/us-mexican-border/bowden-text. May 2007.
Brewer, Jan. "Arizona Immigration Law: Gov. Brewer's Statement." *Azcentral.com* (Arizona's
   home page). http://www.azcentral.com/news/articles/2010/04/23/20100423arizon
   a-immigration-law-brewer-statements-CR.html. April, 23, 2010.
Brice, Alice. "Report: 8 Percent of U.S. Newborns Have Undocumented Parents." CNN. http://
   www.cnn.com/2010/US/08/11/hispanic.study/?hpt=T2. August 12, 2010.

Brzezinski, Zbigniew. "Terrorized by 'War on Terror': How a Three-Word Mantra Has Undermined America." *Washington Post.* http://www.washingtonpost.com/wp-dyn/content/article/2007/03/23/AR2007032301613.html. March 25, 2007.

Buchanan, Patrick J. *State of Emergency: The Third World Invasion and Conquest of America.* New York: St. Martin's Press, 2006.

Cambridge City Council. "Policy Order Resolution." http://www.cambridgema.gov/city-Clerk/PolicyOrder.cfm?item_id=13247. May 8, 2006.

Campese, Gioacchino, and Daniel G. Groody, editors. *A Promised Land, a Perilous Journey: Theological Perspectives on Migration.* Notre Dame, IN: University of Notre Dame Press, 2008.

Campese, Gioacchino. "*Cuantos Más? The Crucified Peoples at the U.S.-Mexico Border.*" In *A Promised Land, a Perilous Journey: Theological Perspectives on Migration,* edited by Gioacchinno Campese and Daniel Groody (271–298). Notre Dame, IN: University of Notre Dame Press, 2008.

Carens, Joseph H. "The Case for Amnesty: Time Erodes the State's Right to Deport." *Boston Review.* http://bostonreview.net/BR34.3/carens.php. May/June 2009.

Carroll, M. Daniel R. *Christians at the Border: Immigration, the Church, and the Bible.* Grand Rapids, MI: Baker, 2008.

President Jimmy Carter, statement, "Refugee Act of 1980 Statement on Signing S. 643 into Law," March 18, 1980.

Chaddock, Gail Russell. "The Canteen Man of the U.S.-Mexico Border." *Christian Science Monitor.* http://www.csmonitor.com/2007/0122/p20s01-ussc.html. January 22, 2007.

Church of Jesus Christ of Latter-day Saints. "The Articles of Faith." *The Official Scriptures of the Church of Latter-day Saints.* http://scriptures.lds.org/en/a_of_f/1/ (accessed May 2010).

Coalición de Derechos Humanos. "Arizona Recovered Remains." http://www.derecho-shumanosaz.net/index.php?option=com_content&task=view&id=20&Itemid=34 (accessed June 2009).

Cornelius, Wayne A., et al. *Controlling Immigration: A Global Perspective.* Stanford: Stanford University Press, 2004.

Crittenden, Ann. *Sanctuary: A Story of American Conscience and the Law in Collision.* New York: Weidenfeld and Nicolson, 1988.

Cunningham, Hilary. *God and Caesar at the Rio Grande: Sanctuary and the Politics of Religion.* Minneapolis: University of Minnesota Press, 1995.

Dawkins, Richard. "Atheists for Jesus." *The Richard Dawkins Foundation.* http://richarddawkins.net/articles/20-atheists-for-jesus?page=1. April 10, 2006.

Deparle, Jason. "Defying Trend, Canada Lures More Migrants." *New York Times.* http://www.nytimes.com/2010/11/13/world/americas/13immig.html?pagewanted=all. November 12, 2010.

Derrida, Jacques. "Hospitality, Justice and Responsibility: A Dialogue with Jacques Derrida." In *Questioning Ethics: Contemporary Debates in Philosophy,* edited by Richard Kearney and Mark Dooley. London: Routledge, 1999.

———. *Of Hospitality.* Stanford, CA: Stanford University Press, 2000.

Desert Invasion-U.S. http://www.desertinvasion.us/index.html.

Dever, Larry A. "Abandoned on the Border." *New York Times.* www.nytimes.com/2011/05/13/opinion/13 Dever.html, May 12, 2011.

Doty, Roxanne Lynn. "*Fronteras Compasivas* and the Ethics of Unconditional Hospitality." *Millenium: Journal of International Studies* 35, no. 1. (2006): 53–74.

———. *The Law into Their Own Hands: Immigration and the Politics of Exceptionalism.* Tucson: University of Arizona Press, 2009.

Ehrman, Bart D. *Jesus Interrupted: Revealing the Hidden Contradictions in the Bible (and Why We Don't Know about Them).* New York: HarperCollins, 2009.

Ellingwood, Ken. *Hard Line: Life and Death on the U.S.-Mexico Border*. New York: Pantheon Books, 2004.

Fanestil, John. "Friendship across Fences: Communion and Civil Disobedience on the U.S.-Mexico Border." *God's Politics Blog*. http://blog.sojo.net/2009/02/11/friendship-across-fences-communion-and-civil-disobedience-on-the-us-mexico-border/. February 11, 2009.

———. "'Good Guys and Bad Guys' on the Border." *God's Politics Blog*. http://blog.sojo.net/2009/02/27/good-guys-and-bad-guys-on-the-border/. February 27, 2009.

Fife, John. "Civil Initiative." In *Trails of Hope and Terror: Testimonies on Immigration*, edited by Miguel A. de la Torre. Maryknoll, NY: Orbis Books, 2009.

Freud, Sigmund. *The Future of an Illusion*, translated by James Strachey. New York: W.W. Norton, 1961.

———. *Civilization and Its Discontents*, translated by James Strachey. New York: W.W. Norton and Company, 1961.

———. *Why War? A Correspondence between Albert Einstein and Sigmund Freud*. Chicago: Chicago Institute for Psychoanalysis, 1978.

Frost, Robert. *The Collected Poems of Robert Frost*. New York: Halcyon House, 1939.

Funk, Robert, Hoover, and the Jesus Seminar. *The Five Gospels*. New York: Harper Collins, 1993.

Galli, Mark. "Blessed Is the Law—Up to a Point." *Christianity Today*, http://www.christianity-today.com/ct/2006/aprilweb-only/114-53.0.html, April 7, 2006.

Gilbert, Robert W. "Curbing Voluntary Return." *Arizona Daily Star*. January 25, 2009.

Gilchrist, Jim, and Jerome R. Corsi. *Minutemen: The Battle to Secure America's Borders*. Los Angeles: World Ahead Publishing, 2006.

———. "An Essay by Jim Gilchrist." http://www.minutemanproject.com/essay.php. September 2008.

Goodell, Roger. "Immigration Debate Gets Religious." *Washington Times*. http://www.washingtontimes.com/news/2007/jan/8/20070108-125514-4201r//?page=all#pagebreak. January 8, 2007.

Hagan, Jacqueline Maria. *Migration Miracle: Faith, Hope and Meaning on the Undocumented Journey*. Cambridge, MA: Harvard University Press, 2008.

Henry, Bonnie. "Byrd Is 'Model of Hospitality' to Border Crossers' Helpers." *Arizona Daily Star*. http://azstarnet.com/lifestyles/article_ed1e40a9-bd7b-588a-8ea0-923de1fd0b96.html. May 17, 2009.

———. "Desert Druid Writes On." *Arizona Daily Star*. http://azstarnet.com/lifestyles/article_44bb6c9b-de27-5a91-b402-259727e10e17.html. May 17, 2009.

Hondagneu-Sotelo, Pierrette. *God's Heart Has No Borders: How Religious Activists Are Working for Immigrant Rights*. Berkeley: University of California Press, 2008.

Hoover, Robin. "Social Theology and Religiously Affiliated Nonprofits in Migration Policy." Ph.D. dissertation, Texas Tech University, 1998.

———. "Remarks of Reverend Hoover." Paper presented at the World Council of Churches Fourth Annual United Nations Advocacy Week, New York City, November 17, 2008.

———. "The Story of Humane Borders." In *A Promised Land, a Perilous Journey: Theological Perspectives on Migration*, edited by Gioacchinno Campese and Daniel Groody (160–173). Notre Dame, IN: University of Notre Dame Press, 2008.

———. "Humane Borders Essays and Opinion Pieces: The Story of Humane Borders." http://www.humaneborders.org/news/news_storymarch05.html. March 2005.

Humane Borders/*Fronteras Compasivas*. http://www.humaneborders.org (accessed June 2009).

———. *Desert Fountain* (Newsletter). January–March 2009.

———. *Desert Fountain* (Newlsetter). July–September 2009.

————. "Humane Borders Fact Sheet." January 2008.

Huntington, Samuel P. *Who Are We? The Challenges to America's National Identity*. New York: Simon and Schuster, 2004.

James, William. *On Some of Life's Ideals: On a Certain Blindness in Human Beings. What Makes a Life Significant*. Folcroft, PA: Folcroft Library Editions, 1974.

Kearney, Richard. *Anatheism: Returning to God after God*. New York: Columbia University Press, 2010.

————, and Mark Dooley, editors. *Questioning Ethics: Contemporary Debates in Philosophy*. London: Routledge, 1999.

Kennedy, Duncan. "Divided View as U.S. Fence Goes Up." BBC News, January 31, 2008.

Kerwin, Donald. "The Natural Rights of Migrants and Newcomers: A Challenge to U.S. Law and Policy." In *A Promised Land, a Perilous Journey: Theological Perspectives on Migration*, edited by Gioacchinno Campese and Daniel Groody (192–209). Notre Dame, IN: University of Notre Dame Press, 2008.

Kobach, Kris K. "Why Arizonans Drew a Line." *New York Times*. www.nytimes.com/2010/04/29/opinion/29kobach.html. April 29, 2010.

Levinas, Emmanuel. *Ethics and Infinity: Conversations with Philippe Nemo*, translated by Richard Cohen. Pittsburgh: Duquesne University Press, 1985.

————. *Of God Who Comes to Mind*, translated by Bettina Bergo. Stanford, CA: Stanford University Press, 1998.

Library of Congress (Thomas). "Secure Fence Act of 2006." http://thomas.loc.gov/cgi-bin/query/D?c109:4:./temp/~c109EvEKo2. January 3, 2006.

Mahoney, Cardinal Roger. "Arizona's Dreadful Anti-immigrant Law." Cardinal Roger Mahoney Blogs L.A. http://cardinalrogermahonyblogsla.blogspot.com/2010/04/arizonas-new-anti-immigrant-law.html. April 18, 2010.

Malkin, Michelle. *Invasion: How America Still Welcomes Terrorists, Criminals, and Other Foreign Menaces to Our Shores*. Washington, DC: Regnery, 2002.

Marosi, Richard. "Mexican Teen Admits Killing U.S. Border Patrol Agent." *Los Angeles Times*. http://articles.latimes.com/2009/nov/21/local/la-me-border-agent21-2009nov21. November 21, 2009.

Marrujo, Olivia Ruiz. "The Gender of Risk: Sexual Violence against Undocumented Women." In *A Promised Land, a Perilous Journey: Theological Perspectives on Migration*, edited by Gioacchinno Campese and Daniel Groody (225–239). Notre Dame, IN: University of Notre Dame Press, 2008.

Martin, Steven. "On Arizona's Draconian Immigration Law: Major Religious Groups Condemn Inhumane Anti-immigrant Law in Arizona." *New Evangelical Partnership for the Common Good*. http://www.newevangelicalpartnership.org/?q=node/38. April 23, 2010.

Massey, Douglass S., Jorge Durand, and Nolan J. Malone. *Beyond Smoke and Mirrors: Mexican Immigration in an Era of Economic Integration*. New York: Russell Sage Foundation, 2002.

Michael Luo. "A Closer Look at the 'Sanctuary City' Argument." *New York Times*. http://www.nytimes.com/2007/11/29/us/politics/29truth.html. November 29, 2007.

McCombs, Brady. "Two Men Praying at Virtual-Fence Site Are Arrested." *Arizona Daily Star*. http://azstarnet.com/news/local/border/article_c997c5a0-0fc0-54a4-b8be-ea4ab7c3735a.html. August 7, 2009.

————. "Focus in Krentz Killing on Suspect in U.S." *Arizona Daily Star*. http://azstarnet.com/news/local/border/article_35ef6e3a-5632-5e58-abe7-e7697ee2f0d5.html. May 3, 2010.

————. "AZ Border Saw Record 252 Deaths in Fiscal '10." *Arizona Daily Star*. http://azstarnet.com/news/local/border/article_c50f048f-acf9-52a9-8863-6e5969360091.html October 5, 2010.

McKinley, Jesse. "San Francisco at Crossroads over Immigration." *New York Times*. http://www.nytimes.com/2009/06/13/us/13sanctuary.html. June 13, 2009.

National Association of Evangelicals. "Resolution on Immigration." http://www.nae.net/resolutions/347-immigration-2009.

Nazario, Sonia. *Enrique's Journey: The Story of a Boy's Dangerous Odyssey to Reunite with His Mother*. New York: Random House, 2006.

Nevins, Joseph. *Operation Gatekeeper: The Rise of the "Illegal Alien" and the Making of the U.S.-Mexico Boundary*. New York: Routledge, 2002.

———. *Dying to Live: A Story of U.S. Immigration in an Age of Global Apartheid*. San Francisco: City Lights Books, 2008.

New York Times. "Water in the Desert." Editorial. August 16, 2009.

———. "Border Fantasies." Editorial. September 22, 2009.

No More Deaths. *Crossing the Line: Human Rights Abuses of Migrants in Short-Term Custody on the Arizona/Sonora Border*. September 2008.

———. "NMD Volunteer Found Guilty of Littering." http://nomoredeaths.org/index.php/Press-Releases/nmd-volunteer-bound-guilty-of-littering.html. June 3, 2009.

———. "Litter or Life? Letters of Support and Media Hits." http://nomoredeaths.org/index.php/Updates-and-Announcements/litter-or-life-letters-of-support-and-media-hits.html. June 16, 2009.

———. "NMD to Put Water on Refuge." http://nomoredeaths.org/index.php/Updates-and-Announcements/nmd-to-put-water-on-refuge.html (accessed July 2009).

———. "Feds Hand Out 13 Littering Tickets." http://www.nomoredeaths.org/index.php/Press-Releases/feds-hand-out-13-littering-tickets.html. July 9. 2009.

———. "Humanitarian Convicted of 'Littering' Sentenced to Community Service, Banned from Refuge." http://www.nomoredeaths.org/index.php/Press-Releases/humanitarian-co…of-littering-sentenced-to-community-service-banned-from-refuge.html. August 12, 2009.

———. "No More Deaths Releases Recommendations for Border Patrol Short-Term Custody Standards." http://www.nomoredeaths.org. August 13, 2009.

President Barack Obama, speech. "Remarks by the President on Comprehensive Immigration Reform," American University School of International Service. July 1, 2010.

Otto, Rudolph. *The Idea of the Holy*, translated by John W. Harvey. London: Oxford University Press, 1958.

Phillips, Marelene H. "Arizona Man Arrested for 'Trying to Save Lives.'" *Huffington Post*. June 4, 2009.

Pedersen, Brian J. "Conviction Has Crossers' Water Supplier Defiant." *Arizona Daily Star*. http://azstarnet.com/news/local/crime/article_1ff7961c-bf46-5d61-8452-a760cb298709.html. June 4, 2009.

Powers, Ashley. "Arizona Immigration Debate at Heart of Littering Case." *Los Angeles Times*. http://articles.latimes.com/2009/aug/13/nation/na-water-immigrants13. August 13, 2009.

Ramos, Tarso Luís, and Pam Chamberlain. "Nativist Bedfellows: The Christian Right Embraces Anti-Immigrant Politics." *The Public Eye Magazine* 23, no. 2 (2008). http://www.public-eye.org/magazine/v23n2/nativist_bedfellows.html.

Rodríguez, Oscar Andrés Cardinal. "A Witness to Hope: Migration and Human Solidarity." In *A Promised Land, A Perilos Journey: Theological Perspectives on Migration*, edited by Gioacchinno Campese and Daniel Groody (xi–xvii). Notre Dame, IN: University of Notre Dame Press, 2008.

Salvatierra, Alexia. "Sacred Refuge." *Sojourners* 36, no. 9 (September/October 2007). http://www.sojo.net/index.cfm?action=magazine.article&issue=soj0709&article=070910.

Samaritans. http://www.samaritanpatrol.org.

Sartre, Jean-Paul. *Being and Nothingness*, translated by Hazel E. Barnes. New York: Washington Square Press, 1992.

———. *Huis Clos*. Paris: Gallimard, 1947.

Seper, Jerry. "16 Illegals Sue Arizona Rancher." *Washington Times*. http://www.washington-times.com/news/2009/feb/09/16-illegals-sue-arizona-rancher/?page=all. February 9, 2009.

State of Arizona Senate. "Senate Bill 1070," Forty-ninth Legislature, Second Regular Session, 2010. http://www.azleg.gov/legtext/49leg/2r/bills/sb1070s.pdf.

Senior, Donald. "Beloved Aliens and Exiles: New Testament Perspectives on Migration." In *A Promised Land, a Perilous Journey: Theological Perspectives on Migration*, edited by Gioacchinno Campese and Daniel Groody (20–34). Notre Dame, IN: University of Notre Dame Press, 2008.

Soerens, Matthew, and Jenny Hwang. *Welcoming the Stranger: Justice, Compassion and Truth in the Immigration Debate*. Downers Grove, IL: IVP Books, 2009.

Stillwell, Cinnamon. "San Francisco: Sanctuary City Gone Awry." *San Francisco Chronicle*. http://articles.sfgate.com/2008-07-16/opinion/17120431_1_sanctuary-city-immi-gration-status-illegal-immigrants. July 16, 2008.

Sullivan, Amy. "Religious Groups Push for Immigration Reform." *Time*. http://www.time.com/time/nation/article/0,8599,1986320,00.html?xid=rss-topstories-polar. May 4, 2010.

Tassello, Giovanni Graziano. "For the Love of Migrants: The Scalabrinian Tradition." In *A Promised Land, a Perilous Journey: Theological Perspectives on Migration*, edited by Gioacchinno Campese and Daniel Groody (124–140). Notre Dame, IN: University of Notre Dame Press, 2008.

Teitelbaum, Michael S., and Myron Weiner. *Threatened Peoples, Threatened Borders: World Migration and U.S. Policy*. New York: W.W. Norton, 1995.

Time. "Nation: Deathtrap (Thirteen Aliens Die in the Desert)." http://www.time.com/time/magazine/article/0,9171,924300,00.html. July 21, 1980.

The New Oxford Annotated Bible. Edited by Bruce M. Metzger and Roland E. Murphy. New York: Oxford University Press, 1989.

UNHCR, Convention and Protocol Relating to the Status of Refugees. http://www.unhcr.org/protect/PROTECTION/3b66c2aa10.pdf.

United States Code, Title 8, "Aliens and Nationality." http://www.law.cornell.edu/uscode/8/usc_sup_01_8.html.

United States Conference of Catholic Bishops, Inc. and Conferencia del Episcopado Mexicano. "Strangers No Longer: Together on the Journey of Hope." http://www.usccb.org/mrs/stranger.shtml., January 22, 2003.

United States Customs and Border Protection. *National Border Patrol Strategy*. Washington, DC: U.S. Customs and Border Protection, 2004.

———. "Tucson Sector Project." http://www.cbp.gov/xp/cgov/border_security/sbi/pro-jects/project_descrip/tucson_project.xml. November 10, 2008.

———. "Ultralight Plane Crashes in Arizona, Smugglers Apprehended." http://www.cbp.gov/xp/cgov/newsroom/news_releases/may_2009/05302009.xml. May 30, 2009.

Van Biema, David. "Does the Bible Support Sanctuary?" *Time*. http://www.time.com/time/world/article/0,8599,1645646,00.html. July 20, 2007.

Vanderpool, Tim. "Requiem for an Arrest: Charges against a Samaritan Activist Are Mysteriously Dropped." *Tucson Weekly*. http://www.tucsonweekly.com/tucson/requiem-for-an-arrest/Content?oid=1092883. October 9, 2008.

———. "The Activist Question: Tensions between Humanitarians and Federal Officials Are on the Rise along the Border." *Tucson Weekly*. http://www.tucsonweekly.com/tucson/the-activist-question/Content?oid=1230781. July 9, 2009.

Vu, Michelle A. "Evangelicals Make Case for Welcoming Immigrants." *Christian Post*. http://www.christianpost.com/article/20090401/evangelicals-make-case-for-welcoming-immigrants. April 1, 2009.

Wallis, Jim. "Arizona's Immigration Bill Is a Social and Racial Sin." *God's Politics*. http://blog.sojo.net/2010/04/21/arizonas-immigration-bill-is-a-social-and-racial-sin. April 21, 2010.

Westerhoff, Caroline. *Good Fences: The Boundaries of Hospitality*. Cambridge, MA: Cowley, 1999.

Wood, Daniel B. "Where U.S.-Mexico Border Fence Is Tall, Border Crossings Fall." *Christian Science Monitor*. http://www.csmonitor.com/USA/2008/0401/p01s05-usgn.html. April 1, 2008.

———. "Arizona's 'Virtual' Border Wall Gets a Reality Check." *Christian Science Monitor*. http://www.csmonitor.com/USA/2008/0402/p12s01-usgn.html. April 2, 2008.

———. "Along the U.S.-Mexican Border, an Erratic Patchwork Fence." *Christian Science Monitor*. http://www.csmonitor.com/USA/2008/0403/p01s02-usgn.html. April 3, 2008.

———. "Billions for a US-Mexico Border Fence, but Is It Doing Any Good?" *Christian Science Monitor*. http://www.csmonitor.com/USA/2009/0919/p02s09-usgn.html. September 19, 2009.

———. "Opinion Polls Show Broad Support for Tough Arizona Immigration Law." *Christian Science Monitor*. http://www.csmonitor.com/USA/Society/2010/0430/Opinion-polls-show-broad-support-for-tough-Arizona-immigration-law. April 30, 2010.

INDEX